The Visualization of a Nation
Tàpies and Catalonia

LEGENDA

LEGENDA is the Modern Humanities Research Association's book imprint for new research in the Humanities. Founded in 1995 by Malcolm Bowie and others within the University of Oxford, Legenda has always been a collaborative publishing enterprise, directly governed by scholars. The Modern Humanities Research Association (MHRA) joined this collaboration in 1998, became half-owner in 2004, in partnership with Maney Publishing and then Routledge, and has since 2016 been sole owner. Titles range from medieval texts to contemporary cinema and form a widely comparative view of the modern humanities, including works on Arabic, Catalan, English, French, German, Greek, Italian, Portuguese, Russian, Spanish, and Yiddish literature. Editorial boards and committees of more than 60 leading academic specialists work in collaboration with bodies such as the Society for French Studies, the British Comparative Literature Association and the Association of Hispanists of Great Britain & Ireland.

The MHRA encourages and promotes advanced study and research in the field of the modern humanities, especially modern European languages and literature, including English, and also cinema. It aims to break down the barriers between scholars working in different disciplines and to maintain the unity of humanistic scholarship. The Association fulfils this purpose through the publication of journals, bibliographies, monographs, critical editions, and the MHRA Style Guide, and by making grants in support of research. Membership is open to all who work in the Humanities, whether independent or in a University post, and the participation of younger colleagues entering the field is especially welcomed.

ALSO PUBLISHED BY THE ASSOCIATION

Critical Texts
Tudor and Stuart Translations • *New Translations* • *European Translations*
MHRA Library of Medieval Welsh Literature

MHRA Bibliographies
Publications of the Modern Humanities Research Association

The Annual Bibliography of English Language & Literature
Austrian Studies
Modern Language Review
Portuguese Studies
The Slavonic and East European Review
Working Papers in the Humanities
The Yearbook of English Studies

www.mhra.org.uk
www.legendabooks.com

STUDIES IN HISPANIC AND LUSOPHONE CULTURES

Studies in Hispanic and Lusophone Cultures are selected and edited by the Association of Hispanists of Great Britain & Ireland. The series seeks to publish the best new research in all areas of the literature, thought, history, culture, film, and languages of Spain, Spanish America, and the Portuguese-speaking world.

The Association of Hispanists of Great Britain & Ireland is a professional association which represents a very diverse discipline, in terms of both geographical coverage and objects of study. Its website showcases new work by members, and publicises jobs, conferences and grants in the field.

Founding Editor
Trevor Dadson

Editorial Committee
Chair: Professor Catherine Davies (University of London)
Professor Stephanie Dennison (University of Leeds)
Professor Sally Faulkner (University of Exeter)
Professor Andrew Ginger
(New College of Humanities at Northeastern University)
Professor James Mandrell (Brandeis University, USA)
Professor Hilary Owen (University of Manchester/University of Oxford)
Professor Philip Swanson (University of Sheffield)
Professor Jonathan Thacker (Exeter College, University of Oxford)

Managing Editor
Dr Graham Nelson
41 Wellington Square, Oxford OX1 2JF, UK

www.legendabooks.com/series/shlc

STUDIES IN HISPANIC AND LUSOPHONE CULTURES

20. *(Un)veiling Bodies: A Trajectory of Chilean Post-Dictatorship Documentary*, by Elizabeth Ramírez-Soto
21. *Photographing the Unseen Mexico: Maya Goded's Socially Engaged Documentaries*, by Dominika Gasiorowski
22. *The Rise of Spanish American Poetry 1500-1700*, edited by Rodrigo Cacho Casal and Imogen Choi
23. *José Saramago: History, Utopia, and the Necessity of Error*, by Mark Sabine
24. *The Cultural Legacy of María Zambrano*, edited by Xon de Ros and Daniela Omlor
25. *Cortázar and Music*, by Nicholas Roberts
26. *Bodies of Disorder: Gender and Degeneration in Baroja and Blasco Ibáñez*, by Katharine Murphy
27. *The Art of Cervantes in Don Quixote: Critical Essays*, edited by Stephen Boyd, Trudi L. Darby and Terence O'Reilly
28. *The Modern Spanish Canon: Visibility, Cultural Capital and the Academy*, edited by Stuart Davis and Maite Usoz de la Fuente
29. *The Novels of Carmen Laforet: An Aesthetics of Relief*, by Caragh Wells
30. *Humanizing Childhood in Early Twentieth-Century Spain*, by Anna Kathryn Kendrick
31. *Gómez Manrique, Statesman and Poet*, by Gisèle Earle
32. *No Country for Nonconforming Women: Feminine Conceptions of Lusophone Africa*, by Maria Tavares
33. *Form and Reform in Eighteenth-Century Spain*, by Carla Almanza-Gálvez
34. *Women and Nationhood in Restoration Spain 1874–1931*, by Rocío Rødtjer
35. *Francisca Wood and Nineteenth-Century Periodical Culture*, by Cláudia Pazos Alonso
36. *Pepetela and the MPLA: The Ethical Evolution of a Revolutionary Writer*, by Phillip Rothwell
37. *Queer Genealogies in Transnational Barcelona*, by Natasha Tanna
38. *Hispanic Baroque Ekphrasis: Góngora, Camargo, Sor Juana*, by Luis Castellví Laukamp
39. *Contemporary Galician Women Writers*, by Catherine Barbour
40. *The Marvellous and the Miraculous in María de Zayas*, by Sander Berg
41. *Twentieth-Century Sephardic Authors from the Former Yugoslavia*, by Željko Jovanović
42. *From Doubt to Unbelief: Forms of Scepticism in the Iberian World*, edited by Mercedes García-Arenal and Stefania Pastore
43. *Franco's Female Prisoners: Writing No / Bodies*, by Holly J. Foss
44. *Memory and Utopia: The Poetry of José Ángel Valente*, by Manus O'Dwyer
45. *Quim Monzó and Contemporary Catalan Culture (1975–2018)*, by Guillem Colom-Montero
46. *Horizontalism and Historicity in Argentina: Cultural Dialogues of the Post-Crisis Era*, by Brigid Lynch
47. *The Visualization of a Nation: Tàpies and Catalonia*, by Emily Jenkins
48. *Naturalism Against Nature: Kinship and Degeneracy in Fin-de-siècle Portugal and Brazil*, by David J. Bailey
49. *Queering Lorca's Duende: Desire, Death, Intermediality*, by Miguel García

The Visualization of a Nation

Tàpies and Catalonia

❖

Emily Jenkins

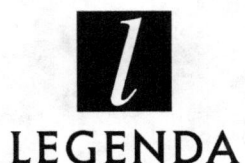

LEGENDA

Studies in Hispanic and Lusophone Cultures 47
Modern Humanities Research Association
2021

Published by Legenda
an imprint of the Modern Humanities Research Association
Salisbury House, Station Road, Cambridge CB1 2LA

ISBN 978-1-78188-419-5 (HB)
ISBN 978-1-78188-422-5 (PB)

First published 2021

All rights reserved. No part of this publication may be reproduced or disseminated or transmitted in any form or by any means, electronic, mechanical, photocopying, recording or otherwise, or stored in any retrieval system, or otherwise used in any manner whatsoever without written permission of the copyright owner, except in accordance with the provisions of the Copyright, Designs and Patents Act 1988, or under the terms of a licence permitting restricted copying issued in the UK by the Copyright Licensing Agency Ltd, Saffron House, 6–10 Kirby Street, London EC1N 8TS, *England, or in the USA by the Copyright Clearance Center, 222 Rosewood Drive, Danvers MA 01923. Application for the written permission of the copyright owner to reproduce any part of this publication must be made by email to legenda@mhra.org.uk.*

Disclaimer: Statements of fact and opinion contained in this book are those of the author and not of the editors or the Modern Humanities Research Association. The publisher makes no representation, express or implied, in respect of the accuracy of the material in this book and cannot accept any legal responsibility or liability for any errors or omissions that may be made.

Trademark notice: Product or corporate names may be trademarks or registered trademarks, and are used only for identification and explanation without intent to infringe.

© Modern Humanities Research Association 2021

Copy-Editor: Dr Ellen Jones

CONTENTS

❖

Acknowledgements ix
List of Abbreviations x

Introduction 1

1 Unchanging in an Era of Change 27
  1.1 From Surrealism to Informalism 27
  1.2 Consistency in an Era of Instability 37
  1.3 Concluding Remarks 46

2 An Icon in the Making 51
  2.1 Achieving an Iconic Status 51
  2.2 Sculpting Catalonia 56
  2.3 How Politics Affect Art 61
  2.4 Concluding Remarks 63

3 A New Foundation and an Old Sock 67
  3.1 Financial and Institutional Support 67
  3.2 'Mr. Tàpies's Unmatched Sock' and Other Public Works 73
  3.3 Concluding Remarks 88

4 The Visualization of a Catalan Nation 93
  4.1 Art, Nationalism, and Identity 93
  4.2 Art and Politics, Direct links 101
  4.3 Concluding Remarks 104

5 The Context of Artistic Content 109
  5.1 Exhibiting Tàpies 110
  5.2 Exhibition Practices, Ideology, and Identity 115
  5.3 Concluding Remarks 126

6 Art as a Nationalizing Tool 131
  6.1 Marketing National Identity 131
  6.2 How Art Affects Politics 140
  6.3 Concluding Remarks 145

Conclusion 151

Appendix: Interview with Toni Tàpies 163

Bibliography 171
Index 187

To Lucas, with love

ACKNOWLEDGEMENTS

'Què fem? On enem? D'on venim?
Però aquí tenim una caixa de llapis de colors.'
Joan Brossa

While this investigation would have been impossible without the guidance and insight of a number of excellent professors, colleagues, friends, and family, I take full responsibility for any errors within this text. When asked about my research, I am met with a number of different reactions. Some ask me what the artwork of Tàpies looks like, others ask why anyone would study Catalan nationalism, and a few say it sounds fascinating. This journey began in 2008 at a FC Barcelona soccer match where the omnipresence of the Catalan flag waving around the stadium stuck me as extraordinary. Growing up in the United States, the only comparison I could contrive was attending a Boston Celtic's basketball game and seeing the audience swaggering their Massachusetts flags. This simply does not happen. Studying art and nationalism in Spain has led me to corners of the country that I never thought I would go. It has been an incredible adventure, particularly as I learned the Spanish language (*de golpe*), and I am indebted to many who have helped me along the way. To Justo Beramendi and Lourenzo Fernández Prieto: thank you for your kindness and for guiding me in Galicia. Your interest in my research has instilled me with a confidence that I lacked before meeting each of you. To my beloved undergraduate professors at Rhodes College: thank you for encouraging me to be evermore curious. To Victor Coonin: thank you for a simple conversation that gave me courage when I needed it most. To Graham Nelson and the Legenda team: for believing in me and this work. To my family and friends: for supporting and loving me unconditionally. To Marcos: for your creativity, endless enthusiasm, and help with the interviews. Finally, to Alex: for your patience and your compassion, for reading all of my work, and for relentlessly pushing me to publish these pages, I truly cannot thank you enough.

E.J., January 2021

LIST OF ABBREVIATIONS

CDC	Convergència Democràtica de Catalunya
CiU	Convergència i Unió
CUP	Candidatura d'Unitat Popular
ERC	Esquerra Republicana de Catalunya
ICV	Iniciativa per Catalunya Verds
MACBA	Museu d'Art Contemporani de Barcelona
MNAC	Museu Nacional d'Art de Catalunya
PCC	Partit Comunista de Catalunya
PCE	Partido Comunista de España
PP	Partido Popular
PSC	Partit dels Socialistes de Catalunya
PSOE	Partido Socialista Obrero Español
PSUC	Partit Socialista Unificat de Catalunya
Reina Sofía	Museo Nacional Centro de Arte Reina Sofía
UDC	Unió Democràtica de Catalunya

INTRODUCTION

> 'We should never forget that imagination has been central to agency for most of human history'.
>
> Umut Ozkirimli[1]

In 1981 the President of the Catalan Government Jordi Pujol expressed his esteem for the artistic activity of Catalonia. He simultaneously praised the Romanesque and modern artists of the region, specifying naming Antoni Gaudí, Joan Miró, Antoni Tàpies, and Salvador Dalí. Pujol idolized this group of men to demonstrate that Catalonia harbours creativity and innovation. The president went on to discuss how the exhibition *Catalunya Avui*, held at the UNESCO headquarters in Paris, would expose Catalan culture to the international audience and enable a better understanding of Spain as well.[2] Reviewing the list of Pujol's acclaimed artists, Tàpies must be the least famous. It is impossible to visit Barcelona without gawking at one of Gaudí's eccentric buildings. His unfinished basilica Sagrada Família is the most visited monument in all of Spain. Similarly, Miró's style with cheerful colours and fantastical figures makes his art instantly recognizable. An established name in the 'Western' canon of art history, Miró's individuality separated him from contemporary circles of artists working to cultivate Surrealism and Dada, however he developed his style parallel to avant-garde movements in interwar Paris. Dalí is internationally known as an artist with a dramatic personality. His paintings with melting clocks are perhaps as equally renowned as his ostentatious moustache. Tàpies's artistic merit is recognized within the art world and his reputation has remained closely tied to that community. His dirty, demanding, ambiguous pictures are not easily read. They are neither jovial like Miró's work nor scandalous like Dalí's. During the mid-twentieth century, however, Tàpies developed a unique language that Catalans continue to celebrate today.

I.I. Goals

Why has Tàpies's art become iconic in Catalonia? In 2009, art historian Katherine Jentleson referred to him as the 'reigning cultural king of post-Picasso Spain'.[3] Looking back with the perspective of an art historian, it is logical to position Tàpies amongst modern masters such as Pablo Picasso, Henri Matisse, Kazimir Malevich, Jackson Pollock, Robert Rauschenberg, and Willem de Kooning. However, what is it that has made his solemn, grimy images beloved in Barcelona? In 1981, as Pujol proclaimed, Tàpies was an honourable figure in the Catalan community. On the day of the artist's death on February 6, 2012 the President of the Generalitat de

Catalunya Artur Mas asserted, 'Tàpies was the artist with the most radically Catalan thoughts, expressions, and references'.[4] This book explores the sociopolitical conditions that enabled Tàpies to effectively replace Miró as the principle reference of visual art in Catalonia.

What were the sociopolitical circumstances that affected the artist's ascent to prominence? While specifically investigating the role that the Generalitat de Catalunya and the Ajuntament de Barcelona played in promoting the artist's work, we can better understand how local institutions chose to support Tàpies, in addition to why they chose to do so. Different organizations have demonstrated dissimilar incentives through their relationships with the artist and his work. For example, the Generalitat appropriated Tàpies in the 1980s and 1990s and fit his work into a Catalan nationalist narrative, while the Ajuntament sought to portray his art as representative of Barcelona's modernity. Other establishments have highlighted Tàpies's Spanish heritage, while literature and media concerning the artist's national identity is variable.

More recent retrospective exhibitions, organized in the twenty-first century, have provoked further questions concerning the perception of Tàpies's art. How does context affect the reception of his artworks? I am particularly concerned with the way that the public could view the artist's aesthetic as conveying certain ideologies without consideration of the history of the maker's life and previous works. This book will examine how exhibitions at the Museu Nacional d'Art de Catalunya (MNAC), Guggenheim Museum Bilbao, Fundació Antoni Tàpies, Instituto Cervantes, and Dia:Beacon have presented the artist and how particular cultural institutions can mould the conception of contemporary Catalan identities. In looking at the way in which works of art are presented to the public, I intend to draw attention to often-unforeseen nuances concerning institutional agendas and the practice of creating exhibitions.

For example, curators do more than simply select artworks that fit into a particular theme; they structure the order and environment in which we experience those works, similar to a pastor who herds a flock of sheep. In turn, this affects our thoughts and sensations concerning the works themselves. I will illustrate this point through the comparison of exhibitions held in Barcelona, Bilbao, and New York in order to demonstrate the extent to which curators can control the perceived meaning of artistic content.

How does political art impact national thought? Murray Edelman's book *From Art to Politics: How Artistic Creations Shape Political Conceptions* demonstrated that art is able to 'excite minds and feelings' differently than other quotidian experiences.[5] Furthermore, art can create new realities, offering alternative perspectives that could lead to previously unperceived possibilities. Through the presentation of visual ideas, art can activate critical thinking, 'energize' democracy, and encourage a rethinking of conventional habits and beliefs.[6] Edelman showed that art is a fundamental aspect of the human experience and it is always political.

While *From Art to Politics* established that art is a significant political force, it did not delve into the relationship between art and nationalism. What is the current relationship between the artwork of Tàpies, nationalisms, and national identities in Catalonia? While Tàpies created many canvases that show his desire to visually express material associated with his homeland, they do not reveal to us that being Catalan is mutually exclusive with being Spanish or even European. This is critical to recognize when observing his art decades after its creation. At the same time, Tàpies's acceptance of certain public projects and, more interestingly, his refusal to create a mural for Madrid's international airport in the early 1990s did reveal the artist's attitude towards high-profile works beyond Catalonia. Through his art and writing, what Tàpies did make clear was his desire for freedom and a democratic government both in and beyond Catalonia. This investigation seeks to consider both the artist's depictions in relation to nationalism and the way that diverse groups from different parts of the globe can come to understand his art in different spaces and different moments in time.

I.2. Historiography

Montserrat Guibernau stated that the Catalan artists Miró, Gaudí, Dalí, Tàpies, and Casals have been converted into icons that play a role in the emotional arguments linked to Catalan nationalism.[7] At different moments throughout history, Catalan nationalists have looked to art and culture in order to support the idea that Catalonia is different from Spain. In *Identitats contemporànies: Catalunya i Espanya*, Borja de Riquer stressed that being Catalan stems from one's identity and is related to the land's 'history, customs, traditions, laws, art, and, essentially, language and culture'.[8] However, that difference is not necessarily problematic. During the debates concerning the drafting of Spain's 1978 Constitution, all of Catalonia's political parties except for the Esquerra Republicana de Catalunya (ERC) accepted the configuration of Catalonia as one of Spain's multiple nationalities. ERC's representative Heribert Barrera objected to characterizing Spain itself as a nation, but his party did not have an issue with Catalonia's political inclusion within the Kingdom of Spain. He stated that Catalonia's future status as an Autonomous Community 'is perfectly compatible with our feelings and aspirations as Catalans'.[9]

Literature concerning the nature of Catalan nationalism is extensive and often emphasizes Catalonia's unique situation as a stateless nation within a multinational state, the historicity of Catalan Courts, and the movement's propensity towards nonviolent mobilization (Balcells, Balfour and Quiroga, Conversi, Crameri, Dowling, Guibernau, Mar-Molinero and Smith, McRoberts, Molinero and Ysàs, Sobrer, and Riquer).[10] However, as both Guibernau and Riquer's quotations have communicated, emotions and feelings are also important factors that have an impact on nationalism and national identity through a process that Alejandro Quiroga explained as the personalization of the nation, the link between nationalism and national identity.[11] Anthony D. Smith shares this perspective, understanding emotions as a sort of primer for nationalism and, by extension, the nonverbal side of national 'fabrication/ invention/ [and] manipulation'.[12] This investigation does not pretend to analyse the different forms or shifting nature of twentieth and twenty-first century Catalan nationalism. Instead, it seeks to identify how the work of Tàpies is, and has been, attached to the idea of Catalonia.

As Alejandro Quiroga and Fernando Molina sketch in 'National Deadlock: Hot Nationalism, Dual Identities and Catalan Independence (2008–2019)', narrative experiences are a part of what connects individuals to the nation.[13] Visual experiences impact that formative narrative, which then plays out in the various spheres of nationalization. Works of art change the way individuals perceive and experience the world around them within any beyond the context of the nation.

Few art historians have examined the relation between the nation and modern art in Spain. Robert Lubar conceptualized Miró's artistic career as moving from a cataloguing of Catalan country life to an exploration of the act of painting and how minimal his subjects could become before they would lose their ideological weight.[14] Lubar expressed Miró's vacillation between the antiquated and the modern as the artist's 'desire to come to terms with traditional Catalan values and international (European) artistic impulses'.[15] Miró's early works show a longing for an appropriate visual language to communicate a contemporary Catalan 'essence'.[16] Robin Greeley reversed Lubar's terms, claiming that Miró's early use of representation to create a modern cultural identity was inverted in the artist's work after 1923; Catalan identity became the subject and the act of representation turned into the agent.[17]

Miró sought to construct a visual notion of what it means to be Catalan. However, Lubar reminded us that the artist's first solo exhibition at Galeries Dalmau in Barcelona was a failure. The public ridiculed and criticized the works of art, which catalyzed Miró's move to Paris shortly after.[18] Barcelona's art patrons proved to be too conservative for the young artist during the first years of his professional career. In 1948, two years before Tàpies's first solo exhibition at Galeries Laietanes in Barcelona, the two artists met for the first time.[19] This encounter brought together two men, of different generations, with similar goals. Both sought to push modern painting to its limits without losing sight of their Catalan identities. The former Director of the Fundació Antoni Tàpies, Manuel Borja-Villel, explained that Tàpies had direct access to a number of Miró's works through the collection of Joan Prats. Furthermore, Tàpies greatly admired Miró's ability to manipulate the materials with which he worked. For Tàpies, Miró's art was both powerful and convincing, an embodiment of both modernity and the avant-garde.[20]

Scholarship concerning Tàpies is limited. American authors often discuss the formal aspects of his art and regard him as a European artist working within Informalism, an artistic movement that developed in the 1940s around the same time as Abstract Expressionism (Lubar, Mayhew, and Fishman).[21] Little work has been done that analyses the social role of Tàpies's work and his foundation in Barcelona. In 1995 Lubar expressed the need for more dedication to Tàpies after what he deemed was a mediocre retrospective exhibition in New York. In a review of the show, the art historian discussed the role that the Catalan artist played in shaping two generations of artists. Through his creation of a unique style and his experimentation with non-traditional media, Tàpies served as a model for younger international artists looking to break away from Surrealism and later Abstract

Expressionism. As Lubar pointed out at the end of the review in a frank and disappointed tone, 'Antoni Tàpies deserves far more'.[22]

While there are countless exhibition essays about Tàpies's works, critical examinations of his creations and their importance (both plastic and social) are far from developed. A couple of the more developed exhibition texts include Lluís Permanyer's from the 1986 *Tàpies y la nueva cultura* and Laurence Rassel's from the 2013 *Tàpies. From Within*.[23] These presentations introduced particular works of each exhibition to the general public. Both are accurate accounts, yet not particularly reflective.

Similarly, many articles published in numerous periodicals have followed Tàpies's long career, but only scratch the surface of the political implications associated with his works of art. While contemporary newspaper articles have not generally addressed this particular topic that I am concerned with, they have provided much insight into the different ways in which the artist was conjured and represented, in order to bolster underlying and even invented arguments that have to do with Catalonia and Spain. For example, *ABC* detailed Tàpies's 1990 Premio Príncipe de Asturias award using a quotation from an artist and member of the jury Javier Mariscal. The newspaper printed Mariscal's statement that Tàpies 'has always made works that are very European, and, above all, very Spanish',[24] without any sort of clarification to what exactly 'very European' or 'very Spanish' artwork actually means. Mariscal also stated that it is impossible to understand the artwork of Miquel Barceló without comprehending Tàpies. While there are countless examples of the proud projection of Tàpies as Spanish or Catalan and sometimes both, little work has been done to investigate how the artist's works of art have been presented in Spain and abroad. Later, I will discuss in greater detail how different sources in the media have interpreted Tàpies's identity.

Director of the Museo Nacional Centro de Arte Reina Sofía (Reina Sofía) Manuel Borja-Villel's 1989 doctoral thesis is the most outstanding study concerning Tàpies and the formal characteristics of his works of art. The unpublished work discussed the Matter Paintings in depth and includes a comprehensive catalogue of exhibitions, publications, and an interview with the artist.[25] Matter painting was a term coined in the 1950s to describe a technique of combining alternative materials (such as sand, mud, marble dust, etc.) with a thick layer of paint in order to achieve a desired texture.[26] Borja-Villel was the first to approach these paintings from an academic perspective. In the same year, he also published an article in *Kalías* that examined the relationship between Tàpies and Surrealism. *Kalías* was a biannual magazine edited by the Generalitat de Valencia and the Institut Valencià d'Art Modern that ran from 1989 to 2002. The magazine printed scholarship on art theory, analysis, and criticism. In the second edition, Borja-Villel argued that Tàpies's affinity with Miró's work did not terminate with the end of his surrealist compositions in the 1950s and he discussed how the Matter Paintings purposefully play with the push and pull between the foreground and the background.[27] This is something that Miró also did, which effectively creates a confusion of conceivable space.

Borja-Villel has not published a tremendous quantity of work concerning Tàpies, however, his writings are the most thoughtful. As he stated in 2009 in an article published in *El País*, Tàpies 'is not a Spanish invention, but an artist whose work is fundamental in order to understand other works of art created during the second half of the twentieth century'.[28] Still, Borja-Villel's examinations stayed close to the works of art and within the conventional boundaries of art history. He has not delved into the social and political ramifications of the work as this book does. Furthermore, although he did discuss Tàpies's recycling of Miró's use of letters and signs in the *Kalías* article, he missed one of the most significant iconographic connections, the cross, which I will elaborate on in the following chapter.

Polígrafa has published the great number of books concerning Tàpies, far outnumbering any other publisher, for example: Alexandre Cirici's *Tàpies: Testimoni del silenci*, José Corredor-Matheos's *Antoni Tàpies: materia, signo, espíritu*, and Andreas Franzke's *Tàpies*.[29] This Barcelona-based company, founded in 1964, has contributed to Tàpies's exposure in and beyond Catalonia through texts written in Catalan, Spanish, and English. Polígrafa also published (together with Fundació Antoni Tàpies) eight volumes of the artist's complete works, available in Catalan, Spanish, English, and French. Many of Polígrafa's publications have addressed Tàpies's connection to Catalonia, especially Pere Gimferrer's 1975 *Tàpies and the Catalan Spirit*. However, more than four decades have passed since the poet from Barcelona wrote this book and this investigation provides an updated, more nuanced, and less partial perspective on the artist's relationship to Catalonia.

European publications have tended to point out the artist's Catalan heritage, biographical history, ethical values, and artistic inspiration (Borja-Villel, Catoir, Cirici, Corredor-Matheos, Dupin, Agustí, Enguita Mayo, Miquel Tàpies, Franzke, Gasch, Gimferrer, Penrose, Permanyer, Rassel, and Tapié).[30] Few investigations have analysed the political implications of Tàpies's art. Barbara Catoir questioned the artist about his personal beliefs in her 1991 *Conversations with Antoni Tàpies* and his responses were almost as ambivalent as his canvases. In addition to examinations of the formal aspects of the artist's works and his artistic career, newspaper articles featuring Tàpies were bountiful, particularly in the early 1990s. While Tàpies himself also wrote extensively about his work, he ultimately said quite little about how to read his pictures.[31] His difficult style and purposeful ambiguity make it challenging to pin down any objective meaning, which is one of the reasons that more scholastic attention should be dedicated to the artist and how his artworks are presented to the public.

In *Tàpies and the Catalan Sprit* Gimferrer boldly announced 'the work of Antoni Tàpies is now at a beginning of a future that belongs to it'.[32] With this statement, the poet demonstrated his regard for Tàpies's work and confidence in his artistic career. Similar to the belated public recognition of works by Gaudí, Miró and the Catalan poet J. V. Foix, Gimferrer predicted in 1975 that Tàpies's work was at the beginning of a similar path.[33] Furthermore, he established a parallel relation that linked Miró and Foix with Tàpies and Joan Brossa as two different generations of avant-garde artists and poets that best represented what he called the 'Catalan spirit'.[34]

Gimferrer, despite his romantic ideas about the essence of Catalonia, accurately pointed out that Tàpies's work ought to be considered using a bilateral perspective in relation to the regional culture; it is important to consider how Catalan culture shaped Tàpies's art *and* how Tàpies's art positions itself in the trajectory of that culture.[35] Gimferrer's analysis is now dated, as he wrote the text under Francoism. After nearly forty years of democracy in Spain, an updated evaluation of the artist's relationship to culture in Catalonia will shed light on the evolving nature of this relation. Recent nationalist activity, including a popular separatist movement, in the region further complicates the exhibition politics surrounding Tàpies's works. New assessments of his compositions are necessary as Spain enters a new era of history. Although the artist passed away in 2012, his visual language has been very much alive in Barcelona in the years following his death. This investigation provides a fresh perspective on Tàpies and the relationship between visual art and national politics.

I.3. Hypotheses

This book opens a new debate concerning the political role of art in society. Using Tàpies and Catalonia as a case study, I propose several hypotheses. First, the artist's work became iconic for a population at a unique moment in time, ironically enabling the artist to prosper during the 1970s. The beginning of Tàpies's career coincided with an era of political repression in Spain and a time when abstraction was internationally recognized as a valuable vehicle for political expression within the art world. This moment was critical in the early formation of the artist and his style; it allowed him to create politically charged, semi-abstract art in the 1950s and 1960s that would become respected around the globe without drawing too much attention from General Francisco Franco's regime. Beginning with his Matter Paintings, Tàpies used art as a means of political communication.

His objectives were not always clear, but as a whole he sought to defend democracy, justice, and freedom through his works of art. Unlike Picasso or Miró, Tàpies lived in Spain during and after the Spanish Civil War (1936–1939). The style that Tàpies developed in post-war Spain allowed him to continue living there because his ideas were not necessarily explicitly expressed in visual terms. Picasso, on the other hand, denounced Francisco Franco and his conservative ideology in his grotesque 1937 etchings titled *Sueño y mentira de Franco*; Picasso was living in France when he made these compositions and he never returned to Spain again. Although Tàpies experienced the war as a young boy, he remained in Catalonia afterwards. The conditions in which he developed his artistic style did not allow him to be as bold as Picasso had been in 1937. Tàpies had to be careful; he astutely avoided concrete political imagery during the 1950s and 1960s while simultaneously developing an inventive body of work that was relevant in an international panorama of visual arts. Tàpies continued to work in the same style throughout the remainder of his artistic career, producing an impressive collection of thousands of artworks that have maintained a tremendous stylistic continuity.

Second, the Generalitat de Catalunya and the Ajuntament de Barcelona played a major role in promoting the artist within the region and sought to present Tàpies as a model Catalan citizen both during and after his lifetime. However, each group did so in their own way. While both bodies championed Tàpies as one of the most reputable living artists in Spain during the 1980s, their reasons for taking interest in the artwork was disparate. Jordi Pujol and his conservative coalition Convergència i Unió (CiU) ran the Generalitat from 1980 to 2003. CiU's nationalist program worked in harmony with the commission and financial support that the Generalitat offered Tàpies during this period. Tàpies's relationship with the regional government was mutually beneficial despite the artist's leftist political views. The Generalitat was happy to promote the internationally acclaimed artist who articulated his Catalan heritage and the artist embraced the institution's initiatives to expose his work. The Ajuntament, on the other hand, was controlled by a socialist party, Partit dels Socialistes de Catalunya (PSC), which promoted Tàpies as a contemporary, vanguard artist with an international profile and encouraged him via financial aid, public commissions, and exhibition publications. The local government was eager to project Barcelona's modernity, especially in the years leading up to the 1992 Olympic Games held in the *Ciudad Condal*. Tàpies and his foundation played a role in the transformation of the city in the years prior to the event. For the Ajuntament de Barcelona, Tàpies's value did not necessarily lie in his Catalan roots, instead he was espoused for his artistic ingenuity, developed during a time when many of Spain's talented artists and intellectuals remained abroad as a result of the war and ensuing dictatorship.

The institutional support that Tàpies received is remarkable. This is most evident through his public works and posthumous exhibitions that have honoured his life and artistic career. Investigating the connection between the artist and these major political bodies is imperative in order to visualize a top-down *and* bottom-up model of cultural analysis in Catalonia. Tàpies's career certainly benefited from the relationships that he built with local and regional governments in Spain. Interestingly, his discernible artistic style was created in response to a lack of a democratic system in Catalonia. The artwork itself ought to belong to a bottom-up conceptualization of culture, however its public exhibition and patronage were often tied to systems of power. The artist's continual representation of his particular style, coupled with an analysis of the nature of institutional support that Tàpies received, amplifies more traditional studies primarily concerning the formal characteristics of his works.

Third, recent shows that have included Tàpies's work are subject to misinterpretation of the artist's ideologies, specifically the representation of art that may concern Catalonia's relationship to Spain. A greater understanding of the artist's life and work is needed in order to preserve the artwork's integrity and to avoid misconceptions in addition to generalizations. The exhibition practices of cultural institutions like MNAC are always political and play an active role in the conception and negotiation of Catalan identity from within and from the outside. Learning at this museum is not limited to visitors living in the region. This institution has also sought to present ideas about art and society to 'foreign' visitors from other parts of Spain, Europe, and beyond. While there does not seem to be a model that could eliminate political sway from public exhibitions, being aware of the underlying structures of power that envelop cultural institutions is an important part of viewing works of art.

Finally, political art is an often-overlooked avenue that channels ideas about historical and contemporary identity. National identity is amongst one of the most powerful (albeit frequently veiled) themes in Tàpies's artwork. It is a theme that continues to resonate with some Catalan citizens that have been seeking new ways to govern themselves during the past decade. In examining the ways in which art can trigger emotional and intellectual responses, a heightened awareness of our own responses to outside stimuli becomes evident. Emotions can be the 'motor behind individual and collective conduct', despite the difficulties that historians may face in their definition and analysis.[36] Furthermore, an analysis of the way in which objects that often trigger emotions are presented also exposes the political power structures that frequently affect how beholders experience works of art.

The scale of a work of art does not have to correlate with its degree of engagement with political affairs. It is true that large artworks that take up political themes do so in a grandiose manner; for example, Picasso's *Guernica* or works by the 'big three' Mexican muralists Diego Rivera, José Clemente Orozco, and David Alfaro Siqueiros. However, size does not determine the quality of engagement with societal concerns that an artwork is able to transmit. Different formats are able to convey various viewpoints. For example, the form of Goya's series of etchings *The Disasters of War* has little in common with any large-scale painting. They are small, detailed, horrific scenes meant for close observation. Physically holding the images close enough to be able to see their detail is part of the experience. *Guernica*, on the other hand, was created for viewers to pass from the right to the left, as it was made specifically for the 1937 International Exposition in Paris where visitors would enter from one side and exit on the other. Reading a Goya etching and a Picasso painting provides entirely different sensations, although both take up themes of war, violence, and brutality.

Many of Tàpies's public works are quite large. However, some of his most potent political works, such as his 2006 cover for the *Estatut d'Autonomia de Catalunya*, are small. This is significant because as a viewer, individuals are more likely to identify with smaller formats. Viewers tend to feel less like an isolated observer when the work of art has a scale that is approachable. Through an analysis of the formal characteristics, ideological subject matter, and forms of exhibition, this book expounds how Tàpies's art is involved in the formation and reformation of national identity and nationalism in Catalonia.

Becoming attuned to the ways in which context affects our perception, conceptualization, and understanding of works of art is imperative in order to think critically about visual languages. The situation of art in particular circumstances can alter our thoughts and imagination. While it is impossible to escape the temporal moment of our own existence, it is necessary to consider how time conditions our perceptions of reality. In *The Politics of Aesthetics*, Jacques Rancière used Victor Hugo's 1862 *Les Misérables* as an example of a narrative that, depending on the reader and how history conditioned their historical moment, has had numerous different interpretations.³⁷ Changing political circumstances affect the way we come to conceptualize works of art, literature included. Rancière outlined the 'problem' that exists between aesthetics and politics: 'there is no criterion for establishing an appropriate correlation between the politics of aesthetics and the aesthetics of politics'.³⁸ Although there is no specific formula to determine how these two concepts are interconnected, their relationship is bilateral. Politics affects aesthetics (and art) and vice versa.

I.4. Methodology

In 'Art, Nationalism and War: Political Futurism in Italy (1909–1944)' Daniele Conversi examined the relationship between the Italian Futurist movement, fascism, and nation-building and inventing.³⁹ This book can be taken as a model of an interdisciplinary approach to achieve a better understanding of the links between art and politics during the twentieth century. The futurists of Italy created their own short-lived political party *Partito Politico Futurista* (1918–1920), which was later absorbed into the *Partito Nazionale Fascista*. Conversi showed that 'the futurists were involved and partook actively in Fascism's most violent exploits' and that the movement was part of a 'broader European phenomenon of the "nationalization of the masses"'.⁴⁰ The study relied more on Futurism's written material and the various forms of media transmission, as opposed to focusing on plastic works of art. Conversi stated that the subject has been exhausted in the context of art historical accounts, characterizing the discipline as having a 'selective propensity to eulogistic accounts', yet its political ramifications had not yet been adequately addressed.⁴¹

Without accusing Tàpies scholars of being 'eulogistic', a similar lack of critical inquiry with respect to the political nature of the artist's work is plain. Although Tàpies himself recognized that 'painting during the Franco regime was less difficult than painting in Nazi Germany or Fascist Italy because they [Francisco Franco and entourage] thought that modern art was not important and that it did not actually influence daily life',⁴² his work is comparable to that of the futurists. While these Italian artists collaborated with Mussolini and his totalitarian regime, Tàpies sought to undermine Francisco Franco's dictatorship, yet both the futurists and Tàpies created a visual language that formed ideological borders concerning the idea of the nation and its reputation.

Another exemplary study concerning the relation between art and politics is David McCarthy's 2015 book *American Artists Against War (1935–2010)*.⁴³ The first chapter outlines how independent artists and the American Artists' Congress found ways to protest 'fascism, militarism, and war' via works of art.⁴⁴ McCarthy stated:

> Their actions were predicated on the deeply held beliefs that art has a role to play in shaping public consciousness in progressive societies and that artists should link creativity with citizenship, to the mutual benefit of both. Art would gain by the broadening of its worldview beyond abstraction,

experimentation, and hermetic symbolism. Citizenship might be improved by providing viewers with points of view that they may not have considered (or encountered), especially when the government and media have reason to shape the interpretation of events.[45]

In other words, American antiwar artists did not necessarily halt any fascist regimes nor put an end to violence and war. However, they did provide a platform for the public to think. This is a valuable lesson because art and images are able to shape 'public consciousness', for better or for worse.[46] Consider, for example how twenty-first century advertisements are saturated with images and sprinkled with words. This is due to a picture's ability to emotionally impact the viewer's conscience quickly, instantaneously even. McCarthy based his argument in twentieth century art from the United States, but the crux of his analysis does not rely solely on that particular time and place; it depends heavily on the relationship between the formal characteristics of the work of art and the beholder's perception and response to visual stimuli.

Catalan politician Joan Guitart shared McCarthy's sentiment concerning art and politics. In the 1980s and 1990s, Guitart was a member of the political party Convergència Democràtica de Catalunya (CDC) and he worked for the Generalitat as Councillor of Education and later Councillor of Culture. Between 1996 and 2004 he served as the President of MNAC's board of trustees. Similar to McCarthy, Guitart believed that art is directly linked to the welfare of citizens. In a discussion concerning the relationship between contemporary art and politics, Guitart told me 'Culture, with a capital C, forms a fundamental part of the wellbeing of people and society, wellbeing understood as the best realization of countries and their citizens'.[47] Both the art historian and the politician agreed that culture and citizenship are correlated and that connection is worth investigating.

In contrast to Conversi's analysis of Futurism's link to Fascism, McCarthy analysed works of art that sought to defy ideologies in support of totalitarianism, violence, and imperialist wars. However, both studies have exemplified the political nature of art and its relevance beyond a frame of reference that restricts the history of art to its relation to other works of art. Rethinking Tàpies using the multidisciplinary scopes of Conversi and McCarthy, which encompass much more than the formal characteristics of works of art, is what distinguishes *The Visualization of a Nation: Tàpies and Catalonia* from previous analyses of the works of Antoni Tàpies.

Art, among the plethora of omnipresent images, signs, and symbols in contemporary culture, is able to selectively aggrandize national, historical narratives. Narratives concerning a nation, whether they deal with a heroic effort on behalf of an individual or a masterpiece created hundreds of years before the establishment of the nation state, can be perpetuated and preserved via images. Similarly, emblems associated with the modern nation are relentlessly propagated, marking particular spaces as linked to the power of the state. However, not all images are representative of historical truths, nor does demarcating a site with a flag or heraldic symbol create a space where only legal activities are carried out. Pictures, signs, and symbols all contribute to the myth of the modern nation as a historically legitimate entity, when in reality it is an invented concept commonly shared and accepted as just.

In *Narrating the Nation: Representations in History, Media and the Arts* Stefan Berger introduced the tremendous ways in which the fine arts have proposed and emphasized ideas concerning the modern nation.[48] Images, similar to other forms of creative expression, do not have to reflect reality. They can put forth new concepts of truth, whose meaning can change in both time and space. The relation between Tàpies's artwork and Catalan nationalism and identity is a central theme of this investigation.

To clarify, the term nationalism is not fixed and can connote different meanings depending on historical circumstances, geographies, etc. Individual identity is also an unfixed concept, susceptible to variation and modification. As Berger expressed in *Narrating the Nation*, 'researchers seeking to understand the national conundrum from a variety of different perspectives are, themselves, not outside the discursive construction of the past but are participating in the process'.[49] The very terms of this investigation are conditioned by the conventional ways in which contemporary societies are organized, as nations. While it is difficult to evade this fact, it is possible to be conscious that nations are constructed entities. They are neither divinely ordained nor everlasting.

For the purpose of this book, I rely on Benedict Anderson's 1983 definition of the nation as 'an imagined political community'.[50] In *Imagined Communities: Reflections on the Origin and Spread of Nationalism*, Anderson defined the nation as 'imagined' because the majority of its members will never come to meet the rest of their 'fellow members' and the idea of community stems from what he characterized as a 'deep, horizontal comradeship'.[51] This conception of the nation is closely linked to the people who feel that they somehow belong to that entity.[52] This idea of belonging creates an us/them dynamic that, in the case of Catalonia, has different versions of 'them' depending on the historical moment and particular circumstance. 'Them' could be those who also live in Spain, but are not Catalan, or those who are not Spanish, or even both. In some instances, Catalan nationalism has not only about articulating what it means to be Catalan, but also what it means *not* to be Spanish.

E. J. Hobsbawm argued in his 1992 *Nations and Nationalism since 1780: Programme, Myth, Reality* that the nation and nationalism are dual phenomena in which nationalism is the reality that creates the myth, or imagined community, also known as the nation.[53] In other words, nationalism is the motor that has propelled the vast spread of the idea of the nation as a legitimate political unit in a relatively short period of time. Hobsbawm relied on Ernest Gellner's 1983 definition of nationalism as 'primarily a principle which holds that the political and national unit should be congruent'.[54] In this sense, Catalonia is an exceptional case, where the nation belongs to another nation, despite a determined degree of legislative autonomy.

Michael Billig elaborated on the term nationalism in his 1995 book *Banal Nationalism*.[55] For Billig, nationalism needed to encompass more than temporary movements stemming from the periphery. Banal nationalism best describes how already established nations reproduce their 'ideological habits'.[56] Billig stressed that banal is not synonymous with benign. Banal nationalism is ubiquitous in 'Western' nations; however, one cannot say that it lacks a propensity towards violence. This idea, as I will later elaborate on in greater detail, has much to do with the signs and symbols that nations appropriate and accumulate in a way that makes their absence seem unimaginable. In terms of art and culture, Billig's concepts help connect the often invisible links between the visual and political realm.

In *National Identity, Popular Culture and Everyday Life*, Tim Edensor stated, 'national identity is processed through the realms of affect and sensuality as much as through cognitive processes of meaning construction and transmission'.[57] Nationalism, the nation, and national identity are linked to an individual's experiences and feelings. In 'Emociones en política. Conceptos, debates y perspectivas analíticas', Ludger Mees pointed out the difficulties that come with methods to analyse emotions and emotional experiences.[58] Despite this dilemma, historians have made advances in incorporating this important component into their investigations. This book also incorporates the intersections between emotions, national identity, and nationalism.

As Quiroga explained in 'The Three Spheres. A Theoretical Model of Mass Nationalization: The Case of Spain', the individual is an 'active subject who "personalizes the nation."'[59] This personalization is what connects the concept of nationalism to that of national identity; it is contingent upon 'attitudes' towards the nation and feelings of belonging to it. While experiences of the past cannot be undone, memories and emotions are malleable.

How is all this related to art? As Berger explained, 'public monuments, the fine arts and music have all been hugely influential in putting forward and emphasizing national narratives'.[60] Art is one way in which images that deal with the nation, nationalism, and national identity are circulated in everyday situations.

For example, on 13 August 2013, MNAC opened an exhibition titled *A Visit to the Romanesque: In company of Antoni Tàpies*. The show worked to connect a cohesive national history though visual art, unifying the past with the present. The objective of this exhibition, as the museum described, was twofold: 'to offer a contemporary look at medieval art, and at the same time to enrich Tàpies's universe with elements linking it to the art of the past'.[61] The image that accompanied the text that announced the show subtly introduced an intermediary figure in the chain of Catalan artists. Hanging from a rope that splits the canvas in half, the red wool peasant's hat (*barretina*) links the art of Tàpies to his compatriot Miró. The earth coloured background, which supports the stagnant pendulum that the rope and hat create, is a recycled medieval piece, which echoes the colours of the Romanesque works celebrated at the museum. Walls, time, and tradition are all themes that Tàpies's *Pintura romànica i barretina* embody. The 1971 artwork, in the context of this 2013–2014 exhibition, recapitulated the idea that the aesthetics of Catalonia are unique and traceable to a distant past. Ideologically bonding contemporary images with those of the past is a nationalist tactic that seeks to disguise a complex national history as a neat fusion of linear history. The image, as MNAC displayed in the exhibition, exemplifies Billig's concept of banal nationalism, as the *barretina* is physically and ideologically tied to a historic work of art from the same imagined community.

Pintura romànica i barretina embodies the central themes of this investigation. Tàpies's unique style, which the French critic Michel Tapié described in the 1950s as 'art autre' [other art], was a response to avant-garde artistic movements developing both in Europe and in the United States during the twentieth century. Geometric Abstraction and Abstract Expressionism were inadequate modes for what Tàpies's creations sought to accomplish. What Tapié once coined as other art, Martine Heredia categorized as Informalism, an artistic style that is not a trend with limits, but an enduring alternative to parallel movements developing after the Second World War.[62] This canvas contains informalist elements: it is minimalist, pared down to a few essential components that are recognizable yet organized in an unordinary fashion. His rejection of conventional beauty in favour of a worn, highly textured, and dirty aesthetic forces the viewer to think beyond the surface of his art. The light brown, decaying background from an original Romanesque piece of little value and an old rope are not necessarily beautiful. However, his commitment to political subjects demonstrates the artist's dedication to support a democratic and peaceful community, which he clarified in a number of his written works and published interviews.[63] Without that artist's written statements, much of his art would be rather unapproachable.[64] His extensive writing, however, bolsters the philosophical depth of his canvases. The red hat has historically been identified with peasants in Catalonia. Here, it is in an awkward position, without an owner, the hat is separated from an ordinary place. It is an anti-portrait. We are left to wonder whose hat that is and why it wound up tied from a rope. Ambiguity is one of Tàpies's trademarks, which he used to invite spectators, allowing them freedom to engage and learn with minimal restraints. *Pintura romànica i barretina* could be a play on Miró's Cap de pagès català paintings. These portraits from 1925 are highly simplified compositions that are just as much about the act of representation as they are about Catalan peasants. Tàpies's picture can also be read as the aftermath of a hanging, the quiet, spooky wake of an intolerable and dramatic means of punishment. The hanging red hat could take on the role of an inert pendulum, frozen in time. The inability to pin down one specific vision of Tàpies's red *barretina* dangling from a rope, and countless other works, is an intentional tactic that seeks to provoke reflection. Informalism, political content, and ambiguity are all elements that run through the extensive oeuvre of Tàpies. Furthermore, themes of time and space are often employed and important in the consideration of different exhibitions of the artist's works, which will encourage new readings of pictures such as *Pintura romànica i barretina*.

Using a theoretical foundation from James C. Scott's *Dominance and the Art of Resistance: Hidden Transcripts*, it becomes clear why Tàpies made thousands of surprisingly similar compositions over the course of his lifetime. Scott's theory concerns power relations and the behind-the-scenes dynamic that exists before a public denunciation against a dominant power.[65] While Scott's examples concern tactics such as coded language, storytelling and rumours, art is a type of visual language that can contribute to the culture of each position within a disparate social situation. Plastic art communicates ideas that can alter opinions, perceptions, and shift perspectives. Read alongside Scott's framework, Tàpies's body of work could be understood as an elusive yet fierce denunciation of the Franco regime. What *Dominance and the Art of Resistance* left out, however, is what happens after a dramatic public rebuke or shift in power. After the death of the dictator, who had led Spain's government for the better part of Tàpies's life, how did his developed transcript change throughout the transition to democracy and into the 1980s? Style is a key component in any artist's work and Tàpies's style, remarkably, did not waver during this period.

Homi Bhabha's theory concerning nations and nationalism has also been a valuable tool for analysis. I have investigated the relationship between Tàpies and Catalan society, the history of the region as well as the artist's ideas concerning its future. The artist, as a member of the Catalan community, used art to communicate his political identity and desires in a strategic manner. While Bhabha looked to literature to demonstrate how the idea of the nation is conceived of and perpetuated in literary terms, his ideas are applicable in fine arts.[66] Tàpies, like Miró before him, engaged with a multiplicity of times, 'Janus-faced' times that contribute to the idea that the nation is a physical (as opposed to ideological) entity that simultaneously looks towards both a grand history *and* unified future, as Tom Nairn suggested.[67] For Bhabha, these double times have been expressed in literature as what he coined as the 'pedagogical' and 'performative', strategic elements that ultimately enable the ability of national myths to flourish in the contemporary imagination. Tàpies made works of art that fuse these elements. This book will illuminate how national tales concerning the past and future of Catalonia have impacted the artist and his work.

I bridge Murray Edelman's discussion of how meaning is produced through the structures of certain spaces and Tim Edensor's argument concerning national spaces and places in order to critically examine public works of art that Tàpies created during the 1990s and into the first few years of the twenty-first century.[68] This is something that has not yet been explored regarding Tàpies's work. It is both an interesting and relevant topic because the artist did not accept just any sort of commission and the location of his exhibitions primed viewers in different ways. Both physical and geographic spaces are critical factors to analyse regarding Tàpies's work. He deliberately chose to show in and around Barcelona while collaborating to create exhibitions beyond his birthplace, most frequently in Paris or New York City. His public works, typically rather large in scale, have created previously nonexistent environments which, in turn, affect the ways in which individuals understand the function of those particular spaces. The formal characteristics of Tàpies's artworks are only part of the bigger picture, which includes the ways in which visual material is accessible to beholders. This book critically examines the content and context of public works and exhibitions and how their spatial distribution and geographic location affect the ways in which the artist's work has been presented to the public.

Concepts that Anderson, Billig, Gellner, Hobsbawm, and Quiroga have worked to define form the foundation of my methodology, which engages with theories proposed by Berger, Billig, Bhabha, Edelman, Edensor, Quiroga, and Scott. Art historical investigations published by Conversi, Lubar, and McCarthy have served as models that critically examine the relations between the visual arts and politics. My method of analysis includes traditional art historical formal analyses of particular works of art, sociopolitical contextualization of those works, and the application of several theories to demonstrate the direct and bilateral relationship between art and politics. This is a way to provide a more comprehensive examination of the art of Antoni Tàpies while situating his body of work outside the traditional art historical perspective. As Sabina Mihelj discussed in *Media Nations*, culture cannot be understood as a 'mere by-product of power relationships'.[69] The study of art and culture should not become isolated from wider sociopolitical contexts.

Finally, the perspective of this investigation stems from Ferran Archilés's and Miguel Ángel del Arco Blanco's works. Both have outlined constructive ways to comprehend history. Archilés emphasized the shared relationships between historical perspective, the cultural arena, and the national experience in an article that examines the languages and experiences of the nation and the processes of nationalization.[70] He explained that culture structures what an individual considers normal, correct, novel, or valuable; culture also structures the way that that person understands their relationship to the abstract idea of the nation. This relates to artistic exhibitions as a form of cultural expression that citizens are exposed to, particularly in metropolitan areas. Culture is not limited to the arts, but also deals with how individuals go about their daily lives and make sense of their experiences. Archilés's ideas help explain why some individuals may perceive a Tàpies show as a form of nationalization, while others may see the same show as having little to do with the idea of the nation.

In a historiographical chapter on Cultural Studies, del Arco wrote how the discipline utilizes particular viewpoints to examine the interactions between culture, power, and society. Historians, he stated, ought to keep this in mind as they write history.[71] While history tends to focus on realities of the past, the interdisciplinary nature of cultural studies allows for greater attention to both historical realities and fictions. In order to accurately represent the past, del Arco expressed that we must take into consideration two narratives: the 'realist' history that is pieced together using primary sources and the world of fiction and imagination which permits reality to seep in.[72] Art engages in both of these realms. However, attention is too often focused on the creative and imaginary aspect of visual culture. I am not solely interested in the imaginative spaces that Tàpies created from unusual materials like marble dust; I also want to explain some of the real political processes that conditioned the ways in which Tàpies worked. This book combines Archilés and del Arco's approaches to analysing history, both of which focus on culture and its polyvalent nature in order to cognize the past.

However, the limits of this sort of analysis have to do with the subjectivity of images and the fact that personal experiences affect how individuals respond emotionally and interpret visual material in different spaces, places, and moments in time. Museums and galleries create a space where visitors can think about and criticize artworks, but visitors may not consider what specific cultural and historical perspectives affect the way that they experience art; they may not reflect on the institution that created the exhibition and how it structures knowledge; finally, they may not separate the 'real' (historical) from the imaginary (fiction) while viewing works of art in a museum setting or controlled environment. In analysing the multiple layers at work in the context of an artistic exhibition, it becomes possible to expose unforeseen or subtle ways in which images impact the conception of beholder's ideas and identities in addition to their relationship to the society in which they live.

I.5. Sources

The Visualization of a Nation: Tàpies and Catalonia is a multidisciplinary study that draws from art history, theories of nationalism, political science, and social theories. Primary sources include artworks, artist statements, interviews, exhibition publications, media publications, public education textbooks, public records, and public surveys. Researching in the archive and library at the Fundació Antoni Tàpies has been an essential part of this investigation. Not only does the library include all of Tàpies's own works and writings, it also includes books and documents from his personal collection. The archive preserves copies of newspaper articles, comics, exhibition material, photographs, and unpublished sketches from various projects. The tremendous quantity of articles from different periodicals, particularly from the early 1990s, is astonishing. Going through many of these publications has been a remarkably time-consuming yet ultimately rewarding experience. Although this archive has been fundamental to this investigation, it lacks much information about Tàpies's public works. I hoped to find documents regarding public commissions, contracts, and preliminary sketches but was disappointed to find that the Fundació Antoni Tàpies does not allow access to much of the information available. Furthermore, some of his public works are not actually accessible to the public. The foundation used to organize visits through Barcelona that would allow people to see such works that pertain to the Generalitat and Universitat Pompeu Fabre, but they no longer do this. The foundation appointed Charles Guerra to Director in 2015, but his time there was short-lived. It will be interesting to see what goes on with this institution under new leadership. At this point in time, the Fundació Tàpies, together with the Tàpies Estate, have been unwilling to grant permissions to publish a number of images of the artist's work within this book. This is disheartening, and somewhat unbelievable as some of the artworks were commissioned by public institutions, and all very telling.

Other archives in the Catalan capital have been fruitful, particularly that of the Museu d'Art Contemporani de Barcelona (MACBA), the Arxiu Fotogràfic de Barcelona, and the Arxiu Històric de la Ciutat de Barcelona. MACBA's archive includes more than a dozen letters and postcards that Tàpies wrote to his friend, a Catalan poet, Joan Brossa. What is remarkable about their correspondences is that they discussed ideas above all else. MACBA also has letters from Brossa to Tàpies, in which he wrote about his thoughts and feelings concerning literary and aesthetic styles. The photographic archive preserves a significant number of original black and white images of the artist and his family, many of which had been published in periodicals during the 1980s and 1990s.

The Centre d'Estudis d'Opinió has published results from their surveys online, which has been a useful way to measure public opinions concerning the nation of Catalonia and how its citizens feel about its relationship to Spain. The Generalitat de Catalunya has sent me information concerning financial contributions that the regional government has made to fund the Fundació Antoni Tàpies, but has not been helpful in answering my questions regarding contracts that were made between the Generalitat and the artist. When asked about information related to commissioned works from the 1990s, civil servants working for the Generalitat were unable to find answers to basic questions. New York art gallery Dia:Beacon, Bilbao's Guggenheim Museum, and MNAC have all provided valuable information and statistics concerning the attendance of various exhibitions.

Secondary sources consist of art historical scholarship, political and social histories of Catalonia, historical and social theories, articles and comics from periodicals, magazine publications, documentaries, websites, and interviews. Academic sources concerning Tàpies are scarce and many of the publications that have accompanied exhibitions and introductory essays in the eight volumes of Tàpies's complete works have been written by just a few different authors (Agustí, Combalía, Enguita Mayo, Permanyer, and Miquel Tàpies). Tàpies often appeared in national periodicals such as: *ABC, Ara, Avui, Diari de Barcelona, El Mundo, El Observador, El País, Punt Diari, El Periódico,* and *La Vanguardia*. International papers also covered some stories about the artist and his work such as *Miami Herald, The New York Times,* and *The Wall Street Journal*. Finally, I have found useful information in magazines such as *Artinfo, The Burlington Magazine, Destino, Goya,* and *Kalías*. These sorts of contemporary accounts have played a major role in my analysis, specifically related to Tàpies's public works. The Fundació Antoni Tàpies has preserved a great quantity of press related to the artist, although I have also accessed many of these periodicals through their online databases.

Documentaries and other films about the life and work of Antoni Tàpies have also informed this investigation. Gregory Rood directed *Tàpies*, which was televised in 1990 in Catalonia and the United Kingdom.[73] The film opens with Tàpies speaking in Catalan about how he believes that art is able to transform people's consciences and vacillates between footage of the artist talking and working. Carolina Tubau directed the 2009 *Te de Tàpies* in collaboration with Televisió de Catalunya.[74] *Te de Tàpies* focuses on the sources that the artist used and how he saw his work as connected to the natural world. Both documentaries have provided insight concerning the way in which Tàpies talked about his work, which is similar, but not exactly the same as the way in which he wrote about his art. Shortly after the artist passed away in 2012, Ateneu Barcelonès organized and filmed a series of lectures, *En record d'Antoni Tàpies*.[75] The act included nearly a dozen different speakers (including artists and politicians, among others), who presented ideas about Tàpies, his art, and his legacy.

On February 4, 2016 I interviewed the artist's son, Toni Tàpies, in Barcelona.[76] I also spoke with the current Director of MNAC, Pepe Serra, and politician Joan Guitart.[77] Before becoming director of MNAC in 2011, Serra had worked: in MACBA's curatorial department, for Fundació La Caixa, in the Generalitat's

Departament de Cultura, and as director of Barcelona's Museu Picasso. Guitart worked in politics from 1978 to 1996. In the Generalitat, he led the department of education from 1980–1988 and the department of culture from 1988–1996. He went on to lead MNAC's board of trustees from 1996–2004, while simultaneously serving as the Vice President of the Fundació Mútua General de Catalunya, a medical insurance company. The conversations I had with Toni Tàpies, Pepe Serra, and Joan Guitart have been vital to this investigation.

Finally, the Biblioteca Nacional and the library at the Reina Sofía in Madrid have been excellent spaces to consult research material. Combining information from several archives and libraries ranging from various disciplines has allowed for a comprehensive analysis concerning Tàpies's work and its social functions.

Still, I was unsuccessful in finding adequate answers to a handful of questions. Most of these questions concern public works of art, contracts, commissions, and financial information. For example, the Arxiu Fotogràfic de Barcelona has a photograph of Tàpies signing an agreement with the Generalitat to create a large-scale work of art in 1989, but I have not been able to find any information concerning the conditions of that contract. Another unanswered question has to do with a proposal on behalf of the Ayuntamiento de Madrid for Tàpies to create a mural for the Madrid-Barajas airport. The artist refused to make the mural, although I have not found a single source that contains more specific details about the project. These types of questions are important for two major reasons: because finding answers will enable a greater understanding of the intersections between art and politics in Spain, and because they involve information about public spending, which ought to be available to the public.

An article from *The New York Times* that discusses new sculptures in Barcelona, as symbols of 'civic pride' provides a hint of insight as to why some of my questions remain unanswered.[78] In 1990, Edward Schumacher claimed in 'Sculptures Are Changing the Look of Barcelona' that the city's public art 'program still has no budget and no formal screening commission [...] The money, taken from different city budgets as needed, is often said to come from what city officials call the 'disaster budget' — a fund to undo what Franco did to the city'.[79] If this was the case, it would explain why some of the contracts and financial information that I am interested in has proved impossible to find. However, there were, at some point, documents concerning Tàpies and the regional and local governments, which I believe still exist somewhere.

Ideally, this book would be accompanied by a number of images of Tàpies's artworks but copyright permission to include them was ultimately withdrawn. The artist's Estate felt strongly that his works should not be reproduced in a volume that did not devote greater space to a history of the Franco regime's suppression of Catalan culture, and to a wider analysis of the resistance of Catalan institutions to Spanish nationalism, past and present. This is not that book. The visual material in question was accordingly removed from the page proofs. However, Tàpies was a highly visible artist and the reader may like to turn to Google from time to time.

I.6. Framework

The Visualization of a Nation: Tàpies and Catalonia is organized chronologically. The first and second chapters cover the early stylistic development of the artist in the 1950s, his mid-career presence in Catalan society as a reputable living artist, and art he created in the 1970s and 1980s with respect to the transition to democracy in Spain (1975–1978).

Before reading Tàpies's visual language, I have found it useful to look back to previous generations of artists working in Catalonia. In the early twentieth century, figures such as Joaquim Sunyer and Joaquín Torres-García established an aesthetic in Catalonia that Miró and Tàpies ultimately sought to reinvent. Furthermore, both did so while engaging with a greater community, the art world, and pushing painting to previously unthinkable frontiers.

There is a tremendous history of painting linked to the Catalan landscape and its inhabitants. Landscape painting worked in tandem with nationalist groups in order to glorify and solidify a cohesive visual representation of the national territory during the nineteenth and twentieth centuries. Ángel Duarte analysed the changing nature of the Catalan landscape after the fall of the Second Spanish Republic in literature for youth education.[80] What once aggrandized the lands of the Catalan people quickly transformed to fit the agenda of the early Franco regime: Spain is part of the historic Mediterranean cradle of civilization and Catalonia is a region within 'immortal Spain'.[81] Works by Joaquim Sunyer and Joaquín Torres-García that include picturesque scenes in the Catalan landscape were established norms that both Miró and Tàpies were working against, effectively disturbing the conventions of art that the *noucentistas* sought to perpetuate well into the twentieth century.[82]

Before Miró's death in 1983, Tàpies had already established himself as the new referential artist in Catalonia. In addition to his growing international status as a European informalist, this phase in Tàpies's career is particularly rich. While he had already found his token style during the 1950s, the artist continued to work consistently within the same framework despite the changing political environment after the death of Francisco Franco in 1975. Chapters 1 and 2 discuss why the artist chose not to evolve his style and how his images project particular political ideologies.

These first chapters primarily focus on the formal characteristics of Tàpies's work, their relation to his personal beliefs concerning society, and his acceptance within Catalonia as a contemporary artist. In 1983 the Ajuntament de Barcelona commissioned the painter to create a three-dimensional monument to honour the life and works of Picasso. Public artworks like this one helped to establish Tàpies's stature in Spain. These sections discuss the importance of the 1984 establishment of the Fundació Antoni Tàpies in the context of art history as well as the composition of the cosmopolitan city of Barcelona. The examination of style, time, and social stimuli in Chapter 1 'Unchanging in an Era of Change' and Chapter 2 'An Icon in the Making' establishes a base for a more specifically political analysis throughout the remainder of the book.

Chapter 3 'A New Foundation and an Old Sock' and Chapter 4 'The Visualization of a Catalan Nation' deal with the relationship between the artist and public institutions. Chapter 3 opens with a discussion of an enormous mural *Les quatre cròniques* (1990), which references Catalan manuscripts written between the late thirteenth and fourteenth centuries. This work is housed in Barcelona's Palau de la Generalitat, the seat of the Catalan government, and often appears in the media behind politicians meeting at a large, round table in front of the painting. Both chapters explore the Catalan government's promotion of the artist both financially and institutionally, concluding with an analysis of Tàpies's cover design for the 2006 Statute of Autonomy, which defines Catalonia as a nation in the preamble. Tàpies's *Les quatre cròniques* and his 2006 cover design are visually vague yet tied to contemporary Catalan politics. Chapters 3 and 4 will examine how the artist's work relates to nationalist narratives concerning the past and future of Catalonia and how different government bodies have looked to the artist in order to promote particular ideas via the visual arts.

Chapter 5 'The Context of Artistic Content' and Chapter 6 'Art as a Nationalizing Tool' discuss twenty-first century exhibition practices including Tàpies's work in and beyond Catalonia. Over the past two decades, the political environment in Catalonia has shifted in a manner that would have seemed rather unimaginable during the final years of the twentieth century. As many Catalan nationalists have been demonstrating a desire to separate from Spain, pressure has been placed on public figures and institutions to take sides. Critically examining the exhibition practices of MNAC, in comparison to other major museums, is essential in order to demonstrate how context affects the reception of art in society. The incessant assault of mass media and advertisement that has dominated twenty-first century North American and European cultures greatly impacts how beholders conceptualize works of art. Looking at the words '*Visca Catalunya*' [Long live Catalonia] scratched on an enormous wood panel in a 2014 exhibition in Bilbao suggests a meaning that is quite different from what that same panel would have signified in Barcelona during the 1970s (*L'esperit català*, 1971). Time and space are equally important in these chapters, as I demonstrate how each affects the ideas that art and exhibitions generate, perpetuate, change, or confirm (*L'esperit català*, 1971).

Chapters 5 and 6 highlight political positioning regarding the presentation of art. They characterize the rather tangled web of politics that engulfs the final years of Tàpies's career and the first post-mortem exhibitions of his works. Both identity and feeling of national belonging are relevant issues in the analysis of public art exhibitions. The original contexts of artworks are simply impossible to recreate, therefore curators work to project meaning concerning numerous already decontextualized objects. For viewers, time is compressed, as they move freely between works that, in the case of some retrospective shows, span several decades. Experiencing art in this manner, along with texts concerning the theme and selected groups within the space, conveys ideas about the value of art, artistic identity, national pride, and personal taste. In a museum setting all spectators are able to openly criticize artworks, but how often do they consider how culture affects their experience or how the organization that created the exhibition plays a role in structuring knowledge? Art can contribute to what Sebastian Balfour and

Alejandro Quiroga defined as 'new layers of identity',[83] that ultimately transform and replace previous, less dynamic individual and social conceptions of the self. These chapters are supported by Stuart Hall's definition of ideology as 'mental frameworks — the languages, categories, imagery of thought, and the systems of representation — which different classes and social groups deploy in order to make sense of, define, figure out and render intelligible the way society works'[84] and how art and institutions relate to the tensions that exist between ideas about: individual and community, private and public, traditional and novel, and national and global.

The final chapter revisits the initial research questions and hypotheses, offering both specific and general conclusions. Furthermore, it provides a theory for future studies relating to the interconnectedness between the visual arts and national ideologies and identities. The scheme, in the case of Tàpies, is cyclical, reinforcing a visual language concerning his own preoccupations. His works of art, in addition to the public commissions and exhibitions that he was involved with, are products of particular social and political circumstances. This is no different from any other artist, in that the conditions under which an artist is born are inescapable. Through the public display of Tàpies's art, he built a visual language distinct from his contemporaries. He repeated that language throughout the course of his life, despite great sociopolitical changes. The institutional support that Tàpies received strengthened his repertoire as an innovative and internationally recognized artist and contributed to the value, both monetary and ideological, of the artist's oeuvre. The vast majority of his artworks, because of their style, are contingent upon the particular historical context of Tàpies's early career. However, the nature of their relationship to politics is reciprocal. They are not a mere effect or reflection of the time and place of their creation, but an active part of an endlessly evolving visual language. Their meanings are purposely unfixed yet undoubtedly political.

I have created a general theory of this concept: art is always political; its exhibition and/or public patronage is also political and facilitates the construction of a visual language made accessible to different audiences; that language is part of how individuals (including artists) understand their relationship to society; the 'meaning' of the language is never static nor fixed and is dependent on an individual's personal experiences; the language is then susceptible to reconstruction, transformation, modification, or replication. Politics are embedded throughout this model, as they are inseparable from the act of making, commissioning, and showing works of art. Similarly, art affects political ideas concerning how society functions and what concepts people consider to be 'normal'. The relationship between art and politics is bilateral, as this book demonstrates. It is my hope that *The Visualization of a Nation: Tàpies and Catalonia* starts a new chapter of academic work concerning the political nature of the artist's works because, as Lubar stated over two decades ago, Antoni Tàpies deserves far more.

Notes to the Introduction

1. Umut Ozkirimli, *Contemporary Debates On Nationalism: A Critical Engagement* (New York: Palgrave Macmillan, 2005), p. 205.

2. Jordi Pujol, *Discurso en la sede la UNESCO en París, con motivo de la exposición Catalunya Avui* (23 March 1981), pp. 115–17.
3. Katherine Jentleson, 'Antoni Tàpies: An Artist's Odyssey in the Age of Franco', *Artinfo*, 2 July 2009.
4. 'Artur Mas: "Tàpies ha sido el artista más radicalmente catalán en su pensamiento, su expresión y sus referentes"', *El Periódico*, 6 February 2012, accessed 10 January 2016, http://www.elperiodico.com/es/noticias/ocio-y-cultura/artur-mas-sido-artista-mas-radicalmente-catalan-pensamiento-expresion-sus-referentes-1393521. All translations from Catalan or Spanish texts are my own unless otherwise noted.
5. Murray Edelman, *From Art to Politics: How Artistic Creations Shape Political Conceptions* (Chicago: The University of Chicago Press, 1995), p. 143.
6. Edelman, *From Art to Politics*, p. 144.
7. Montserrat Guibernau, 'Nationalism and Intellectuals in Nations without States: the Catalan Case', *Working Papers 222* (Barcelona: Institut de Ciències Polítiques i Socials, 2003), p. 25.
8. Borja de Riquer, *Identitats contemporànies: Catalunya i Espanya* (Vic: Eumo, 2000), p. 219.
9. Carme Molinero and Pere Ysàs, *La cuestión catalana: Cataluña en la transición española* (Barcelona: Crítica, 2014), p.239.
10. Albert Balcells, *Catalan Nationalism* (New York: St. Martin's Press, 1996); Sebastian Balfour and Alejandro Quiroga, *The Reinvention of Spain* (Oxford: Oxford University Press, 2007); Daniel Conversi, *The Basques, the Catalans and Spain: Alternative Routes to Nationalist Mobilisation* (Reno and Las Vegas: University of Nevada Press, 1997); Kathryn Crameri, *Goodbye Spain?: The Question of Independence for Catalonia* (East Sussex, England: Sussex Academic Press, 2014); Andrew Dowling, *Catalonia Since the Spanish Civil War: Reconstructing the Nation* (Portland, OR: Sussex Academic Press, 2013); Montserrat Guibernau, *Catalan Nationalism: Francoism, Transition and Democracy* (London: Routledge, 2004); Clare Mar-Molinero and Angel Smith, eds, *Nationalism and the Nation in the Iberian Peninsula: Competing and Conflicting Identities* (Oxford: Berg, 1996); Kenneth McRoberts, *Catalonia: Nation Building Without a State* (Oxford: Oxford University Press, 2001); Molinero and Ysàs, *La cuestión catalana*; Josep Miquel Sobrer, *Catalonia: A Self-Portrait* (Bloomington: Indiana University Press, 1992); and Riquer, *Identitats contemporànies*.
11. Alejandro Quiroga, 'The Three Spheres. A Theoretical Model of Mass Nationalization: The Case of Spain', *Nations and Nationalism* 20:4 (2014), 693.
12. Ludger Mees, 'Emociones en política: Conceptos, debates y perspectivas analíticas', *Emoción e identidad nacional: Cataluña y el País Vasco en perspectiva comparada*, Géraldine Galeote, Maria Llombart Huesca, and Maitane Ostolaza, eds, (Paris: Édicions Hispaniques, 2015), pp. 25–45 (p. 40). See Anthony D. Smith, *Chosen Peoples: Sacred Sources of National Identity* (Oxford: Oxford University Press, 2003).
13. Alejandro Quiroga and Fernando Molina, 'National Deadlock. Hot Nationalism, Dual Identities and Catalan Independence (2008–2019)', *Genealogy*, 4.15 (2020): 1–18 (p. 2).
14. Robert Lubar, 'Joan Miró before "The Farm," 1915–1922: Catalan Nationalism and the Avant-garde' (unpublished doctoral dissertation, New York University, 1988) and 'Miró's Linguistic Nationalism', *Cent Anys de Miró, Mompou i Foix* (Barcelona: Universitat de Barcelona, 1994).
15. Lubar, 'Joan Miró before "The Farm"', p. xvii.
16. Rosalind Krauss and Margit Rowell, *Joan Miró: The Magnetic Fields* (New York: Solomon R. Guggenheim Museum, 1972), p. 84.
17. Robin Greeley, 'Nationalism, Civil War and Painting: Joan Miró and Catalanisme in the 1930s' (Paper presented at the University of Michigan, 1996), 76. Greely also analyses both Spanish and Mexican nationalism via an examination of surrealist paintings during the civil war in Spain and Maria Izquierdo's paintings that affectively provided an alternative to the popular 'big three' muralists in post-revolutionary Mexico. See: *Surrealism and the Spanish Civil War* (New Haven: Yale University Press, 2006) and 'Painting Mexican Identities: Nationalism and Gender in the Work of María Izquierdo', *Oxford Art Journal*, 23.1 (2000), 51–72.
18. Lubar, 'Joan Miró before "The Farm," 1915–1922: Catalan Nationalism and the Avant-garde', p. 116.

19. Barbara Catoir, *Conversations with Antoni Tàpies* (Munich: Prestel-Verlag, 1991), p. 24.
20. Manuel Borja-Villel, 'Antoni Tàpies: Pintura matérica y surrealismo', *Kalías* 2 (October 1989: 82–95), 83–85.
21. Robert Lubar 'Antoni Tàpies Recent Works', (New York: Pace Gallery, 1993) and 'Tàpies: New York', *The Burlington Magazine*, 137.1105 (1995); Jonathan Mayhew 'Valente/Tàpies: The Poetics of Materiality', *Anales de la literatura española contemporánea*, 22.1/1 (1997); George Fishman, 'Antoni Tàpies elevates consciousness and conscience in PAMM exhibit', *Miami Herald*, 13 March 2015, accessed 23 March 2015, http://www.miamiherald.com/entertainment/visual-arts/article14061947.html.
22. Lubar, 'Tàpies. New York', p. 273.
23. Lluís Permanyer, *Tàpies y la nueva cultura* (Barcelona: Polígrafa, 1986); Laurence Rassel, *Tàpies From Within 1945–2011* (Barcelona: Fundació Antoni Tàpies, 2013).
24. 'Antoni Tàpies galardonado con el Príncipe de Asturias de las Artes por su 'riesgo creativo y capacidad innovadora', *ABC* (Sevilla), 19 May 1990, 61, accessed 13 June 2016, http://hemeroteca.abc.es/nav/Navigate.exe/hemeroteca/sevilla/abc.sevilla/1990/05/19/061.html.
25. Manuel Borja-Villel, 'Antoni Tàpies: The "Matter Paintings"' (unpublished doctoral dissertation, City University of New York, 1989). There is a version of the unpublished text in the Fundació Antoni Tàpies Library.
26. 'Matter Painting', *Tate*, accessed 17 May 2015, http://www.tate.org.uk/learn/online-resources/glossary/m/matter-painting.
27. Borja-Villel, 'Antoni Tàpies: Pintura matérica y surrealismo', 84; 91–92.
28. Barbara Ceus, 'Tàpies, más allá de la pintura', *El País*, 18 May 2009.
29. Alexandre Cirici, *Tàpies: Testimoni del silenci* (Barcelona: Polígrafa, 1974); José Corredor-Matheos, *Antoni Tàpies: materia, signo, espíritu* (Barcelona: Polígrafa, 1992); Andreas Franzke, *Tàpies* (Barcelona: Polígrafa, 1992).
30. Manuel Borja-Villel, 'Antoni Tàpies: The "Matter Paintings"' and *Fundació Antoni Tàpies* (Barcelona: Edicions de l'Eixample, 1990); Catoir, *Conversations with Antoni Tàpies*; Alexandre Cirici, *Tàpies: Testimoni del silenci*; José Corredor-Matheos, *Antoni Tàpies: Materia, signo*; Jacques Dupin, *Matiere d'infini* (Tours: Farrago, 2005); Anna Agustí, Nuria Enguita Mayo and Miquel Tàpies, *Tàpies. Obra completa: Volum 8è. 1998–2004* (Barcelona: Polígrafa and Fundació Antoni Tàpies, 2006); Andreas Franzke, *Tàpies*; Sebastian Gasch, *Tàpies* (Madrid: Dirección General de Bellas Artes, 1971); Pere Gimferrer, *Tàpies and the Catalan Spirit* (Barcelona: Polígrafa, 1975); Roland Penrose, *Tàpies* (Barcelona: Polígrafa, 1977); Permanyer, *Tàpies y la nueva cultura*; Rassel, *Tàpies From Within 1945–2011*; Michel Tapié, *Antoni Tàpies* (Milan: Fratelli Fabbri, 1969).
31. Catoir, *Conversations with Antoni Tàpies*.
32. Gimferrer, *Tàpies and the Catalan Spirit*, p. 82.
33. Ibid., 81.
34. Ibid., 36.
35. Ibid., 31.
36. Mees, 'Emociones en política: Conceptos, debates y perspectivas analíticas', p. 37.
37. Jacques Rancière, *The Politics of Aesthetics* (New York: Continuum, 2004), p. 62.
38. Ibid., p. 62.
39. Daniele Conversi, 'Art, Nationalism and War: Political Futurism in Italy (1909–1944)' *Sociology Compass*, 3.1 (2009), 92–117.
40. Ibid., p. 106; pp. 93–94.
41. Ibid., p. 92.
42. Jentleson, 'Antoni Tàpies'.
43. David McCarthy, *American Artists Against War (1935–2010)* (Oakland: University of California Press Books, 2015).
44. Ibid., p. 16.
45. Ibid., p. 16.
46. Ibid., p. 16.
47. Interview with Joan Guitart, 12 July 2016.
48. Stefan Berger, Linas Eriksonas and Andrew Mycock, eds, *Narrating the Nation: Representations in History, Media and the Arts* (New York: Berghahn Books, 2008), p. 9.

49. Berger et al., *Narrating the Nation*, p. 4.
50. Benedict Anderson, *Imagined Communities: Reflections on the Origin and Spread of Nationalism* (London: Verso, 1983), p. 5–7.
51. Ibid., p. 6–7.
52. For alternative, contested definitions of nationalism see: Ozkirimli, *Contemporary Debates On Nationalism*, p. 15.
53. E. J. Hobsbawm, *Nations and Nationalism Since 1780: Programme, Myth, Reality* (Cambridge: Cambridge University Press, 1992), p. 9–10.
54. Ernest Gellner, *Nations and Nationalism*, (Oxford: Blackwell, 2006).
55. Michael Billig, *Banal Nationalism*, (London: Sage, 1995), p. 6.
56. Ibid., p. 6.
57. Tim Edensor, *National Identity, Popular Culture and Everyday Life* (New York: Berg, 2002), p. 140.
58. Mees, 'Emociones en política: Conceptos, debates y perspectivas analíticas', p. 36.
59. Quiroga, 'The Three Spheres', p. 693.
60. Berger et al., *Narrating the Nation*, p. 9.
61. Museu Nacional d'Art de Catalunya, *Tàpies: From Within*, accessed 21 July 2014, http://museunacional.cat/en/tapies-within-3.
62. Martine Heredia, *Tàpies, Saura, Millares: L'art informel en Espange* (Paris: Presses Universitarires Vincennes, 2013), p. 8.
63. See Antoni Tàpies, *Complete Writings Volume I. A Personal Memoir: Fragments for an Autobiography* (Barcelona: Fundació Antoni Tàpies, 2009), *Complete Writings Volume II. Collected Essays* (Barcelona: Fundació Antoni Tàpies, 2009), *El tatuaje y el cuerpo: Antoni Tàpies conversaciones con Manuel Borja-Villel* (Barcelona: Rosa Cúbica, 2005); and Catoir, *Conversations with Antoni Tàpies*.
64. Tàpies, in an interview with Barbara Catoir, spoke about why he decided to begin writing about his work: 'the reason why I took up the pen was that I wanted to state my point of view in a Catalan magazine at a time when the entire cultural life of Barcelona was dominated by a single prominent critic, Alexandre Cirici [...] to show young artists and younger people in general who were interested in art that Cirici's pontifications were not the only legitimate options'. Catoir, *Conversations with Antoni Tàpies*, p. 108.
65. James C. Scott, *Domination and the Arts of Resistance: Hidden Transcripts* (New Haven, CT: Yale University Press, 1990).
66. Homi Bhabha, *Nation and Narration* (New York: Routledge, 1990).
67. Tom Nairn, *The Break up of Britain: Crisis and Neo-Nationalism* (London: New Left Books, 1977).
68. Edelman, *From Art to Politics*; Edensor, *National Identity, Popular Culture and Everyday Life*.
69. Sabina Mihelj, *Media Nations: Communicating Belonging and Exclusion in the Modern World* (New York: Palgrave Macmillan, 2011), p. 10.
70. Ferran Archilés, 'Lenguajes de nación. Las "experiencias de nación" y los procesos de nacionalización: propuestas para un debate', *Ayer*, 90.2 (2013), p. 100.
71. Miguel Ángel del Arco Blanco, 'Un paso más allá de la historia cultural: los *cultural studies*', Teresa María Ortega López, ed., *Por una historia global: El debate historiográfico en los últimos tiempos* (Granada: Universidad de Granada, 2007), p. 20.
72. Ibid., 13.
73. *Tàpies*, Gregory Rood, dir., BBC and TVE Catalunya, 1990.
74. *Te de Tàpies*, Carolina Tubau, dir., Televisió de Catalunya, 2009.
75. *En record d'Antoni Tàpies*, Ateneu Barcelonès, 3 March 2012.
76. Interview with Toni Tàpies, 4 February 2016. See Appendix A.
77. Interview with Pepe Serra on 27 June 2016 and Joan Guitart on 12 July 2016.
78. Edward Schumacher, 'Sculptures Are Changing the Look of Barcelona', *The New York Times*, 4 September 1990, accessed 27 August 2016, http://www.nytimes.com/1990/09/04/arts/sculptures-are-changing-the-look-of-barcelona.html.
79. Ibid.
80. Ángel Duarte, 'El catalán en su paisaje: Algunas notas sobre los usos del imaginario del paisaje catalán, y catalanista, en el primer franquismo', *Historia y Política*, 14 (2005), p. 165–90.
81. Duarte, 'El catalán en su paisaje', p. 187.

82. Torres-García reworked the French murals of Puvis de Chavannes in order to decorate the Saló de Sant Jordi in the Palau de la Generalitat de Catalonia. His fresco *Catalunya Eterna* (1912–1916) presents the image of ancient civilization, calling on Greek and Roman architectural and philosophical motifs to project an aura of excellence. However, Torres-García quickly abandoned this new century style, in favour of a more spontaneous, dynamic aesthetic that could depict the curiosities of the sights, sounds, smells, and rhythms of urban Barcelona. Torres-García's break with the *Noucentisme* pictorial agenda coincided with the first 1917 publication of his 'Art-Evolution' in *Un Enemic del Poble*. It is unclear whether this break prompted the essay, or if the essay announced his severance. Another possible stimulus for this stylistic shift could have been the artist's interactions with his compatriot Barradas who moved to Barcelona in 1916. Having spent time in Italy before moving to the Iberian Peninsula, Barradas appropriated stylistic techniques from the futurist work that he saw there. Together, Barradas and Torres-García developed a fusion of Futurist and Cubist approaches to represent the city of Barcelona. They called this new method *Vibrationisme* [Vibrationism].
83. Balfour and Quiroga, *The Reinvention of Spain*, p. 204.
84. Stuart Hall, 'The Question of Cultural Identity', in *Modernity: An Introduction to Modern Societies*, ed. by Stuart Hall (Cambridge, MA: Blackwell, 1996), p. 26.

CHAPTER 1

Unchanging in an Era of Change

> Tàpies's greatest achievement was *la coherencia*, in his works of art as well as his discourse.
>
> JOAN GUITART[1]

This chapter focuses on style and the indirect implications of politics made visible through art. Tàpies infused political ideology and cultural identity into his art before, during, and after the transition to democracy in Spain. Surprisingly, the formal characteristics of his artwork are tremendously consistent despite major sociopolitical transformations after the death of Franco in 1975. Was he 'successful' in communicating what he desired in visual terms? Not always. However, his characteristically dull and dirty compositions, upon which he established his international artistic career, did position Tàpies among the most admired of Catalan painters during the 1970s and 1980s. 'Unchanging in an Era of Change' explores the stylistic uniformity of the artist. The first section outlines the artist's early career and how he developed a groundbreaking style that stemmed from experimentations with Surrealism and the iconography of fellow Catalan artist, Joan Miró. The second section compares artworks created during the final five years of the Franco dictatorship with others made during and after the transition. The objective is to present an in-depth analysis of Tàpies's style using a holistic perspective in order to explain why his art looks the way that it does and how personal and sociopolitical circumstances shaped Tàpies's early career.

1.1. From Surrealism to Informalism (1946–1956)

In order to assess Tàpies's style during the height of his career as a visual artist in the 1970s and 1980s, it is useful to first consider some of his early works. Before delving into some of the most productive years of his life, looking at a few of his first compositions will establish a foundation for the observation of art created during an era of great political change in Spain. This section highlights a handful of drawings and paintings that Tàpies created in the early stages of his career and serves to help situate the main concerns of this chapter, style, and artworks produced during the 1970s and 1980s.

There is a great distinction between Tàpies's earliest works and what art historians refer to as his 'Matter Paintings'[2] of the 1950s. In his doctoral thesis, Manuel Borja-

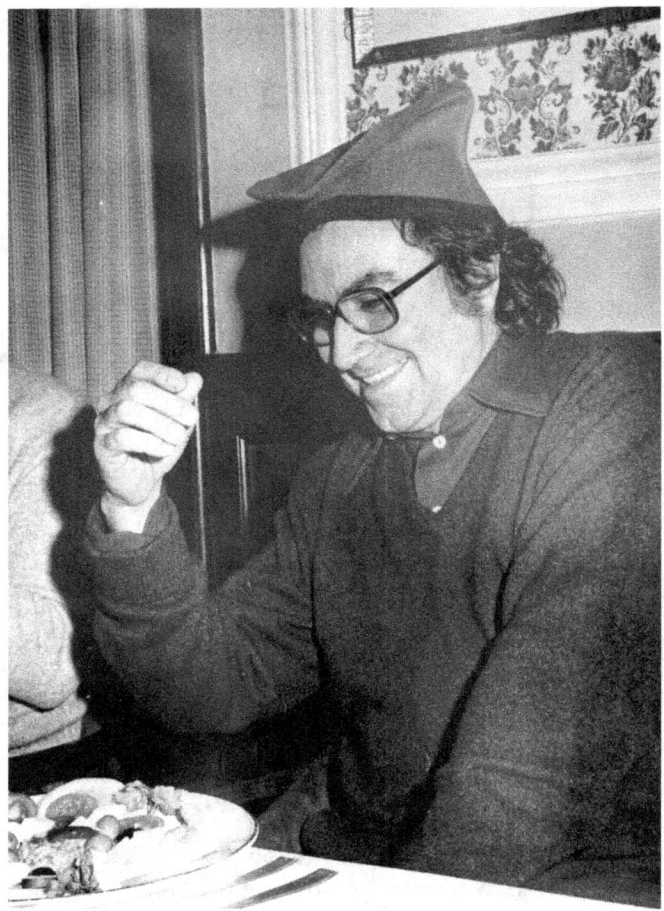

Fig. 1.1. Photograph of Antoni Tàpies wearing a *barretina*, *Diario de Barcelona* 14 March 1976, Arxiu Fotográphic de Barcelona

Villel discussed the rupture between Tàpies's 'surrealist' compositions made from 1946 to 1953 and the origins of his trademark style from 1953 to 1956. At the beginning of his artistic career, Tàpies formed part of a group publishing an avant-garde magazine Dau al Set [Seventh Side of the Die], composed of the philosopher Arnau Puig, the poet Joan Brossa, and a number of other visual and musical artists, founded in 1948 in Barcelona. Tàpies's involvement in this group certainly shaped some of his first artistic creations, not unlike Miró's relationship with avant-garde circles before the Spanish Civil War. This is most evident in his works before 1954, as they often demonstrated affinity with surrealist and dadaist art. For example, *Els solcs* depicts a head in profile with two outstretched arms; one is holding wheat and the other is clutching a sickle to cut it. A red blob connected to the top of the head is a stylized *barretina*. The wonky figure is practically floating in a flat, unrealistic landscape made from shapes in shades of gold and yellow. Four red stripes cut through the bottom of the canvas, simultaneously signifying the rows of crops in a tilled field and the stripes of the Catalan flag. This painting has little to do with Tàpies's mature works. It is an example of his early attraction to Surrealism, a style in which he quickly abandoned.

One of the reasons that Tàpies moved away from surrealist compositions was his friendship with Brossa, one of the founders of Dau al Set. The two men often exchanged ideas, some of which are preserved as written correspondences. During the early 1950s Brossa and Tàpies wrote numerous letters and notes discussing artistic exhibitions, gallery tendencies, and future plans. One particularly intriguing postcard that Tàpies wrote on Christmas Day in 1950 has an image of Joan Miró's 1947 *L'oiseau comète et l'ombrelle fleurie*.[3] On the back side of the card, he wished Brossa happy holidays and explained that he had written to him ten days ago, but the mail was returned to him. The most interesting component of this card is the artist's signature. Tàpies replaced the first letter of his last name 'T' with a pair of perpendicular lines intersecting to create four equal quadrants, '+'.[4]

This sign, which Tàpies prolifically replicated in later works, is prominent in his newspaper collage *Creu de paper de diari* (1946–1947) and his painted self-portrait (1950). Catoir, speaking about the collage, claimed that this form 'takes on an ambivalent symbolic significance', yet she referenced the ancient art of orientation and the four points of the compass.[5] The crossed lines of *Creu de paper de diari*, in Borja-Villel's opinion, symbolized the fusion of the material and spiritual world, the physical realm represented in the form of a horizontal line and the ideological (or spiritual) via the vertical line.[6] Tàpies was rather elusive when speaking about iconography in his own work. He discussed his early affinity for working in an 'automatic, unconscious way'.[7] At the same time, he has said that when he used a certain symbol, it was because it gave him pleasure.[8] Art historians have verbalized various interpretations of the '+' symbol in Tàpies's work. Some have seen it as a self-referential mark, like a signature, referring to the first letter of Tàpies or Teresa, his wife; others have attributed to it a meaning that deals with the convergence of spiritual and physical domains.[9] I argue that those two crossed lines are a reference to Miró and a pair of paintings that he made many years earlier, while working in Paris.

In 1925 Miró worked on a series of paintings that demonstrate his commitment to experimentation in the process of art making. These images titled *Cap de pagès català* are paired down to a handful of signifying essentials. In the first, the *barretina* is connected only through a thin black line to the figure's beard, shown as a triangular series of squiggly lines symmetrically centred on the canvas. Rosalind Krauss characterized the round, beady eyes as 'radiating lines of vision' because of the various vectors that converge at their cores.[10] Krauss also pointed out that these eyes are unequal in size, reading the painting as a 'visual pun' that the artist created to the effect of an 'imperceptible recession in space'.[11] This is characteristic of Miró's body of work at this time, as he was toying with different modes of vision with a number of different canvases. For example, the second painting also works to disrupt any normative sense of visual space and depth through the mark

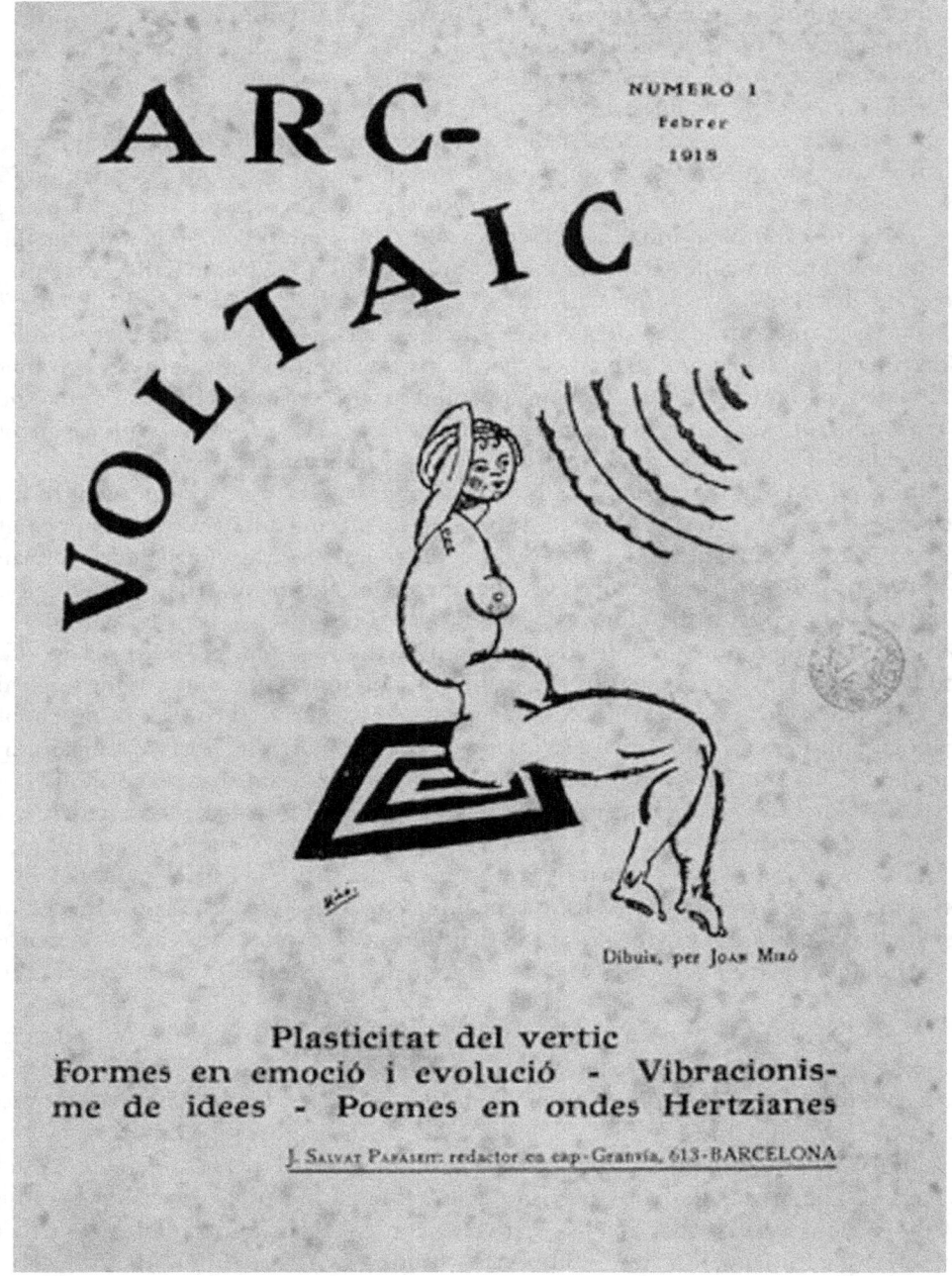

Fig. 1.2. Joan Miró, cover illustration of *Arc-Voltaic*, February 1918, Barcelona

of the horizon line that doubles as an indicator of the peasant's face. Robin Greeley convincingly argued that these images are about Miró's explorations within the act of picture making, 'the figure becomes the site of pictorial experiments as to how insubstantial a painted mark can be before it collapses under the significatory weight placed on it'.[12] Both *Cap de pagès català* paintings open and close the depth of the canvas, depending on how the viewer reads the horizontal axis. At one point it signifies the infiniteness aspect of the horizon, but the same mark simultaneously grounds the floating peasant's head. These canvases are intentionally ambiguous, provoking questions concerning their content and the processes of their creation.

It was in Paris where Miró found a style that simultaneously worked against the conservative formalism of the *noucentistas* and illustrated his sense of Catalan identity.[13] The forms of these 'pictorial experiments' from 1925 are radically different from Miró's illustrated works completed in Barcelona before he moved to Paris. Spending time abroad most likely changed his own conception of himself, his identification as a Catalan and as a Spaniard naturally would have become more central to his being once experiencing life amidst 'others' in Paris. Greeley distinguished an important transition point in the body of Miró's work that cuts between his works from Barcelona, for example the cover of *Arc-Voltaic* (1918, figure 1.2), and these paintings he made in France that flirt with abstraction. She summarized Robert Lubar's argument — that the artist's early works demonstrate Miró's search for an appropriate visual language to convey a contemporary Catalan 'essence' — in order to show that Miró reversed the relationship between subject and object a few years after he left Barcelona. 'In the post-1923 paintings, the terms of Lubar's claim get inverted. What might early on be described as Miró's use of representation in the service of building a modern Catalan national identity, become [sic] nationalism in the service of representation'.[14] Miró recognized this battlefield as an unfixed, transformative space that ought to be addressed in equally dynamic ways. In 1918, this took the form of a female nude as a means of attack against *noucentisme* aesthetics. In 1925, his subject matter became secondary to the modes of representation, as Greeley argued.[15] After arriving in Paris, Miró no longer saw it as his primary task to combat *noucentisme* ideology. Instead, he confronted the act of painting itself, the primacy of the material, and the representational status of the sign. He pinned the face of the Catalan peasant to this project.

Miró's objectives changed from confronting a dominant ideology to facing the medium in which he was working, which demonstrated his drive to discover an appropriate way to visually communicate his ideas. This artist's commitment to contemporaneity did not cease in 1925. As Greeley has argued in *Surrealism and the Spanish Civil War*, the 1930s presented a new challenge for Miró to face through painting. She showed that he was ultimately unable to find a singular style 'through which to address the cataclysm enveloping in his country [and this] suggests his ambivalence as to how to think visually about his own identity as a Catalan'.[16] During the civil war in Spain, Miró worked and reworked his compositions, but he was simply unsuccessful in creating an image that ignited organized political action. His struggles speak to the importance that he placed on plasticity and on contemporaneity in terms of his artistic style and its relationship to the horrors of war taking place in his homeland. His contribution as a working artist was the visualization of his personal beliefs, accessible to an international audience via the Parisian art world. The *Cap de pagès català* paintings announce Miró's impulse to internationalize himself and his art. Instead of taking on a rather simple problem concerning the direction of contemporary art in Barcelona, his Catalan head canvases tackled the methods of painting itself.

Tàpies's recycling of the two crossed lines, as seen in Miró's *Cap de pagès català* paintings, function symbolically in multiple ways. The lines work as a signature identifying its maker, due to their ubiquitous use in other works. They also work to align Tàpies with Miró based on an ideological, as opposed to a purely visual, level. In 1920 Miró wrote a letter to his friend, also a Catalan painter, Enric Cristòfor Ricart that clarifies his mentality towards modernity and national identity:

> I do not know what it is that makes people who lose contact with the world's brain fall into a slumber and become mummies. No painter in Catalonia has arrived at maturity.... You have to be an International Catalan; a homespun Catalan is not, and never will be, worth anything in the world.[17]

Miró's opinions were clear and direct. National culture is worthless if it exists in a vacuum. If the vision of a flourishing Catalan future is solely introspective, then it will remain stagnant and underdeveloped. Catalan leaders must direct their attention to the cultivation of their civilization without losing sight of the increasingly globalized society developing around them. For Miró, this meant approaching painting with an experimental and progressive attitude. In Barcelona, it meant exhibiting Catalan culture as vital and valuable beyond its territorial boundaries.

Interestingly, Miró's ideas about art and its role in society, found in a letter from 1920, are quite close to those of Tàpies half a century later. Miró's thoughts about art are echoed in Tàpies's 1971 essay 'Avant-Garde and the Catalan Spirit'. He wrote that a great artist

> with an ardent sense of what is ours and of the respect due to it, wants to recover and seek to perpetuate that ancestral song that invites the whole world to make the Catalan spirit its own, to become 'Catalanist'. Because for him this means, simply, keeping eternally alive that essential drive, in both love and war, in favor of humanism, democracy and freedom[18]

In accord with the ideas of Miró, Tàpies set out to reinvent what these thoughts might look like. Just as Miró did before him, Tàpies rejected the soft, balanced, harmonious style of the *noucentistas*. In favour of an anti-aesthetic, he found the beautiful side of the ugly, the mundane, and the unremarkable. What Tàpies reused from Miró, albeit taking on an entirely different appearance, was a simple pair of crossed lines. Lines which, as we have seen, signify much more than the first letter of the artist's first name. They signify the processes of visual representation and the artist's ability to create and manipulate ideas in space.

In an undated letter, Brossa wrote to Tàpies stating that he had finally superseded his surrealist phase and that his poetry was moving in a new direction

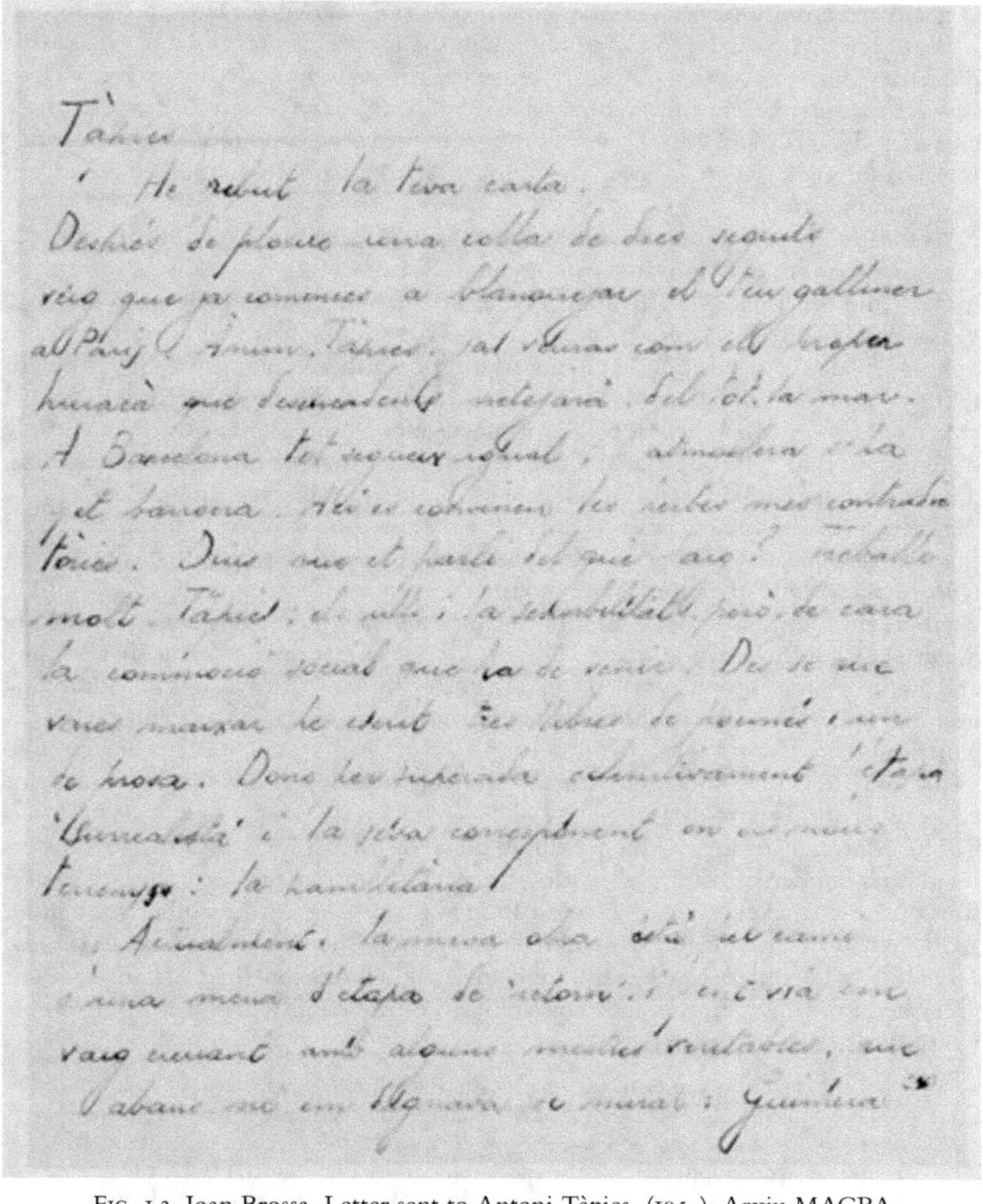

Fig. 1.3. Joan Brossa, Letter sent to Antoni Tàpies, (195–), Arxiu MACBA

(figure 1.3).[19] The letter is probably from 1950 or 1951, considering the content and the quantity of their written correspondences during these years. Furthermore, Tàpies also abandoned the surrealist style shortly after, between 1953 and 1954. Brossa's comments likely had much to do with that decision. In the undated letter, the poet also thanked Tàpies 'for the Mirós', stating that seeing them made an impact on his heart.[20] This could refer to actual artworks that Tàpies gave to Brossa as a gift or, more likely, photographic reproductions of Miró's latest art shown in Paris, as both Miró and Tàpies were living in the French capital at the time. Finally, the letter concluded with a powerful reminder. Brossa wrote, 'do not forget, Tàpies, that art is a spiritual means of contact between people'.[21] The letters between these two men demonstrate several points: both were concerned about one another's style (visual and poetic), both admired the work of Miró, and both considered art a form of communication.

Ironically, Tàpies founded what art historians would later call Informalism via surrealist experimentation and iconography. Surmounting Surrealism, for Brossa in 1951 and for Tàpies shortly after, established new frontiers for both literary and visual culture in Catalonia. In the case of Tàpies, during his transition between quasi-surrealist compositions and his Matter Paintings, colour was swapped for texture. During this change, Tàpies ditched one of the most important formal characteristics of Miró's work, bright primary colours, in order to obtain an entirely different aesthetic through an incongruous palette and through surface texture. Tàpies later explained in an interview with Catoir that he was 'allergic' to colour, that it is overused in advertising, and that he wanted to achieve a chromatic effect that exists 'beneath the superficial appearance of reality, the colour of dream and fantasy, the colour of visions, the colour of emptiness, the colour of space'.[22] One example that demonstrates this desire is *Terra i pintura* (1956). It is a cluster of earthly material affixed to a wood panel. The colour is a mixture between concrete grey and light caramel brown with no focal centre. Instead of toying with automatic gestures and the surrealist notion that the unconscious is the principal element generating creation, Tàpies avoided bright colours in search for a more organic visual experience, combined with an alluring texture, as his main vehicle for expression in this work.

The Matter Paintings, which exhibit the style that Tàpies decided to stick to for the remainder of his long artistic career, are unmistakably tied to the life and times of their maker. Antoni Tàpies i Puig was born on 13 December 1923 in an apartment on Carrer Canuda in Barcelona. In 1966 he wrote *A Personal Memoir: Fragments for an Autobiography*, although the original version (in Catalan) was not published until 1977. In this autobiographic account he recalled a memory from his youth that is tied to a specific image:

> From the day after the proclamation of the Republic [14 April 1931] I hold the persistent vision of the garden of a villa facing our house with a large object covered with sheets and tied with ropes. They told me that the inhabitants of that house were supporters of the monarchy and had recently placed on their garden fountain the royal coat of arms, which they now hurried to hide under those sheets so the Republican sympathizers wouldn't break and destroy it. I thought those monarchists were members of a sinister sect, and the image of that cabalistic object now bundled like a kind of gigantic package has remained with me as the symbol of something forbidden and wicked.[23]

At the age of seven, it is implausible that Tàpies understood, at the time, the magnitude or complexity of the sociopolitical changes that occurred during his youth. In a single decade he lived through the fall of General Miguel Primo de

Rivera's dictatorship (1923–1930), the termination of the monarchy, the declaration of the Second Spanish Republic and its short-lived democratic government (1931–1939), the break out of a long and bloody civil war and Francisco Franco's subsequent dictatorial rule (1936–1975). Before Tàpies had turned sixteen-years-old, the Republic had fallen to rebel leader Francisco Franco and his military regime, marking the end of the war on 1 April 1939. The young artist's adolescence straddled a devastating national conflict and the early years of what would become a long dictatorship. Both had a great impact on Tàpies's attitude towards politics and his homeland.

In *A Personal Memoir*, he also expressed his contempt for the Franco regime, in addition to the numerous spaces and places crippled due to the persecution of the use of his native language:

> Destruction and death brought on by war, hundreds of thousands of executions, people left to die in prison [...] Even though it was not publicized, we knew that Franco had said that, if necessary, he would order the death of Spain. For us especially that genocide was unleashed not only onto our political rights, but upon all that was Catalan. Our language was totally forbidden in the press, in official acts, on the radio, on advertisements and public signs, even in church. The regime went so far as to forbid Catalan in private correspondence. All our cultural institutions were eliminated, our songs banned, as were our dances, the names of our squares and streets, our schools, our monuments, theater, giving our children Catalan names, our anthem, our flag.[24]

The repercussions of war-torn Barcelona and the repressive subjection that followed is not something that is easy to erase from memory. As Michael Richards argued, the end of the war ushered a period 'darker still than the conflict itself', as violence continued long after the final battle.[25] The new regime's use of repressive force was directed at civilians, who suffered the worst of the violence, while guerrilla fighters sought refuge in rural towns and villages.[26] In 1940s Spain, hunger and poverty were prolific, conditions that were magnified by a post-war economic repression. While Tàpies's family did not experience economic hardship, it is a past that remained engrained in his mind, as seen in his writing and in his art. Through art making, Tàpies dedicated his life to combating what the Franco dictatorship effectively undermined: ideological freedom and alternative cultural and national identities.

Although Franco's official rhetoric propagated a unified, Catholic Spain, his regime employed regional symbols and traditions as a means of promoting internal and external tourism. As Pablo Giori outlined, 'bullfighting, soccer, *la sardana* [a dance], and human towers were used separately by Francoists, the opposition, and Catalan nationalists, depending on the place and time'.[27] The 'classic' *barretina* was even adopted by Madrid's politicians during the end of the dictatorship.[28] This sort of appropriation on behalf of the regime contributed to what Borja de Riquer characterized as a form of government 'riddled with contradictions and contrasts'. Similarly, Xosé Manoel Núñez Seixas discussed this side of the dictatorship, expressing 'Franco's contradictory capacity to promote local and regional identities complementary to the national identity'.[29]

Tàpies recalled that during the first decade of the dictatorship, access to information concerning foreign avant-garde art was limited. 'In Spain there was not a word about content, about motivations, about social function, about the politics of art... Here those questions were carefully concealed [...] The clichés dictated that art had nothing to do with politics, or religion, or philosophy'.[30] Meanwhile in the United States, the artists belonging to the New York School experimented with Abstract Expressionism. The Parisian art scene remained split between Surrealist groups and academic schools. In 1948 the international group CoBrA (titled after the cities of Copenhagen, Brussels, and Amsterdam) formed amongst artists and intellectuals with a desire to critique capitalist societies. The visual language of the group took after the styles of Paul Klee and Joan Miró while characterizing abstraction as aseptic and falsely detached.[31] Less than a decade later CoBrA had dissolved, but the new group Situationist International upheld similar values and strategies to present a biting critique of advanced capitalism and its effect on human relations. Those loyal to the Situationist International saw art and politics as inextricably linked and sought to denunciate consumer culture.[32] While Tàpies was not directly linked to this group of social revolutionaries, his Matter Paintings worked in a similar fashion. They purposefully cantered on mundane, undervalued material, lacking flashy objects and colours associated with 'spectacle' and advertisements.[33]

Even though Tàpies participated in national art exhibitions, such as the Bienales Hispano-Americanas held in the 1950s, exhibiting internationally was fundamental for his career. Tàpies was not part of the group El Paso, formed in 1957 in Madrid with the agenda of re-establishing avant-garde art in Spain, as it had essentially vanished since the onset of the Civil War. Another Spanish group that ran parallel to Tàpies's career, although the two did not share a relationship, was the Grupo de Cuenca. This circle formed around the artist Fernando Zóbel and his establishment of the Museo de Arte Abstracto Español de Cuenca in 1966. During this period, Tàpies was primarily showing in Catalonia and abroad. He would not begin to seriously expand his gallery exhibitions to the rest of Spain until the late 1970s.

In Franco's Spain, art was being used as a tool to project a certain image to an international audience. Contemporary art at the Bienales was shown to other countries as a facade, suggesting that Spain was *not* under a fascist regime and that nontraditional artists were *not* labeled 'degenerates' and persecuted as they were in Nazi Germany.[34] However, art was not seen as a serious means of expression existing beyond the realm of aesthetics. Tàpies wrote an anecdote about Franco's attitude towards avant-garde artists in Spain between 1951 and 1952:[35]

> I have a photograph showing Franco, surrounded by important people, standing in front of one of my paintings at one of the Bienales Hispano-Americanas [the first, in Madrid between October of 1951 and February of 1952]. At the end of the group, half hidden, covering his face to hide from photographers, stands Llorens Artigas. They are all laughing. According to Llorens, someone, perhaps Alberto del Castillo, was telling Franco: 'Your excellency, this is the hall of the revolutionaries'. And it seems Franco joked: 'If this is the way they carry out the revolution...'.[36]

Beginning with the Matter Paintings of the 1950s, Tàpies found a style that allowed him to continue to work in Spain without flaunting his anti-Francoist posture.[37] His art, albeit often discretely, is closely linked to his political beliefs, as this chapter will further elaborate. As Cirici described, Tàpies's participation in the Bienales was 'thanks to a cryptic system of signs in abstract painting, that censorship couldn't touch'.[38] Remarkably, this style long outlived the dictator, who died on 20 November 1975. Tàpies continued to work in this manner because, even after the death of Franco, it was a way to remind beholders of the importance of values such as freedom and humanism, values that had been robbed from countless citizens after the fall of the Second Republic.

1.2. Consistency in an Era of Instability (1970–1987)

By the 1970s, Tàpies had become the new reference of Catalan visual art, replacing the aging artists of the previous generation including Miró and Dalí. Gimferrer wrote in 1975 that 'the work of Antoni Tàpies is now at a beginning of a future that belongs to it'.[39] While the artist began his professional career in the late 1940s and began producing his most recognizable style in the mid 1950s, it took several decades for Tàpies to establish his work in a country suffering the lingering effects of a destructive war and lengthy dictatorship. During and after the transition to democracy, following the death of Franco, Tàpies's style did not change.[40] His art continued to work against the conservative cultural policies of the former regime that sought to suffocate alternative national identities under the guise of national unity.[41] During and after the transition to democracy in Spain, Tàpies continued to reinvent his oeuvre, albeit in his style of the past.

For example, three works that are analogous in terms of style but were created under disparate political circumstances are: *Creu ocre i blanc sobre marró* (1971), *Blanc amb deus creus* (1976), and *Gran pintura amb X i +* (1981). Tàpies created the first at the end of the Franco dictatorship, the same year as the Assemblea de Catalunya met to consolidate a resistance movement that would work towards establishing a democratic Spain. He made the second painting during the transition, one year after the dictator's death. During this year, the government was in a fragile state as the newly appointed Prime Minister Aldolfo Suárez began to set in motion the Law for Political Reform. This legislation was approved by the Francoist Cortes in 1976 and also by popular referendum in 1977, enabling Suárez to work towards establishing a parliamentary democracy in Spain. The third picture dates from three years after the ratification of the 1978 Spanish Constitution. At this time, Catalonia was officially an Autonomous Community and the resilience of Madrid's new democratic government was proved after a failed coup d'état on 23 February 1981. At the age of fifty-five, this became the first national democracy in which Tàpies could participate. However, this major change is *not* reflected in the style of his art.

Creu ocre i blanc sobre marró includes a wonky, white square and cross floating in the bottom third of a dark brown canvas. The large white cross, or '+' symbol, has a second pair of perpendicular lines scratched into the centre, creating a second, darker and equally hasty looking cross. The white square has the initials of Tàpies's three children (Antoni, Clara, and Miquel) scraped over the surface of the paint. Nothing in the canvas is grounded; both the square and large cross exist in an unnatural, indecipherable space. Similarly, *Blanc amb deus creus* consists of a sloppy layer of white paint, partially dripping down towards the bottom of the rectangular base. Four short, thin, black lines radiate from each corner, slicing them around 45 degrees. Equally spaced between these lines at the top, arranged like the title of a book, are two pairs of perpendicular lines. Although Tàpies's self-proclaimed allergy to colour creates a great divide between his art and that of Miró's, these crosses and his play on perspective in this painting is remarkably similar to the elder artist's experimentations like *Cap de pagès català*.[42] Not only did Tàpies appropriate the slender, stark cross-shaped markings of Miró, in *Creu ocre i blanc sobre marró* and *Blanc amb deus creus* he was also toying with the depth of the picture, just like Miró. The sign refuses to allow the viewer to read into the depth of the canvas in the traditional sense. There is no conventional perspective; rather, we are provided with fragments of hovering horizons that pull our eyes from one side to the other like a seesaw. The segments of orthogonal lines pragmatically placed in each corner of *Blanc amb deus creus* create the ghost of a focal point in the centre, where the lines would converge if they were to continue towards infinity. The depth of the canvas is simultaneously never-ending, and flat like the cover of a book, depending on how the viewer imagines those four seemingly unimportant lines.

Beyond Miró, both *Creu ocre i blanc sobre marró* and *Blanc amb deus creus* resonate with Kazimir Malevich's 1918 *Suprematist Composition: White on White*. The colour white, for Malevich, was pared with the idea of infinity, and his theory on art that dealt with 'pure' feelings accessible through non-objective art.[43] *Suprematist Composition* is a sombre yet hopeful canvas, created as the First World War came to an end. Relatedly, *Creu ocre i blanc sobre marró* includes an imperfect, white square like that of Malevich, and *Blanc amb deus creus* is an optimistic image of floating forms in a calm sea of white.

Gran pintura amb X i + also echoes both Miró and Malevich's artworks. Tàpies's canvas is not white but the soft, golden colour is emotive, while the pair of perpendicular lines (Miró's Catalan peasants) are designated to the two upper corners. His continual use of broad colour fields and non-objective forms was resolute before, during, and after the transition to democracy. Objects in the materials world, however, were not always absent from Tàpies's compositions. In fact, he often incorporated everyday, worn, tattered, or dirty items into his creations. Comparing another set of artworks, made under distinct historical conditions in Spain, confirms Tàpies's unwavering stylistic commitment despite the immense changes of the 1970s and 1980s. *Tela i tisores* (1970) displays a pair of scissors affixed in the middle of a light coloured cloth or sheet. The scissors are closed and pointing downward, towards the painted outline of a large foot amidst stray splatters of paint. The weight of the scissors pulls on the material, creating wrinkles stemming from the two upper corners that lead the eyes towards the scissors. Meaning, in this artwork, is unfixed. There is no single interpretation that this work can uphold based purely on visual evidence. However, it does show beholders that the boundaries of art are not limited to the conventional conception of what is beautiful or attractive. It is the antithesis of the seductiveness of an oil painting. Tàpies believed that art ought to instigate thought and reflection. *Tela i tisores* is purposefully ambiguous yet uncannily familiar.

In a later work, Tàpies used an open pair of scissors as a stencil to recreate the axis of a vertical and horizontal line for the poster announcing the 1977 exhibition *ACC 1 Art Català Contemporani: Brossa, Miró, Tàpies* at the Museu de Granolliers. The negative space left when he removed the scissors is the colour of a cardboard box, and since it is significantly lighter than the matte black that surrounds it, the figure (or lack thereof) is pushed to the foreground. A third work that also includes scissors does not depart from his previously established style; *Empremta de tisores* (1987) likewise employs a pair of open scissors, this time angled in the form of an 'X' imprinted in white on a grey background with straight lines radiating from each corner. The lines, formed from scratching through the surface of wet paint, do not converge at a centre point; instead, the top two create a 'V' shape, which is linked with a short, vertical line to an inverted 'V' below. Several nonsensical signs or letters are scratched through a white label at the top, revealing a layer of light orange below. The canvas works on a sentimental as opposed to a symbolic level through its texture, symmetry, and style.

Tàpies struck a balance between non-objective and familiarity throughout his career. What unifies these three works is the aura in which the artist created via style. In a newspaper article titled 'Tàpies para escépticos' [Tàpies for Skeptics], Luis Alemany pointed out that when looking at the artist's work, 'you have to get rid of the analytic gaze, understand that we are before an open field of colliding emotions [...] it is a question of suggestion, not analysis'.[44] Throughout his long career, Tàpies worked to refine this style, a style that does not seek to solve anything yet suggest everything.

The extraordinary thing about Tàpies's work is the stability of his art over time. Separate works that were created under vastly different situations are unified through the sensation that they transmit. While each individual canvas may not yield easily to analysis, the luxury of hindsight allows for an analytical approach to understanding Tàpies's pictures. There is no major stylistic change amongst artworks that he created during the final five years of the Franco regime, the transition, and after the signing of the 1978 Constitution. However, the 1971 Assemblea de Catalunya, ensuing uncertainty after Franco's death, the first democratic elections in 41 years, and the drafting of a new Spanish Magna Carta were all events that could have prompted an alteration of artistic practices.

The Assemblea de Catalunya was formed in opposition to Franco's regime, seeking a new democratic system, amnesty for those arrested during the dictatorship, and an autonomous status for Catalonia, as part of the Spanish State. Approximately three hundred people gathered in Barcelona to celebrate the act composed of members from clandestine political parties, cultural associations, syndicates, and individuals. The group did not seek separation from the State but major political reforms.[45] Tàpies made a painting memorializing the event, *7 de novembre* (1971), which now hangs in the Palau del Parlament de Catalunya. Similar movements against the regime increased in popularity in the early 1970s throughout Spain. Sebastian Balfour explained that 'Barcelona became the capital of the opposition to the dictatorship' during these years.[46] The Partit Socialista Unificat de Catalunya (PSUC) had turned into what Carme Molinero and Pere Ysàs characterized as 'the primary political anti-Francoist formation', although other groups throughout Spain also mobilized in acts of resistance. The Partido Comunista de España (PCE) and Madrid's university student riots held some of the most active initiatives before the dictator's death in November 1975.[47] Activism in the form of student protests also established strongholds in Valencia, Zaragoza, and Bilbao.[48] Finally, labour movements also played a role in the push towards a new political system in Spain.[49]

After Arias Navarro failed to transform the nation into a democracy that would not wholly upset Franco's followers, King Juan Carlos I appointed Aldolfo Suárez as Prime Minister of Spain on 3 July 1976. The following year, Suárez would continue to lead Spain, as the first democratically elected Prime Minister since the Spanish Civil War. He made the decision to legalize the PCE on 9 April 1977, a few months after members of an ultra-right, anti-Communist group killed five lawyers in the centre of Madrid in an act of terror.

In the final days of 1978, Spain held a referendum concerning the adoption of the new Constitution. At the time, more than 91% of voters were in favour of the law that would establish a constitutional monarchy in the Kingdom of Spain. On 18 December 1979, Catalonia and the Basque Country were granted the status of Autonomous Communities. The newly ratified Constitution allowed certain privileges to these regions, along with Galicia, as historical nationalities (*nacionalidades históricas*), which enabled their swift transition to becoming Spain's first three Autonomous Communities. The failure of an attempted military coup in February 1981 in the Congress of Deputies demonstrated the resilience of the nascent government, although numerous scholars have characterized the early years of the new democracy as 'fraudulent' and a perpetuation of Francoism.[50] Nevertheless, King Juan Carlos I made a nationally televised speech in the aftermath of the failed coup, publicizing his support for the strength of the current legal system. Later that year, the creation of further autonomic pacts paved the way for future transfers of power. Spain would go on to create seventeen regional governments corresponding to its autonomous communities that had been outlined during the transition.[51]

Surprisingly, Tàpies did not seem to have a pictorial response to such stimuli, his images remained the same. His works throughout the 1970s and 1980s radiate a resolute energy that is as if the constantly changing nature of the world around him had been suspended or locked in time. His treatment of a pair of crossed lines or a pair of old scissors (that create the same shape when open) has always been the same. He was not preoccupied with things, rather, he was interested in how things are able to trigger sentiments or memories and provoke ideas. The logic behind Tàpies's commitment to his unique aesthetic (or antiaesthetic) style was shared between the realm of politics and that of modern art. Two realms that are *not* antithetical, as I will later elaborate.

In *Domination and the Arts of Resistance* James Scott addressed the dynamics of power relations, public actions and private, or hidden, transcripts. 'Taking a long historical view, one sees that the luxury of relatively safe, open political opposition is both rare and recent'.[52] Forms of disguised resistance are more common, yet not so easy to detect. Scott deemed this type of opposition 'infrapolitics' because it inhabits an intermediary space between the whispered ideas shared amongst friends and the bold performances of public protest or denunciations, for example, the act of spreading rumours, telling folktales, squatting, sabotaging crops, etc. Infrapolitical actions are not direct, outward proclamations; they take the form of veiled and often anonymous resistance in order to protect the agents from potentially violent reactions. If and when subordinate groups seize an opportunity to act publicly, Scott emphasized the importance of the roles that hidden transcripts and disguised resistance play beneath the surface.[53] In other words, while action tends to enjoy the limelight, bold demonstrations against authority are often the culmination of a web of forces that would otherwise remain unnoticed. *Domination and the Arts of Resistance* illustrated the error in solely examining breakthrough moments, 'it is to focus on the visible coastline of politics and miss the continent that lies beyond'.[54] In analysing change or lack thereof, it is imperative to consider the landmass from which the shore has been made.[55]

In considering the work of Tàpies through the lens of Scott, his objectives as an artist and a citizen become sharper. As early as the 1950s, Tàpies began to work in a style that was purposefully ambiguous. He was working within Scott's realm of 'infrapolitics' and his art could be characterized as occupying a space somewhere in-between recognizable protest and secrets shared behind closed doors. His almost entirely abstract canvases from this time are very difficult to apprehend based solely on their physical appearance. Instead of depicting ideas, they show sensations — often sombre, grim sensations. This style stemmed from Tàpies's experiences and his desire to communicate his thoughts visually. Art historian and Universitat Autònoma de Barcelona Professor Maria Lluïsa Borrás stated in *Destino* that his works 'are not the artistic creations that we used to refer to, but an endeavour to communicate'. At the time, Borrás was working as Miró's secretary; she assisted in the early formation of the artist's foundation and later collaborated on an unedited documentary about Tàpies in 1981. She concluded the *Destino* article with an explanation that contemporary culture and art are present, regardless if one sees it or not, and no 'terrestrial power' can change that fact.[56]

For example, in 1974 Tàpies created a series of works in honour of Salvador Puig Antich, an anarchist and active member of the Iberian Liberation Movement who was sentenced to death by the Franco regime after a skirmish with the *Guardia Civil*. Puig Antich was twenty-five years old when he was found guilty of shooting a civil guard without any solid evidence. Despite pleas for clemency on behalf of the Pope and foreign ambassadors, the young man was strangled to death with a garrotte.[57] Although Puig Antich was an anarchist, the PCE used the event, along with the execution of Heinz Chez, as a motive to create propaganda against the regime and others sought to keep Puig Antich's memory alive, converting him into a sort of national martyr.[58]

Without the title *A la memòria de Salvador Puig Antich*, Tàpies's canvas seems to have little to do with this issue. A small, colourful sample of paints is glued above a black sweater neatly folded into a right angle. Several streams of grey paint drip from the sleeve of the upside-down sweater. The neckline is frayed, with a few strands of fabric recalling the method in which Puig Antich was killed. This atypical memorial is about what is missing (the body of the deceased) and its ascension to another, more colourful, realm. The formal characteristics of this example do not point directly to any particular political position. The title is what attaches its meaning: the remembrance of man sentenced to an inhumane death. Without the title, the work is entirely unclear. For this reason, the work fits into Scott's infrapolitical realm; the style of *A la memòria de Salvador Puig Antich* is like a visual version of a code used to subvert those in positions of power.

Another artwork that is both stylistically ambiguous yet anti-Francoist, albeit created after the dictator's death, is *11 de setembre* (1977). Franco had named Prince Juan Carlos I as his successor and after the dictator died, Juan Carlos took on the title King of Spain. The new king, after trying to perpetuate the dictatorial regime for nearly six months, began a process that would transform the Francoist government into a democratic monarchy.[59] During this process, Juan Carlos was cautious not to upset a range of different groups, most importantly the military. After the appointment of a provisional government led by Aldolfo Suárez in 1976, delegates elected in June of the following year would begin to draft the Spanish Constitution that would create a type of federal system. On 11 September 1977 Barcelona hosted the largest demonstration in post-war Europe, to show support for the Statute of Autonomy of Catalonia that would become law two years later.[60]

Tàpies's picture titled after that particular day is blood red, with various forms painted over each other. At the bottom is a small page of a calendar with the date 11 September typed in bold ink. The Catalan holiday (referred to as the *Diada*) dates to the late nineteenth century and has been celebrated in remembrance of the events of 1714, when the Bourbon King Filipe V defeated Barcelona's troops in defence of the Hapsburg dynasty's claim to the throne.[61] Franco had banned the celebration of the holiday and, not surprisingly, the day became even more important for Catalan citizens to acknowledge during and after the transition to democracy. Without the small scrap of paper with the calendar date, the image is an accumulation of layered markings without any dominating focal point. Attaching that little paper at the bottom entirely changes the picture's implication: what would have been an abstract collection of signs turned into a statement concerning the importance of that particular date and year. While the title of Tàpies's image is clear, he did not express what one should do on 11 September or why that day is worth remembering or celebrating. The canvas also lies in Scott's infrapolitical zone because of the tension that exists between the clarity of the title and the opacity of the picture.

A post-transition example of this same style at work, another artwork that can be situated in Scott's infrapolitical realm, is *Efecte de drap* (1980). This mixed media composition is exactly what the title claims, the effect of cloth. The various values of light and dark in this picture are formed from the weight of the fabric, pinned up at the two upper corners. Heavy, black letters are scribbled in a straight line across the bottom, ending with the number eight. Upon first glance the image seems nonsensical, the letters do not seem to spell any particular word and the cloth is an ordinary, banal material. However, considering this work together with the history of the artist's experience in pre-war Barcelona, the image becomes more potent. Tàpies's remembrance of his neighbour's garden fountain with monarchist symbols cloaked in sheets during the Second Republic stuck in his mind as a 'symbol of something forbidden and wicked'.[62] *Efecte de drap* is not about the picture itself; it is about what is *behind* the image, what the material is covering up. While Tàpies's rendition is not quite a tromp l'oeil depiction of fabric, it does invite the curious viewer to touch. This is a trope that artists from Diego Velázquez to Paul Cézanne employed, activating the sense of touch via masterly painted fabrics. *Efecte de drap* is a sensuous image that is politically charged yet ambiguous. It leaves us to wonder both what the cloth feels like and, equally importantly, what it is concealing.

It is possible that this canvas is a metaphor for the transition itself. With a backdrop of the Spanish left's disillusion with the pace of political reforms and the lack of rupture from the Francoist politics of the past, *Efecte de drap* could visualize a parallel process. Tàpies may have wanted to draw attention to the act of covering up, as opposed to eliminating, an object. This would fit into the context of the *desencanto* [disenchantment], a profound pessimism that clashed with the optimism of the *consenso* [consensus] surrounding the creation of the new Spanish Constitution. From 1977 to 1982 many of those who participated in acts of resistance during the early 1970s felt deeply dissatisfied with the processes of the recent political reforms led by political elites.[63] *Efecte de drap* could have provoked viewers in 1981 to think about camouflaging or masking things so that they are not able to be seen.

A la memòria de Salvador Puig Antich, 11 de setembre, and *Efecte de drap* are potent representations that contain political implications, cleverly engaged with avant-garde artistic trends. The first was made in response to Francoist politics the year before the dictator died. The second dealt with a Catalan celebration, which the former regime had banned. Finally, the third has a personal link to Tàpies's childhood memory and hidden symbols that he knew to be dangerous. Despite major political reforms that were made in Spain during the late 1970s, Tàpies continued to create compositions in his style of the past. Just because the dictator had passed away, did not mean that his politics automatically disappeared. Tàpies was not simply against Franco; he was against the dictator's unjust actions and beliefs. By the 1980s, the artist no longer needed to fight against Franco but those who sought to perpetuate Francoism during and after the transition to democracy.[64]

Tàpies created several artworks that are much less ambiguous in terms of ideological and political content. These works include subject matter that is more direct, however they maintain a stylistic similarity with the rest of his art since the mid 1950s. For example, his 1971 *L'esperit català* and 1976 poster for the PSUC both combine words within each picture to signify meaning. The former includes the Catalan word for liberty scratched in the upper portion and below is the phrase long live Catalonia. The image is chaotic with a number of other words etched into the surface that is spattered with bloody handprints. The ladder includes thin black, messy handwriting with a number of unlinked words and phrases such as 'Catalunya = Llibertat' and 'XL anivarsari'. The lower portion of the poster contains the title in small text, *PSUC: per Catalunya, la Democràcia i el Socialisme*. This artwork demonstrates Tàpies's support for the party, which planned to celebrate its fortieth anniversary in 1976, but both the Spanish and French governments prohibited the celebration. As a response, 160 intellectuals and artists publicly displayed their respect for the Catalan communists who had been imprisoned, forced into exile, or given their lives during and after the Civil War. It was both a celebration of PSUC's anniversary and a demonstration signalling that there would not be a democratic government in Catalonia or Spain without the political participation of a future, legal, communist party. Tàpies was one of the artists that signed his name in support of the PSUC on this day.[65] Four years later, PSUC became the third leading power in the first elections of the Catalan Parliament since the end of the Civil War. *L'esperit català* and the poster use the colours of the Catalan flag; they both have a golden yellow background with four red, vertical stripes signalling the *senyera*. The use of the word liberty in each work is significant in its reference to contemporaneous events. In 1971 the slogan 'liberty, amnesty, and a statue of autonomy' was developed in the Assemblea de Catalunya. In 1976 the phrase was used in demonstrations as a way of communicating citizens' desires for the establishment of a new, democratic government in Spain. However, the party's allure for Tàpies was not limited strictly to the party's political objectives. Tàpies shared the PSUC's idea that Catalonia was a community 'culturally and politically differentiated [from Spain] since the Middle Ages'.[66]

Tàpies was a Catalan nationalist and desperately wanted democracy in Spain. He often communicated this via his works of art. Additional examples that include unmasked political content include posters Tàpies made for: an event celebrating popular Catalan songs, the denunciation of capital punishment in Spain, the Liberty March in 1976, and the Congress of Catalan Culture of 1977. The primary objective of the previous year's Congress of Catalan Culture was to establish an initiative for linguistic and cultural 'normality', which participants felt 'was essential to the full recovery of Catalonia's national identity'.[67] Through his already established style, and the inclusion of punctuated words and phrases, Tàpies made concrete expressions of his thoughts. At times, these images appear difficult to comprehend, while other examples were more straightforward.

On 4 February 2016 I interviewed the artist's son Toni Tàpies in his gallery in Barcelona. I asked about his father's relationship with the PSUC, because Tàpies had written in 1976 that it is not necessary to enter or exit any political party if you carry it with you.[68] Toni replied:

> My father was never a militant of any political party because he wanted to maintain his liberty of thought, what happened is that during the Franco dictatorship the PSUC in Catalonia was a very active party, very active in the defence of democracy, very active in the defence of social rights, and very active in defending the recuperation of regional autonomy of the Catalan nation as well; my father agreed with all of these causes, and while he never officially

joined the party, he did have good friends who participated in the clandestine group during this period. They sometimes asked him if he would make a poster, or donate an artwork to sell to help finance the organization, and he always did it [...] at that time, the PSUC was like the centre of the resistance, in favour of democracy for Catalonia in Spain.[69]

Although Tàpies was not officially linked to the PSUC, via his artworks, personal relationships, and publications, it is evident that he shared much in common with the group, which was formed in 1936 from four political parties representing the Catalan left. Amongst which was the Partit Comunista de Catalunya (PCC) a regional branch of the PCE, which Fernando Nistal González characterized as the 'principle enemy of Franco's regime'.[70] The communist party organized illegal meetings and orchestrated acts of resistance ranging from student riots to boycotts. The PCE was not legally recognized as a political party until 1977. Juan Andrade discussed how the party was well organized with many militants during the early 1970s, however, shortly after the PCE was legalized in Spain, it suffered an 'internal crisis' for various reasons.[71]

On 13 June 1976, the same year that he made the PSUC poster, Tàpies published an article in *Avui* that demonstrated his feelings towards art and contemporary political life, 'it is not simply the way of speaking, the technique of making or communicating (although these also count) but, above all, is the way of being and the way of thinking'.[72] Even though not all of his artworks demonstrate such direct words or imagery like that of *L'esperit català* and his PSUC poster, Toni Tàpies confirmed that his father often found ways of expressing himself through his paintings.

If we are to read the consistency of Tàpies's style as unmarried to political changes in Spain then we are to miss the point. Beginning in the mid 1950s, the artist created a trademark style and stuck to it throughout the transition to democracy partially *because of* changing political circumstances. In 1976 Tàpies published another article in *Avui* describing that once an artist develops their own form of creation it is not a reason to settle; he stated, 'when an artist finds his or her voice, it is to execute it with continuity, to deploy it and extend it to everyone, it needs to be like the constant guard, an always attentive and durable symbol, as useful in the conquest of the conscience and of liberty'.[73] It was not a self-imposed rule that his works must look alike, but that they ought to be connected, they ought to embody moral and liberal values, and they ought to be like resilient representations of those principles. He achieved this via style. Another article in *Avui* dating from 1977 discussed the difference between an 'authentic cultural life', which was repressed under Francoism, and the 'parody of "culture"' which involves the limitation of mobilization.[74] In other words, Tàpies was advocating for the support and livelihood of 'authentic' culture, which involves social and political engagement in contrast to culture that unconditionally accepts the status quo. Tàpies thought of Miró as a 'precious example' who demonstrated the roles in which art and the artist could play in the development of social life.[75] For this reason, he admired both the work and commitment of Miró.

The creation of the 1978 Constitution ushered a new age for Spain, but it did not erase or undo memories from the past. This is evident in Tàpies's stylistic vow to his former compositions. He wanted his work to be in defence of human rights, liberty, and peace because those were the values he sought to uphold. However, this sort of art does not always stand alone. It is nearly impossible to unpack one of Tàpies's pictures without reading his written statements, investigating titles, or situating it in a greater historical context. His art is dependent upon extraneous information because he created a style that does not easily yield to immediate understanding based solely on visual evidence.

Nevertheless, the new democracy in Spain did in fact impact the artist and his work. What it did was cause him to cement his style, which was created to defend his political beliefs 'in favour of humanism, democracy and freedom'.[76] During the middle of his artistic career, Tàpies maintained tremendously consistent in terms of style, which he later continued to reproduce throughout the remainder of his life. While discussing this topic with Toni Tàpies, he agreed with my analysis. Tàpies's works do not look exactly the same, but their style is absolutely continuous. Toni Tàpies emphasized that in addition to his father's stylistic stability, he also had profound 'social and political convictions that he always defended from the beginning to the end, and I think that you can see that throughout his entire oeuvre'.[77]

1.3. Concluding Remarks

Much of Tàpies's art is indirectly political. The visual evidence he has given to us is not always explicit, but further information allows for a greater understanding of what he wanted to achieve as an artist and as a citizen. The style that Tàpies created and replicated over the course of decades is the product of a particular moment in time and a response to both international trends in artistic practices and national politics. As is true for all artists, Tàpies's personal and sociopolitical circumstances shaped the ways in which he sought to communicate his own visual language. Memories from the past and desires for the future are components that have maintained a coherent presence in his oeuvre.

This chapter has shown how a single artist developed his career under the Franco dictatorship. Even after the transition to a democratic Spanish government, Tàpies kept working in a comparable manner. Although state and local power systems dramatically changed with the ratification of the 1978 Constitution, that shift was not reflected in Tàpies's art. However, his stylistic consistency was related to the changing sociopolitical context in Spain. First, it was a style that worked for him within the international art world, one that he pioneered, which previous generations of artists had not fully explored. Second, it was a way for Tàpies to continue to assert his position against political oppression, in favour of freedom and democracy. Tàpies's consistency was a deliberate contrast to the dramatic social and political changes that he experienced growing up in the Catalan capital. In the 1970s and 1980s that personal style became more visible to the public via national and international exhibitions as well as public commissions in and around

Barcelona. During this period, Tàpies achieved an iconic status in Catalonia, which the following chapter will explore in greater depth.

Notes to Chapter 1

1. Interview with Joan Guitart, 12 July 2016.
2. For more on Tàpies's early Matter Paintings, see Borja-Villel, 'Antoni Tàpies: The "Matter Paintings"'.
3. Antoni Tàpies, letter to Joan Brossa, 25 December 1950, BROSSA_CORRES_PER_JB_BROSSA_00046_019, A.JBR.03528.020, L'Arxiu del Centre d'Estudis i documentació MACBA.
4. Both in December of 1950 and November of 1951, Brossa wrote letters to Tàpies using the '+' symbol with the remaining letters of the artist's last name. The gesture could affirm (or possibly poke fun) at Tàpies's own letters to Brossa and artworks containing the same sign (for example his 1950 self-portrait or his exhibition posters for the Galería Layetanas from the same year).
5. Catoir, *Conversations with Antoni Tàpies*, p. 27.
6. Borja-Villel, *Fundació Antoni Tàpies*, p. 23.
7. Catoir, *Conversations with Antoni Tàpies*, p. 74.
8. Ibid., p. 74.
9. See Jeremy Roe, *Tàpies* (New York: Parkstone Press Ltd., 2006), p. 69; Catoir, *Conversations with Tàpies*, p. 27; Borja-Villel, Fundació Antoni Tàpies, p. 23.
10. Krauss and Rowell, *Joan Miró: The Magnetic Fields*, p. 84.
11. Ibid., p .84.
12. Greeley, 'Nationalism, Civil War and Painting: Joan Miró and Catalanisme in the 1930s', p. 25.
13. In 1906, Eugeni d'Ors i Rovira defined *noucentisme* through a series of daily columns in the newspaper *La Veu de Catalunya*. The main goal of the movement, with its title referencing the new century, was to develop a cohesive Catalan identity based on a collective culture. Backed by the right-winged party the *Lliga Regionalista*, *noucentisme* started as an idea around which the people of Catalonia would work to modernize their shared territory without losing sense of their Mediterranean heritage. D'Ors wrote about the social and civic responsibilities of art and culture in *La Veu*. Lubar, 'Joan Miró before "The Farm," 1915–1922: Catalan Nationalism and the Avant-garde', p .5.
14. Greeley, 'Nationalism, Civil War and Painting: Joan Miró and Catalanisme in the 1930's', p .5.
15. Ibid., p. 5.
16. Greeley, *Surrealism and the Spanish Civil War*, p. 8.
17. Lubar, 'Joan Miró before "The Farm," 1915–1922: Catalan Nationalism and the Avant-garde', p .183.
18. Tàpies, *Complete Writings Volume II. Collected Essays*, p. 160.
19. Joan Brossa letter to Antoni Tàpies, (195–), L'Arxiu del Centre d'Estudis i documentació MACBA.
20. Ibid., p. 4.
21. Ibid., p. 4.
22. Catoir, *Conversations with Antoni Tàpies*, p. 95.
23. Tàpies, *Complete Writings Volume I. A Personal Memoir: Fragments for an Autobiography*, p .75.
24. Ibid., p .169.
25. Michael Richards, *After the Civil War: Making Memory and Re-making Spain since 1936* (Cambridge: Cambridge University Press, 2013), p. 99.
26. Ibid., p. 126. See also Sebastian Balfour, *Dictatorship, Workers, and the City: Labour in Greater Barcelona Since 1939* (Oxford: Claredon Press, 1989); J. M. Sole i Sabaté, *La represión franquista en Cataluña 1938–1953* (Barcelona: Edicions 62, 1985); and José Antonio Vidal Castaño, *La memoria reprimida: Historias orales del maquis* (Valencia: Universidad de Valencia, 2004).
27. Pablo Giori, 'Castells, sardanes i toros. Les disputes culturals dels nacionalismes durant el franquisme', *Segle XX. Revista Catalana d'historia*, 7 (2014: 13–32), p. 25.
28. *ABC*, 23 March 1974, accessed 5 September 2016, http://hemeroteca.abc.es/nav/Navigate.exe/

hemeroteca/madrid/abc/1974/04/23/001.html.
29. Xosé Manoel Núñez Seixas, 'La región y lo local en el primer franquismo', *Imaginarios y representaciones de España durante el franquismo* (Madrid: Velázquez, 2014), pp. 127–54 (p.150). See also: Andrea Geniola 'Erudición y particularismo: Sobre la oferta 'regional' franquista', VII Encuentro de Investigadores del Franquismo, Santiago de Compostela, 2011.
30. Tàpies, *Complete Writings Volume I. A Personal Memoir: Fragments for an Autobiography*, p. 169.
31. Hal Foster et al., *Arte desde 1900: Modernidad antimodernidad posmodernidad* (Madrid: Ediciones Akal, 2006), p. 391.
32. Ibid., pp. 391–92.
33. One of the Situationist International's key theories: Guy Debord, *La société du spectacle* (Paris: Buchet-Chastel, 1967).
34. José Miguel Cabañas Bravo, 'La primera Bienal Hispanoamericana de Arte: Arte, política y polemica en un certamen internacional de los años cincuenta' (unpublished doctoral dissertation, Universidad Complutense de Madrid, 1991), p. 49.
35. There were three Bienales celebrated between 1951 and 1956 in Madrid, Havana, and Barcelona. Two attempts at a fourth failed and the exhibition was later reinstated in 1963 as *Arte de América y España*. For more on the Bienales Hispano-Americanas and the 'contrabienal' or 'anti-bienal' exhibitions created in opposition of the politics of the organization, Franco's regime, see Cabañas Bravo, 'La primera Bienal Hispanoamericana de Arte'.
36. Tàpies, *Complete Writings Volume I. A Personal Memoir: Fragments for an Autobiography*, p. 326.
37. In 1966, Tàpies attended in the clandestine anti-Francoist meeting, La Caputxinada, in the neighborhood of Barcelona's Sarriá. Molinero and Ysàs, *La cuestión catalana*, p. 24.
38. Cabañas Bravo, 'La primera Bienal Hispanoamericana de Arte: Arte, política y polemica en un certamen internacional de los años cincuenta', p. 45.
39. Pere Gimferrer, *Tàpies and the Catalan Sprit*, p. 82.
40. Some scholars define the end of the transition as occurring in: 1981 after the failed coup, 1982 after the Partido Socialista Obrero Español (PSOE) won general elections, or 1986 after Spain became a member of the European Economic Community; however here I discuss the transition not as a historical frame of reference but a process, the transition to a democratic state which took place between 20 November 1975 and 6 December 1978.
41. For more on the 'Chamelion-like' nature of Spanish nationalism since the new democracy see Balfour and Quiroga, *The Reinvention of Spain*.
42. Tàpies stated in an interview with Catoir, 'I think that advertising has given us a surfeit of colour. I'm positively allergic to colour'. Catoir, *Conversations with Antoni Tàpies*, p. 95.
43. Kasimir Malevich, 'Suprematism', *Theories of Modern Art* (Berkeley: University of California Press, 1968), p. 341.
44. Luis Alemany, 'Tàpies para escépticos', *El Mundo*, 7 February 2012, http://www.elmundo.es/elmundo/2012/02/07/cultura/1328613795.html.
45. See also: Montserrat Guibernau, *Per un catalanisme cosmopolita* (Barcelona: Angle, 2009), pp. 35–36; José Luis de la Granja Sáinz, Justo G. Beramendi, and Pere Anguera, *La España de los nacionalismos y las autonomías* (Madrid: Síntesis, 2001); and Josep Maria Sòria, 'Naixement i mort de l'Assemblea de Catalunya', *La Vanguardia*, 6 November 2011.
46. Balfour, *Dictatorship, Workers, and the City*, p. 191.
47. Fernando Nistal González, *El papel del Partido Comunista en la Transición* (Madrid: Centro de Estudios Políticos y Constitucionales, 2015), p. 81 and Richards, *After the Civil War*, p. 254. See also Carme Molinero, coord., *La Transición treinta años después* (Barcelona: Península, 2006), pp. 31–40; Molinero and Ysàs, *La cuestión catalana*, p. 147–52; and Nicolás Sartorius and Alberto Sabio Alcutén, *El final de la dictadura: La conquista de la democracia en España: Noviembre de 1975–junio de 1977* (Madrid: Temas de Hoy, 2007), pp. 145–95.
48. Sartorius and Sabio Alcutén, *El final de la dictadura*, p. 156.
49. Borja de Riquer, 'Social and Economic Change in a Climate of Political Immobilism', *Spanish Cultural Studies* (Oxford: Oxford University Press, 1995), p. 269.
50. Gonzalo Pasamar, '¿Cómo nos han contado la Transición? Política, memoria e historiografía (1978–1996)', *Ayer*, 99 (2015), 225–49 (p. 249; p. 229).

51. Richards, *After the Civil War*.
52. Scott, *Domination and the Arts of Resistance*, p. 99.
53. Ibid., p. 99.
54. Ibid., p. 199.
55. Ibid., p. 202.
56. Maria Lluïsa Borrás, 'Antoni Tàpies o una nueva cultura', *Destino* (12 June 1971), p. 60.
57. Javier Angulo, 'Puig Antich, caso reabierto', *El País*, 3 September 2006, http://elpais.com/diario/2006/09/03/eps/1157264817_850215.html and Richards, *After the Civil War*, p. 254. See also: Pau Casanellas, *Morir matando: El franquismo ante la práctica armada, 1968–1977* (Madrid: Catarata, 2014).
58. Nistal González, *El papel del Partido Comunista en la Transición*, p. 93. Examples seeking to perpetuate the memory of Puig Antich: Francesc Escribano, *Compte enrere: La història de Salvador Puig Antich* (Barcelona: Edicions 62, 2001); Jordi Panyella, *Salvador Puig Antich, caso abierto* (Barcelona: Lectio, 2015); *Dies de transició Salvador Puig Antich: Dotze hores de vida: l'execució de Puig Antich* (Televisió de Catalunya and Vernal Media, 2006), documentary film.
59. Richards, *After the Civil War*, p. 264. See also Sartorius and Sabio Alcutén, *El final de la dictadura*.
60. Daniele Conversi, 'The Smooth Transition: Spain's 1978 Constitution and the Nationalities Question', *National Identities*, 4.3, (2002), 226–27; Conversi goes on to discuss how the Transition took on a 'smoother process' than other plausible strategies. This later affected how nationalist groups have historically sought recognition as opposed to complete separation. See also Carme Molinero and Pere Ysas, *La cuestión catalana: Cataluña en la transición española* (Barcelona: Crítica, 2014).
61. David Martínez Fiol, 'La construcción mítica del 'onze de setembre' en la cultura política del catalanismo durante el siglo XX', *Historia y Política*, 14.221 (2005).
62. Tàpies, *Complete Writings Volume I. A Personal Memoir: Fragments for an Autobiography*, p. 75.
63. Giulia Quaggio, *La cultura en transición: Reconciliación y política cultural en España, 1976–1986* (Madrid: Alianza, 2014), pp. 190–95.
64. See Pasamar's historigraphical essay '¿Cómo nos han contado la Transición?'. For Francoism in the nacent democracy, see pp. 227–31.
65. Carme Molinero and Pere Ysàs, *Els anys del PSUC: el partit de l'antifranquisme (1956–1981)* (Barcelona: L'Avenç, 2010), p. 227.
66. Molinero and Ysàs, *La cuestión catalana*, p. 220. See also Molinero and Ysàs, *Els anys del PSUC*, p. 185.
67. Josep-Anton Fernández, 'Becoming Normal: Cultural Production and Cultural Policy in Catalonia', *Spanish Cultural Studies: An Introduction*, ed. by Helen Graham and Jo Labanyi (Oxford: Oxford University Press, 1995), p. 343.
68. Antoni Tàpies, *La realidad como arte: por un arte moderno y progresista* (Murcia: Comisión de Cultura del Colegio Oficial de Aparejadores y Arquitectos Técnicos, 1989), p. 84.
69. Interview with Toni Tàpies, 4 February 2016.
70. Nistal González, *El papel del Partido Comunista en la Transición*, p. 81. See also Juan Andrade, *El PCE y el PSOE en (la) transición: La evolución ideológica de la izquerda durante el proceso de cambio político* (Madrid: Siglo XXI de España, 2012); Ferran Gallego, *El mito de la transición: la crisis del franquismo y los orígenes de la democracia (1973–1977)* (Barcelona: Crítica, 2008); and Molinero and Ysàs, *Els anys del PSUC*.
71. Andrade, *El PCE y el PSOE en (la) transición*, p. 379. See also Molinero, *La Transición treinta años después*, pp. 91–93.
72. Tàpies, *La realidad como arte*, p. 82.
73. Ibid., p. 85.
74. Ibid., p. 128.
75. Ibid., p. 265.
76. Antoni Tàpies, *Tàpies in Perspective* (Barcelona: Museu d'Art Contemporani de Barcelona and Actar, 2004), p. 226.
77. Interview with Toni Tàpies, 4 February 2016.

CHAPTER 2

An Icon in the Making

This chapter addresses both indirect and direct links between politics and art. The objective is to explain Tàpies's increasingly iconic status in Spain during the 1970s and 1980s and how politics affects the production of art and artistic practices. The first section examines when and why Tàpies became one of Catalonia's most distinguished cultural icons. The following section investigates how he began to create public works without compromising his already-established style. 'An Icon in the Making' concludes with an elucidation of how the realm of the political is an important agent in that of the processes of making and showing art.

2.1. Achieving an Iconic Status

When and why did Tàpies become an icon of culture in Catalonia? Somewhere between Pere Gimferrer's 1975 statement 'the work of Antoni Tàpies is now at a beginning of a future that belongs to it'[1] and Jordi Pujol's 1981 speech at the UNESCO headquarters positioning Tàpies amongst some of the most renowned artists of the twentieth century, Tàpies's reputation soared, ultimately leading to important public commissions in the 1980s. The reason for his success had much to do with the space and time in which he developed his career. Tàpies's style was a rejection of *nouncentista* aesthetics, bright colours prevalent in commercial advertisement, and geometric abstraction. However, Barcelona was the location in which he became familiar with these modes of representation; it is also where he met Brossa and Miró. When one of Europe's most prominent artistic centres was in a state of transition, with many artists and intellectuals leaving Paris to reestablish themselves in New York City after World War II, Tàpies was holding on to the desire for an avant-garde south of the French capital. His involvement with the group Dau al Set beginning in 1948, and his ensuing nonconformist attitude towards the visual arts is unthinkable in another place or moment in time. The place and time (late 1940s Catalonia) gave shape to Tàpies's pictorial career, for better or for worse. This particular moment was peculiar in that the artist's ambiguous, yet political, semi-abstract, unorthodox, and even unpleasing compositions were recognized and valued on the international level. It was a moment when geometric abstraction was no longer novel and Abstract Expressionism was taking off in New York City. Many European artists and intellectuals flocked to the United States during and after World War II, but Tàpies held on to the idea that a serious artistic environment could still thrive in Europe. By the mid 1950s, major galleries on both sides of the Atlantic Ocean represented Tàpies.

The Martha Jackson Gallery, in New York City, held a solo exhibition in 1953. Tàpies made his first trip to the United States for the opening, where he signed a contract with the gallery.[2] Three years later, Galerie Stradler celebrated a one-man show, presenting Tàpies to the Parisian art scene for the first time. By 1975, galleries from a dozen different countries had hosted important solo exhibitions of the artist's work.

Showing in international locations such as New York City, Paris, or Dusseldorf was quite different than exhibiting works within Spain. One reason is that Tàpies's Catalan identity was, in foreign locations, unproblematic. However, in the Iberian Peninsula beholders would have been more aware of tension between the two labels and would have also considered their own identification as similar or different to that of Tàpies. For example, the opening words of Sebastian Gasch's 1971 book on Tàpies (part of the series *Artistas Españoles Contemporáneos*) highlighted the artist's nationalist behaviours. 'The painter Antoni Tàpies, just like Joan Miró, always writes his name in Catalan and when speaking accents his last name with great emphasis, according to Catalan grammar'.[3] Beyond Spain, particularly in the United States, publications did not highlight these types of nuances. Tàpies's international audience naturally paid less attention to identity politics than his innovation within the art world.

By the end of the Franco dictatorship, he had created a tremendous body of work and continued to display new works around the globe. However, for four consecutive years between 1975 and 1978, Tàpies showed artworks in various Madrid galleries.[4] This is remarkable considering that he had only exhibited works in Madrid on three prior occasions in 1953, 1966, and 1973.[5] In Spain's capital, his identity as a Catalan artist was more visible and was naturally pitted against other national and international contemporary artists during this period. Even after the 1970s, Tàpies did not show very often in Madrid. Luis Figuerola-Ferretti commented on this fact during a rare exhibition at the Galería Antonio Machón in 1985: 'Informing the public, in this case *madrileños*, about the current trajectory of an artist of such international relevance like Tàpies, especially because Madrid has not dedicated a rigorous program to show his recent works, is what this gallery offers us today and it is fascinating'.[6] The infrequency with which Tàpies decided to display works in Madrid is remarkable during the 1970s, he often preferred to show in Catalonia or abroad instead of in Madrid. This certainly stemmed from his love of his place of birth, but also from his animosity towards Spain's capital during Francisco Franco's lifetime. This explains why he would have been more open to showing in Madrid after the dictator's death in 1975.

Meanwhile, in Barcelona, Tàpies remained active in galleries Maeght and Artema and the Fundació Joan Miró held an important retrospective of the artist's work. *Antoni Tàpies (Obra 1956–1976)* first opened in Saint-Paul-de-Vence, France between July and September of 1976 at the Fondation Maeght. The exhibition was then sent to Barcelona and shown at the Joan Miró's foundation between October and December of the same year. The catalogue of the Barcelona exhibition included Tomàs Llorens's notes on the artist's paintings in Catalan and in Spanish, biographical information, and a list of previous exhibitions.[7] Llorens pointed out several important aspects of Tàpies's oeuvre that would have been relevant for visitors with a background in art history as well as the general public. He demonstrated that instead of asking about *what* the artwork means (or what a particular aspect of the picture stands for), we should ask *how* it produces meaning.[8] How do the formal elements of the artwork (colour, tone, line, form, texture, perspective, fracture) trigger associations, memories, and emotions? Furthermore, he discussed Tàpies's intentional ambiguity and his balance between unclear elements and random markings, describing him as having a *'voluntad de engaño'* [desire to deceive].[9] Llorens's notes on the retrospective *Antoni Tàpies (Obra 1956–1976)* illustrate a remarkable understanding and sensibility towards the artist's style, previously unseen in critical and art historical texts concerning Tàpies.

This is the future that Gimferrer was referring to. Although Tàpies had already established an international reputation before 1975, this year was a turning point in his career. It was the end of an era and the beginning of Tàpies's iconic status as a renowned contemporary artist on the national and international level. Showing works in Madrid engaged a new audience previously unexposed to his recent works. However, support from Madrid never matched that of Barcelona, neither from artistic nor political institutions. Part of the reason for this distinction had to do with the artist's visibility and his dedication to projects based within Catalonia. Another factor is that much of the literature on Tàpies is written in Catalan, which worked to bolster his acclaim as a working artist. In a 1981 speech bridging these two realms at the UNESCO headquarters, Jordi Pujol asserted Tàpies as the youngest in line of several generations of avant-garde artists hailing from Catalonia. His proud proclamation positioned Tàpies as the latest visual artist of reference in the region. He was the new Miró. Despite Tàpies's opposition of the conservative government led by the CiU coalition, the Generalitat awarded the artist with the highest recognition of the institution in 1983. The President of the Generalitat presented Tàpies with a gold medal in acknowledgement of his artwork and his hundreds of exhibitions. Aware of the artist's orientation towards leftist politics, Pujol expressed that in one hundred years nobody would remember the name Jordi Pujol but that Antoni Tàpies, through his art, will live on. He did so using an analogy involving the prestige of Pope Julius II verses Michelangelo, with the glory and legacy in favour of the artists.[10]

Why did Pujol and CiU appropriate Tàpies as the leader of the Catalan artistic elite? Part of the answer to this question deals with the artist's nationalist discourse, which echoed that of Miró. The Generalitat's support for Tàpies reflected their interest in cultivating a narrative of Catalan cultural nationalism that would link Miró to Tàpies as the most recent Catalan master painters. The question as to how Catalan government institutions figured into Tàpies's success as an artist is addressed in later chapters.

The media also played a significant role in moving Tàpies into the upper echelons of contemporary Catalan figures. The caption 'Antoni Tàpies, one of the mythical artists of this generation' was published with an interview in *La Vanguardia* in 1981.[11]

The term 'mythical' gives the artist idealized and divine status. The same year, Tàpies created a poster for the 1982 World Cup celebrated in Spain. Various artists representing regions that would host the matches were selected to make an image announcing the event.[12] In Catalonia, Tàpies's image included a foot kicking a ball with a cross through the middle in black, sloppy paint on a leftover newspaper with the title 'Barcelona 82' above. Miró also made a poster for the event, which had no resemblance to that of Tàpies.

The following year, Tàpies had another exhibition at the Fundació Joan Miró. The *Diario de Barcelona* published a photograph of Tàpies holding his granddaughter Teresa in his arms at the show with a pair of his posters hanging in the background on 23 December 1983 (figure 2.1). Two days later, on Christmas day, Miró passed away. The next day, Tàpies published an article in *La Vanguardia* that praised Miró's pictorial accomplishments, 'a new vision of the world, a way of understanding life, a way of living more fully and justly, with which goes included, evidently, both our individual and national liberty. And it is not surprising that in this sentiment, Miró was profoundly tied to the need to defend our Catalan spirit, our liberties, our culture'.[13] National liberty, for Tàpies in this moment, meant protecting the 1979 Statute of Autonomy of Catalonia in the newly established democratic Kingdom of Spain. This statement also demonstrates Tàpies's commitment to principal elements within the discourse of Catalan nationalism: Catalan 'spirit', liberty, and culture.

In a conversation about this particular publication, Toni Tàpies substantiated the meaning of his father's words:

> I would say that for my father in 1983, just as before, defending Catalonia's national liberty was, in a way, practically synonymous with defending the democracy in Spain [...] For my father, when he defended the recuperation of national rights in Catalonia, it was similar to defending the recuperation of democracy not only in Catalonia but also in Spain.[14]

Tàpies's sentiments towards Catalonia mirrored those of Miró, although their ways of expressing their feelings were remarkably distinct. Nevertheless, the two artists were often seen as analogous to one another. For example, in Lluís Permanyer's 1986 *Tàpies y la nueva cultura*, he voiced that everything Tàpies touched turned to gold, knowingly echoing the words of the renowned arts promoter Joan Prats who had previously expressed the same concerning Miró.[15]

Tàpies's iconic status in Spain grew in the 1970s and 1980s despite the fact that he was working within the same style he had developed during the previous two decades. The transition to democracy, Miró's death, and the artist's stylistic peculiarity were all factors in his professional success. Tàpies's decision to consistently show works in Madrid between 1975 and 1978 expanded his audience in an era of great change. Exhibiting art in Spain's capital, a rapidly transforming city, during this period was not a coincidence, but rather an ideological manoeuvre. Hamilton Stapell characterized the changing mood of Madrid during the late 1970s as moving from 'a gray and lifeless former home of the dictator to an open and proud place' that would later become 'known around the world for its vibrancy'.[16] Resonating with Madrid's anti-Franco student movements that advocated for amnesty and a

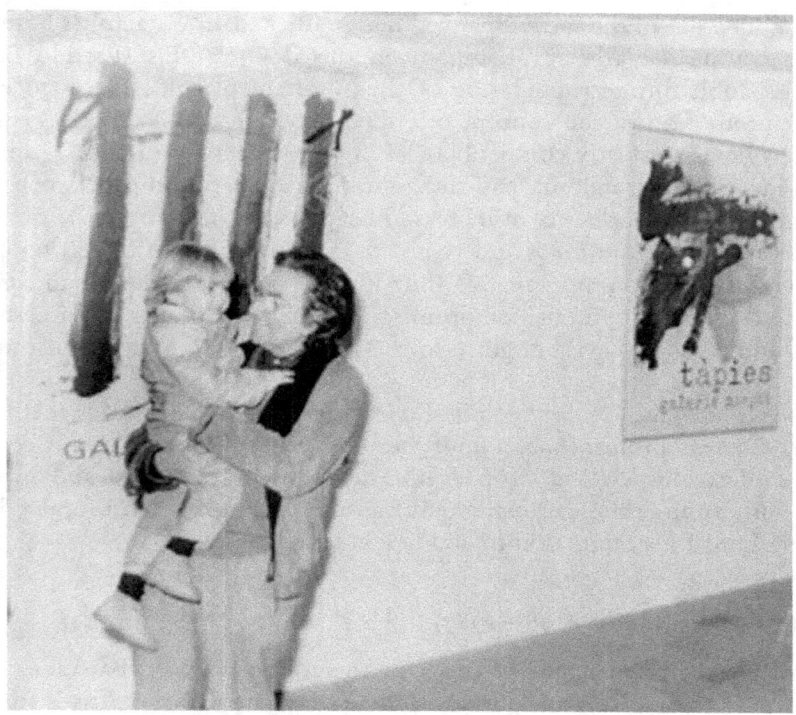

Fig. 2.1. Photograph of Antoni Tàpies holding his granddaughter Teresa at the Fundació Joan Miró, *Diario de Barcelona*, Barcelona, 23 December 1983, Arxiu Fotogràphic de Barcelona

democratic political system, Tàpies's pictures gave shape to parallel ideas concerning his desire for the future of Spain.[17]

Additionally, creating works beyond the traditional exhibition pieces that reach a large national and international audience, such as the 1982 World Cup poster, helped expand Tàpies's exposure and reputation beyond the Iberian Peninsula. At home, the death of Miró in the early 1980s left a void that Tàpies abruptly filled. The number and scale of public commissions that Tàpies undertook in the early 1990s demonstrates the role he played as the foremost living visual artist in Spain at the time. Before his death in 2012, Tàpies had become one of Catalonia's most prestigious artists with his own foundation dedicated to the study and exhibition of modern art. Tàpies, like Miró before him, also aspired to foment the visual arts in Barcelona through the creation of Fundació Antoni Tàpies. Although the two men's artworks had little in common aesthetically, their ideas about the role of art and culture in society were quite similar. Each worked in a different style that was, and continues to be, unique. Style is what first distinguished Tàpies within the international art world and it is also what gave his work continuity throughout his long career.

In 1988, in an exhibition publication from the Ajuntament de Barcelona, *Tàpies els anys 80*, Tàpies was described as 'the most illustrious of contemporary Spanish painters'.[18] The use of the term 'Spanish' here, rather than 'Catalan', is noteworthy, although not particularly surprising given the PSC-PSOE's (Partido Socialista Obrero Español) uninterrupted rule of the Ajuntament since the 1979 elections and their promotion of the concept of a dual national identity, both Spanish and Catalan, as being perfectly compatible. Twenty-first century discourse concerning national identity in Catalonia has antagonized the relationship between Spanish and Catalan identities, due to an increase in support for radical Catalan nationalist groups. However, in the 1980s and 1990s, the compatibility of these two concepts was ubiquitous and unproblematic. Individuals could consider themselves both Spanish and Catalan without compromise. For many, this has remained true to this day, while others have bought into the idea that these two identifications are mutually exclusive.

Another interesting element of the *Tàpies els anys 80* publication is that it sought to bolster Tàpies's prominence, amplifying the arena in which he was considered 'the most illustrious' to the state level. The following sections, and subsequent chapter, will examine the increasing political support that the artist received, which also strengthened his reputation in and beyond Catalonia.

2.2. Sculpting Catalonia (1983–1989)

In 1983 Tàpies finished major projects for the Ajuntament de Barcelona and the Ajuntament de Sant Boi de Llobregat. These were two of the artist's first major public works in Catalonia and their success led to a number of future large-scale commissions. In 1984 he initiated the long process of creating a foundation in his own name. Tàpies began to physically leave his mark as a contemporary artist in Barcelona in the early 1980s in three dimensions and he did so without straying away from his already established individual style.

In Barcelona, Tàpies created a controversial sculpture dedicated to Pablo Picasso, a decade after his 1973 death. *Monument homenatge a Picasso* consists of antique objects and furniture arranged inside a glass cube with gentle streams of water flowing down each side. The pile of encapsulated material was meant to connote familiar objects of comfort, everyday furnishings typical in early twentieth century bourgeoisie homes. The iron rods that slice through the material create a metaphor for Picasso's anticonformist attitude towards both art and life.[19] Tàpies admired both Picasso and Miró, who had passed away months after the sculpture was completed, and he considered each of them as masters in a double sense: for their international artistic merit *and* their regard for social issues. Their works were 'inseparable from ethics and politics',[20] just as Tàpies envisioned his own work. On a white cloth hanging horizontally inside the cube, Tàpies scribbled in Catalan a Picasso quote concerning *Guernica*, his 1937 mural condemning the German aerial bombings of the Basque town during the Spanish Civil War. 'A painting is not intended to decorate a drawing room but is instead a weapon of attack and defence against the enemy'.[21] The famous quotation speaks about the social power and responsibility of art. For Picasso, art was not supposed to be lovely images that make beholders feel warm inside. Instead, he wanted to use art as a means of communicating ideas, important ideas about contemporary life and current events. The composition of *Guernica*, and the tremendous number of preliminary sketches Picasso made before executing the work, demonstrates the artist's abhorrence towards those responsible for the bombing of innocent civilians during the Spanish Civil War. The mural was not meant to be beautiful; it was meant to raise consciousness and funds for the Republicans during the war.[22]

Tàpies's monument, located on Passeig de Picasso near Parc de la Ciutadella, created a polemic when it was first installed. While some saw the new piece as an authentic work of contemporary art, others saw it simply as an ugly sculpture.[23] Newspapers published numerous opinion pieces weighing in on the sculpture with titles such as 'A Polemic Monument', 'The Destruction of Comfort as Homage to Picasso', and 'First Stone'. The latter is a response *not* to the literal first stone laid to commence construction, but to one of the first critics metaphorically throwing a rock at the sculpture in disapproval.[24] Arguments on both sides of the debate assuredly augmented Tàpies's reputation in Barcelona as a living artist. In an *El País* article discussing the polarized public opinion, art critic and professor at the Universitat de Barcelona Victoria Combalía expressed how contemporary art was taught to young students and experienced as a natural component of the urban environment in other countries. She concluded with the desire that, in two or three decades, everyone would be able to appreciate the value of the monument and its artistic merit.[25] An anonymous critic stated that the monument is nice for an exhibition and/or museum but that it is not appropriate for the street, and another claimed that anyone who liked the project was absolutely crazy.[26] The Ajuntament de Barcelona took a risk in commissioning this high-profile work of art. The vast majority of Tàpies's works are difficult, ambiguous, nonconventional, polemic even. Nevertheless, important politicians attended the inauguration in support of the sculpture, including the Mayor of Barcelona, Pasqual Maragall (figure 2.2). There was also an exhibition at the Facultat de Belles Arts of the Universitat de Barcelona which led viewers through a multimedia demonstration of the processes of the creation of the monument. The display included biographical information for both Picasso and Tàpies, preliminary sketches of *Monument homenatge a Picasso*, videos, photographic documentation, technical plans, and literature concerning the project. It is likely that photographs of the installation of the monument were included in this exhibition. A particularly ironic image, now in the Arxiu Fotogràphic de Barcelona that could have been included in the exhibition, is a photograph of the central parts of the sculpture covered in tarps and tied with ropes, to protect the work from the elements (figure 2.3). The picture echoes the image of the wrapped fountain from Tàpies's youth.

Monument homenatge a Picasso is a work of art that essentially aligns Tàpies with Picasso, in its refusal to compromise style in order to appease critics or the public eye. As Rafael Santos Torroella discussed in an article published in *La Vanguardia*, the style of the monument is not different from previous Tàpies works publicly shown in museums and galleries.[27] Furthermore he arrived at the crux of the artist's

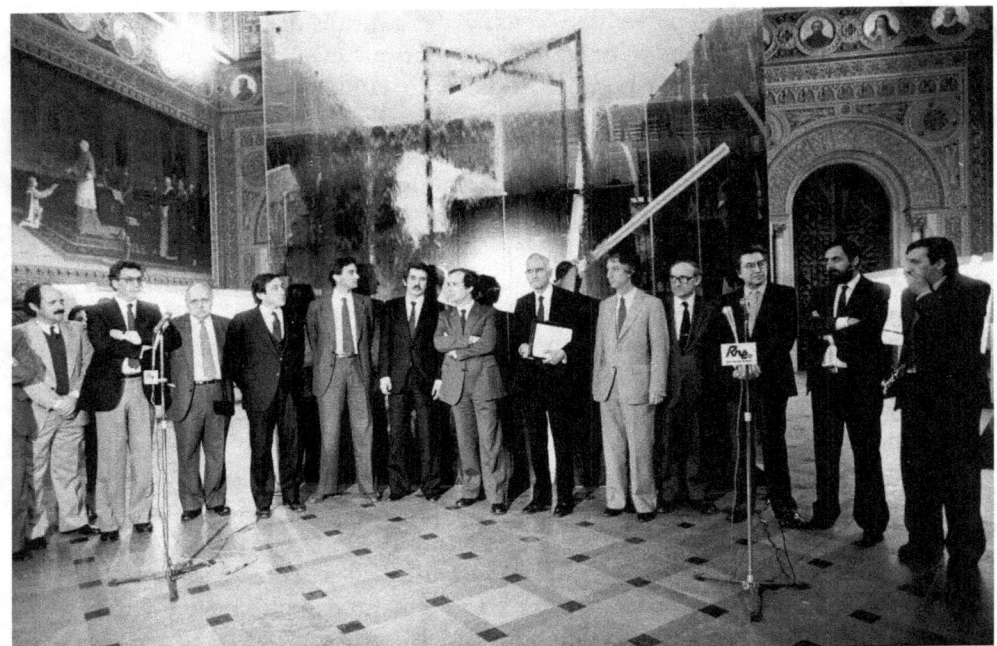

FIG. 2.2. Photograph of the inauguration of *Monument homenatge a Picasso* at the Universitat de Barcelona, *Diario de Barcelona*, Barcelona, May 3, 1983, Arxiu Fotográphic de Barcelona

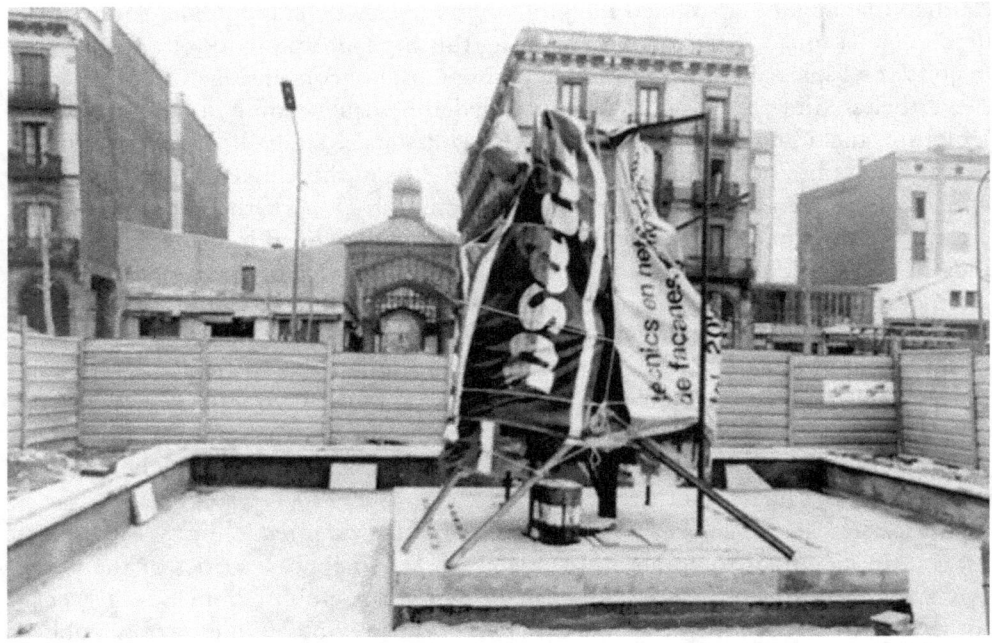

FIG. 2.3. Photograph of the installation of *Monument homenatge a Picasso, Diario de Barcelona*, Barcelona, March 11, 1983, Arxiu Fotográphic de Barcelona

desires: Tàpies made ambiguous works of art in order to engage viewers; he wanted his art to instigate thought and to provoke ideas. As Tàpies wrote in his memoirs, 'these images, as most works of art, have never been an end in and of themselves, they should rather be viewed as a springboard, as a means to reach farther ends'.[28] Similar to many artists of his time, what we see is not an idyllic, picturesque representation of the material world. Instead, artists like Tàpies, Rauschenberg, Malevich, de Kooning, etc., have given us something more challenging. They have inspired us to think, discuss, debate, reconsider, and repeat. Nothing about *Monument homenatge a Picasso* is concrete. On the contrary, it is visibly transparent but also a bit blurry. It is meant to spur contradicting thoughts and generate a productive tension in memory of an artist who set an exceptionally high standard to which future generations of artists would aspire.

Tàpies revealed another public project in Sant Boi de Llobregat, a suburb of Barcelona, in 1983. His mosaic *11 de setembre* in the town's Plaza Catalunya commemorates the historic *Diada* celebrated in the plaza in 1976, the year following Franco's death. This 'traditional' holiday celebration was a preamble to a demonstration on the same day the following year in Barcelona of over a million citizens crying for 'liberty, amnesty, and a statue of autonomy' for Catalonia.[29] The Ajuntament de Sant Boi de Llobregat wanted to present the site as a 'permanent symbol of Catalan identity and democracy'.[30] At the time, PSC's Xavier Vila was the Mayor of Sant Boi de Llobregat. Tàpies's mosaic design on the ground of the plaza memorializes the date of the first nonclandestine *Diada* since 1938. The work consists of four lines, representing the bars of the Catalan flag, terminating in the shape of arrows pointing to the future. The date '11 setembre 1976' is laid amongst the bars. Both elements were made from earthy green and brick-coloured tiles amidst a lightly coloured marble background. The outlines created from the composition pleasingly echo the organic lines formed from the shade of nearby trees.

In March of 1983, close to 20,000 people attended the inauguration in Sant Boi de Llobregat of the donated artwork. Several politicians attended the act where Maria Aurèlia Capmany presented the integration of Catalonia as a model for a cohesive Europe, illustrating that in Sant Boi people from diverse backgrounds have come together as one community. The head of the Ministerio de Sanidad y Consumo and member of the PSC, Ernest Lluch, publicly recalled his presence in the same plaza in 1976 and characterized that moment as both historical and emotional. Then he expressed his gratitude in Spanish to the non-Catalans that were also present on that historic day for their support during 'the most difficult hours' in Catalonia.[31]

An inventory of Sant Boi's contemporary art collection indicates that there is another artwork from 1983 with the same title (*11 de setembre*) that forms part of the municipal's collection of paintings. Two Tàpies lithographs are also on the list (*Suite de Campins 2*, 1983 and *Suite de Campins 3*, 1984) along with a single Miró, (*Personaje solar*, 1974) and dozens of other works.[32] The titles of Tàpies's work that belong to Sant Boi are more closely linked to other works he made for the Generalitat, as opposed to works for the Ajuntament de Barcelona. Their connection to Catalan nationalism is resolute. While Maragall's PSC in Barcelona sought to use Tàpies as a symbol of the city's modernity, Sant Boi's leaders decided to use Tàpies to demarcate a space of historic value to both Catalans and those who celebrated the *Diada* there in 1976. Sant Boi named a public school in honour of the artist in 1986. During the 1980s Tàpies began creating large-scale public installations in Catalonia. With new commissions from local government institutions, his work became more visible to both residents and tourists of the region. *Monument homenatge a Picasso* became the focus of critical attention in the media and *11 de setembre* has permanently politicized the ground of Sant Boi's Plaza Catalunya.

The 1984 establishment of the Fundació Antoni Tàpies set forth with a plan to create a base in the centre of Barcelona to amplify the artist's exposure and provided a space for contemporary art exhibitions. The same year, Tàpies decided that the best location for the newfound organization would be the historic Casa Montaner i Simón, an old publishing house located on Carrer d'Aragó and half a block from Passeig de Gràcia.[33] Located in the heart of Barcelona's l'Eixample neighbourhood, the property's central location and historic design fit well with the newfound project. However, the future home of Fundació Antoni Tàpies required serious attention. A major renovation was necessary. The architect Lluís Domènech i Montaner had designed the structure in 1879 and it became one of Barcelona's first Modernist buildings. In the inicial phases of repairing the old space, the foundation received support from public institutions in Catalonia. In *Fundació Antoni Tàpies*, Miquel Tàpies, the artist's youngest child, wrote about his father's collaboration with the President of the Generalitat de Catalunya, Jordi Pujol, the Councillor of Culture, Joan Rigol, and the Mayor of Barcelona, Pasqual Maragall during the process.[34]

In an *El País* article published on 14 March 1987, Maragall expressed that Tàpies's project would convert the building into one of the 'epicentres of Barcelona's modernity'.[35] This statement fit with the PSC and Ajuntament's project to project the *Cuidad Condal* as a modern, progressive place. The articulation of Barcelona and Spain's 'modernity' would later become magnified as the city began preparations to host the 1992 Olympic Games. Tàpies, for the Mayor of Barcelona in the late 1980s, was a figure whose projects could help position Barcelona as one of Europe's most cultivated cities.

The renovations of the casa Montaner i Simón were made possible with funding from the Ajuntament, Generalitat, and the Spanish Ministerio de Cultura. In 1987, important contracts were signed with these bodies that set the plan in motion.[36] Fundació Antoni Tàpies, however, is a private entity. The artist was theoretically able to organize the project as he wished. In the late 1980s he began to model a sculpture to adorn the top of the building and he established the major goals of the foundation: to further the understanding of contemporary art and culture, to periodically show Tàpies's own works, and to build a library of art and design with a global perspective. Through temporary exhibitions, seminars, symposia, publications, film sessions, etc. the foundation would seek to further the study of art and culture in relation to, and beyond, the art of its founder. While preparing the building to open to the public would take several years, Tàpies had found a charming space for his latest project in the casa Montaner i Simón. The following chapters will examine the 1990 inauguration of the Fundació Antoni Tàpies and the building's crowning sculpture, in addition to a number of other public projects completed in the 1990s.

2.3. How Politics Affects Art

During the renovation of the foundation's new property, the Ajuntament de Barcelona organized an exhibition titled *Tàpies els anys 80* in collaboration with the Universitat de les Illes Balears.[37] Held in a fifteenth century Gothic building whose facade forms part of the maritime wall in Palma de Mallorca, *la Llotja*, the show focused on the artist's works during the first eight years of the 1980s. Portable white walls were used to hang the artworks in the enormous building. The high ceilings provided room for Tàpies's large canvases to breathe. The accompanying publication discusses the artist's commitment to social issues, albeit in an unconventional manner. 'Tàpies shows a great spiritual fortitude of the weak against the ample, uniform presence of power. He clashes brutal activism with passive, mute paintings'.[38] While it is not always evident in every picture the artist made, he worked, like Picasso and Miró before him, with an intense devotion to *both* politics and culture. For all three artists, pictures were not meant to 'decorate apartments', as Picasso famously stated. The work of these artists is socially engaged, provocative, and far from neutral. However, these individuals gained recognition in the art world for making politically charged images that also pushed the conventions of representation to a new level: Picasso with his cubist creations, Miró with his floating figures, and Tàpies with his chromophobic canvases. The combination of political content and visual experimentation was, for these three artists, their contribution to a much larger debate concerning contemporary issues. Why did they each work in this way? Experiencing art is completely different from reading, listening, or conversing. Art is a visual mode of representation, encountered in space, rather than time. Art does not rely on any conventional order to lead to understanding, like words on a page and sentences in a paragraph. For this reason, it is often susceptible to debate concerning content and meaning. This friction that art produces yet tends not to solve, especially in ambiguous works like Tàpies's, provokes thought and conversation. The artist, in this case, is not a divine figure but like the moderator of a debate, instigating active participation in the conceptualization of particular social and political issues that require immediate attention. Through politically engaged art, culture and politics become inseparable properties bound to a picture that, once exhibited in public, is rarely unbiased.

In the context of the *Tàpies els anys 80* exhibition it is made clear that politics affects art both directly and indirectly. The direct connection comes from the public funds that were used to organize the exhibition. The Ajuntament de Barcelona supported the event and subsequent publication, both financially and symbolically. The indirect link between politics and art stems from the artist's conception of his own identity within historical and contemporary society and how he channelled that into the creative process. In a way, this type of indirect agency is unavoidable. What makes his artwork interesting, however, was his ability to take historical and sociopolitical issues and present them in a visual, non-verbal manner.

For example, *Gran diptic roig i negre* (1980) consists of two large, irregular blocks of colour, one black and the other a shade of ivory. In the centre of the diptych the two are hastily united via crisscrossing lines of bright red. The suture binds two disparate entities, but the stitches are the colour of blood. Ambiguous yet clearly political in its connotations, this canvas makes the viewer wonder what two contrasting blocks were sewn together with blood. Tàpies's *Gran diptic roig i negre* gets a powerful message across, albeit an unclear message, in a matter of seconds, whereas a story concerning two dissimilar entities brought together through bloodshed and violence would have taken several minutes to tell. This canvas, shown in *Tàpies els anys 80* demonstrates the artist's desire to present political topics, while leaving the decision-making up to the audience. It is not an instructional work of art, pointing to a concrete conclusion or predetermined destination. Instead, it presents themes for further reflection such as polarity and suture.

More concrete examples of links between politics and art are evident in Tàpies's *A la memòria de Salvador Puig Antich* and *11 de setembre*. The former shows us the artist's stance through its title, indicating Tàpies's sympathies with the anarchist accused of murder and sentenced to death via an antique killing device. This is an indirect example, as Tàpies positioned himself in response to an event carried out by the Francoist dictatorship. The latter is an enormous visual reminder, in a public space, of a historical date that has come to represent the resilience of the Catalan community. It is direct, although the artist donated his time spent on the design, the Ajuntament de Sant Boi de Llobregat sought out Tàpies for the project because of his iconic status and commitment to perpetuating the notion of a unified Catalan culture.

In examining a particular artwork, it is not always evident that there is a direct or indirect link to the realm of politics. For example, the 1989 ink, gouache and collage on paper titled *La bota i el mitjó* does not have any overt reference to civil affairs. The picture consists of various black marks: some are partially transparent, sprayed on like graffiti, some are heavy, jet black lines hastily slapped on the paper, and some are thinner, more defined, yet also applied with a sense of haste. Two flat forms in the shape of a foot and knee with the colour of a brown paper bag are glued over the black marks. The image is not clear. However, it is obvious is that Tàpies made it. Besides the small signature on the bottom left, the darkest and most prominent aspect of the work is the cross in the middle. This symbol works to immediately identify the artist. By 1989, Tàpies had already created a repertoire of vague and non-traditionally beautiful pieces, and this collage belongs to that body of work. As an individual image it may not signify much in terms of political ideology. However, it exists as a part of a larger group, a collection with a consistent style, developed during a specific historical moment and forever tied to the early struggles of the artist to represent himself as both an international and a Catalan artist working under a repressive regime. This trademark style that Tàpies created during the early years of his career is very much political in its enigmatic subject matter and lacklustre colours. Even though *La bota i el mitjó* was made fourteen years after the death of Franco, the style binds it with prior works developed during particular political conditions, which prevented the artist from freely expressing himself. It is indirectly political for its symbolic content and stylistic similarity to former compositions.

Beyond analysing individual works of art, it is also worthwhile to examine entire bodies of works. Politics indirectly affected Tàpies's style during the transition to democracy, in that his resilience to change further legitimized his previous works. His desire for liberty and love for the unconventional in art did not diminish once new political freedoms were established in Spain. His art did not mirror political society. Instead, his art demonstrates a complex relationship with the past, present, and future 'imagined community' to which he identified himself as belonging.[39]

Tàpies actively negotiated his political ideologies in visual terms. Did Tàpies instigate measurable political change? Not quite. However, if we are to read success in terms of a binary structure (the opposite being failure) we cannot say that he failed to address real political situations through works of art. He sought to do so through visual ideas. Politics is intrinsically tied to any creative act made public. Tàpies knowingly embraced this fact, and sought to reproduce his personal viewpoint in terms of matter in space rather than words in time. His artwork does not seek definitive conclusions or concrete courses of action. Instead, it aims at instigating thought and reflection, a habit or skill that is increasingly undervalued in a world saturated in the shiny, seductive advertisements that accompany capitalist societies. Tàpies was not a militant of a political party, but he did contribute to 'the continent that lies beyond'[40] the discernible politics (Scott's visible shoreline) of a politically unstable Spain. The following chapter will outline more concrete, direct links between politics and art, most prominently through financial support and commissions from public institutions that the artist received during the final decade of the twentieth century and into the first years of the twenty-first century.

2.4. Concluding Remarks

In a discussion concerning cultural studies, Miguel Ángel del Arco Blanco explained how the discipline employs certain perspectives to examine the interactions between culture, power, and society. He suggests that historians should keep this in mind as they write history.[41] History is often bound to the trappings of the past, while the multifaceted nature of cultural studies permits for a greater attention to both historical facts and fictions. Del Arco expressed that in order to represent the past, we must take into consideration two narratives: the 'realist' history that is pieced together using primary sources and the world of fiction and imagination which permits reality to seep in.[42] Art engages in both of these realms. However, attention is too often focused on the creative and imaginary aspect of visual culture. Picasso is said to have once stated, 'everything you can imagine is real'.[43] This is important to remember when considering the work of Tàpies. He created fictions that are not isolated from reality. Art, as a mere part of a wider culture, is always engaged with power and politics, directly or indirectly.[44]

This chapter, together with the previous one, shows that the production of art is a political process. Tàpies created a unique style in the 1950s and decided to keep working with it in order to demonstrate his ideological commitment to particular values. Politics had a direct effect on the artist's production because of his personal experiences, desires, and understanding of his own personal identity as a Catalan and anti-Francoist. He became an artistic icon in Catalonia under specific circumstances. His international success as an avant-garde artist working in an almost abstract style bolstered his reputation at home. Further support came from local and regional governments via public commissions, awards, and financial patronage. The regional government found Tàpies's art appealing to create visualizations that were congruent with the CiU's nationalist narrative that depicted Catalonia as a nation since the Middle Ages. The Ajuntament also found the artist useful in order to rebuild Barcelona as a modern, cultivated European city in the final decade of the twentieth century. Both the Generalitat's conservative coalition and the Ajuntament's socialist party found ways to use the art of Tàpies, as the following chapter will explain in greater detail. The artist achieved an iconic status while maintaining an unwavering artistic style that he continued to use throughout the 1990s. The proceeding chapters will focus on how particular public institutions have promoted the artist and how a selection of different cultural centres have presented his works of art.

Notes to Chapter 2

1. Gimferrer, *Tàpies and the Catalan Spirit*, 82.
2. Catoir, *Conversations with Antoni Tàpies*, 140.
3. Gasch, *Tàpies*, 7.
4. Catoir, *Conversations with Antoni Tàpies*, 146–47.
5. Ibid., 140–47.
6. Luis Figuerola-Ferretti, 'El arte en Madrid: La pintura actual de Tàpies', *Goya*, 184 (January–February 1985), 261.
7. *Antoni Tàpies (Obra 1956–1976)* (Barcelona: Fundació Miró, 1976).
8. Ibid., 20.
9. Ibid., 21–22.
10. Joaquín Luna, 'Tàpies recibió sin ningún recelo la Medalla de Oro de la Generalitat', *La Vanguardia*, 7 October 1983, 18.
11. *La Vanguardia*, 5 February 1981, 68.
12. *La Vanguardia*, 14 June 1981, 49.
13. Antoni Tàpies, *La realidad como arte*, 266.
14. Interview with Toni Tàpies, 4 February 2016.
15. Permanyer, *Tàpies y la nueva cultura*, 20.
16. Hamilton Stapell, *Remaking Madrid: Culture, Politics, and Identity after Franco* (New York: Palgrave Macmillan, 2010), 39.
17. Javiera Errázuriz, 'El movimiento estudiantil madrileño durante el curso 1975–1976: Auge y agotamiento de un actor fundamental en lucha contra el franquismo', *Ayer*, 99 (2015): 216. See also Stapell, *Remaking Madrid: Culture, Politics, and Identity after Franco*.
18. *Tàpies els anys 80* (Barcelona: Ayuntamiento de Barcelona, 1988), 9.

19. 'Proyectos y Realización del Monumento a Picasso, de Tàpies', *Butlletí de la Facultat de Belles Arts de la Universitat de Barcelona*, May 1983, 1.
20. Anfosso, 'La destrucción del confort como homenaje a Picasso', *Diario de Barcelona*, 9 February 1982.
21. Fundació Antoni Tàpies, Tribute to Picasso, accessed 22 July 2016, http://www.fundaciotapies.org/site/spip.php?rubrique646.
22. Gijs van Hensbergen, *Guernica: The Biography of a Twentieth-Century Icon* (New York: Bloomsbury Publishing, 2004).
23. Victoria Combalía, 'Un monumento polémico', *El País*, 21 March, 1983, 22.
24. R. Santos Torroella, 'Primera Piedra', *La Vanguardia*, 5 April 1983, 7.
25. Combalía, 'Un monumento polémico', 22. It is safe to say that Combalía's hopes for the future have not yet been realized because art is an undervalued subject and often synonymous with crafts in Spain's current public educational system. Understanding Modern and Postmodern art is often contingent upon a sound background in both art and social history, two subjects that math and science, in the increasingly popular 'bilingual' educational curriculum, often take precedent.
26. Glòria Picazo, 'Tàpies: vestigis d'allò que existí', *Nous Horitzons*, March–May 1983, 30. Combalía, 'Un monumento polémico', 22.
27. Santos Torroella, 'Primera Piedra', 7.
28. Tàpies, *Complete Writings Volume II. Collected Essays*, 107.
29. Tradition is in quotation marks because, like many national events commemorating historical events, it has evolved into a nationalizing movement that has little to do with the actual historical circumstances it presupposes. For more on the historic transformations and implications of the celebration of the *Diada* since the late nineteenth century until 2005, see Martínez Fiol, 'La construcción mítica del "onze de setembre"'. More recent acts on 11 September in Barcelona have included enormous manifestations and isolated acts of enmity such as the burning flags and images of the King Juan Carlos I of Spain in 2008 and 2013. 'La Audiencia Nacional investigará la quema de fotos del Rey durante la Diada', *El País*, 14 October 2013, accessed 11 November 2020, http://politica.elpais.com/politica/2013/10/14/actualidad/1381756290_943397.html.
30. J. Ll. D., 'La plaza de Cataluña de Sant Boi de Llobregat nace como "símbolo permanente de la catalanidad y la democracia"', *El País*, 14 March 1983.
31. Ibid.
32. 'Fons municipal d'art contemporani', accessed 11 November 2020, http://www.santboi.cat/Publio89.nsf/.
33. Borja-Villel, *Fundació Antoni Tàpies*, 12.
34. Ibid., 13.
35. Juan José Navarro Arisa, 'El Ayuntamiento de Barcelona cede a Tàpies un edificio que albergará la fundación del artista', *El País*, 14 March 1987, accessed 28 August 2016, http://elpais.com/diario/1987/03/14/cultura/542674807_850215.html.
36. Ibid., 14.
37. 'Tàpies: els anys 80', Universitat de les Illes Balears, accessed 2 June 2015, http://canal.uib.cat/canals/Tapies-els-anys-80.cid237087?categoryId=100135&showMonth=166774.
38. 'Tàpies demuestra el gran poder espiritual de la impotencia frente a la ampulosa y uniformada presencia del poder. Al brutal activismo le opone él la pasividad y sus cuadros mudos'. *Tàpies els anys 80*, 75.
39. Benedict Anderson's term works to demonstrate the constructed nature of a national population and how individuals imagine themselves as part of a community although they may never know or even see the vast majority of others that belong to the same group. *Imagined Communities*. Later studies concerning nationalization and national identity consider everyday experiences and emotions as fundamental in the creation of a national population. See Billig, *Banal Nationalism* and Edensor, *National Identity, Popular Culture and Everyday Life*. Finally, Quiroga offers a theoretical model that considers both the official national discourse and the everyday experiences and how they work in nations where two or more nationalities are contested in 'The Three Spheres'.

40. Scott, *Domination and the Arts of Resistance*, 199.
41. Del Arco Blanco, 'Un paso más allá de la historia cultural: los *cultural studies*', 20.
42. Ibid., 13.
43. Alexandra George, *Constructing Intellectual Property* (Cambridge: Cambridge University Press, 2012), 10.
44. See Mihelj, *Media Nations*, 10.

CHAPTER 3

A New Foundation and an Old Sock

> Why wouldn't Tàpies make a living off of *antifranquismo*? It is a known, profitable enterprise.
>
> LUIS APOSTUA[1]

This chapter looks at the role that the Generalitat de Catalunya and the Ajuntament de Barcelona played in supporting Tàpies thorough public commissions and financial support of his foundation towards the end of his artistic career. The relationship between the art world and that of politics is bridged through an analysis of artworks created specifically for public and semi-public spaces. I refer to both spaces as accessible to the public, however private entities govern semi-public locations such as the Fundació Antoni Tàpies. The nature of the relationship between art and politics is curious, particularly when considering the thoughts and emotions of a third party, the public. 'A New Foundation and an Old Sock' explains how Tàpies's work is bound to the institutions that support it. The first section focuses on the 1990 inauguration of the Fundació Antoni Tàpies in Barcelona and a Catalan nationalist mural that the artist made for the Generalitat during the same year. The following section introduces several public projects that Tàpies made during the last decade of the twentieth century, including the planning of a controversial project that politicians weighed in on, and which was eventually halted after months of debate. Finally, the concluding remarks concern the nature of public funding and the creation of works of art, the main theme of this chapter.

3.1. Financial and Institutional Support

Upon joining the European Economic Community in 1986, Spain was considerably behind other European nations in terms of gross domestic product per capita. Through this incorporation, to which would later become the European Union, the value of the Spanish currency, the *peseta*, increased. In the early 1990s, during a global recession, Spain supported the push for a common European currency. Before the 1992 Olympic Games, Barcelona poured money into a host of projects to prepare the city for the event.[2] Despite the fluctuating state of the economy during final decade of the twentieth century, Catalan local and regional governments supported public arts initiatives. By the late 1990s the country was already

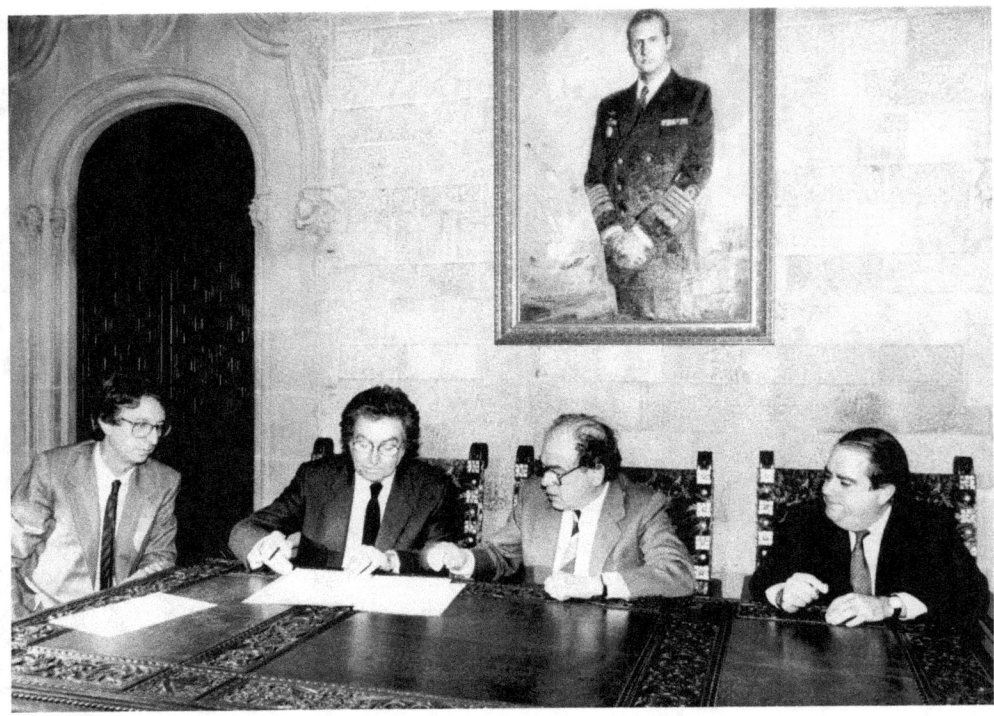

Fig. 3.1. Photograph of Tàpies signing documents at the
Palau de la Generalitat, Barcelona, 16 March 1989, Arxiu Fotográphic de Barcelona

recovering from the recession, employment rates were on the rise, and property values were going up. Once the euro began circulation in the Eurozone in 2002, the Basque Country, Catalonia, and Madrid were reaching high employment rates and the Spanish economy was healthy again.[3]

In 1990 Tàpies finished a mural for the Sala Tarradellas in the Palau de la Generalitat titled *Les quatre cròniques*. There is a photograph that documented the artist signing a contract to create paintings for the Sala Màdico, currently known as the Sala Tàpies; sitting next to Tàpies on the left side of the image, which was taken on 16 March 1989 (figure 3.1), was Joan Guitart, the Generalitat's Councillor of Culture at the time. However, the specific terms of the contract are unknown and the economic compensation for the project has not been published. The Generalitat decided to change the location of *Les quatre cròniques* in 2006, relocating it to a prominent room used for meetings and regularly accessible to the media (figure 3.2). Toni Tàpies could not recall the specifics of the commission, but he assured me that his father, when he was asked to make works such as this one, would have chosen the subject matter. He explained that the Generalitat asked for a work to fit in a specific space, but they would not have specified what, exactly, he should paint.[4] The two-by-six meter painting often appears in the background of twenty-first century news reports concerning official matters of the Generalitat and high-profile

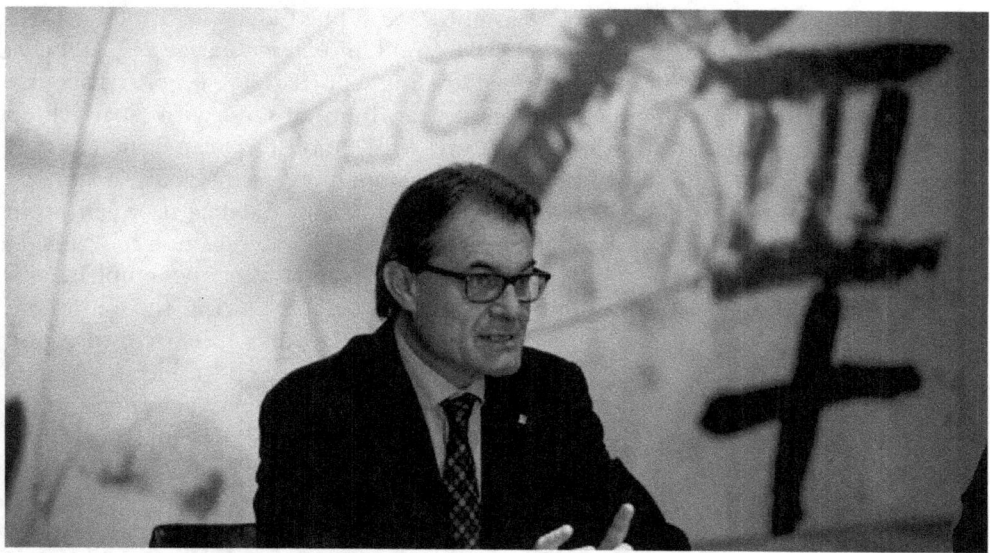

Fig. 3.2. Photograph of Artur Mas discussing the unofficial referendum in Catalonia with Tàpies's *Les quatre cròniques* (1990) in the background, Barcelona, 11 November 2014

figures that visit the government building because of its current location in the Sala Tarradellas. Similar to his mosaic design in Sant Boi de Llobregat, this work takes on a Catalan theme.

The mural consists of four panels, which could clarify why the short text on the back of the photograph refers to murals in plural, each dedicated to a medieval biographical manuscript written in Catalan. Reading from left to right, the first is dedicated to King Jaume I and his thirteenth century *Llibre dels Fets*.[5] The second is about Bernat Desclot's 1288 account *Llibre del rei en Pere d'Aragó e dels seus antecessors passats* in addition to his 'great deeds and conquests'. The next concerns the chronicle of nobleman Ramon Muntaner and his expeditions (1325–1328), represented in the mural with the four red bars of the Catalan flag and Muntaner's benevolent phrase '*què us dire?*' [what shall I tell you?]. The fourth and final panel is about the autobiographical work of King Pere III (1382–1385), which contains an allegorical, biblical text. As a whole, the *Les quatre cròniques* is consistent with Tàpies's style discussed in the previous chapters. There are legible markings and symbols, yet the entirety of the picture gives an effect via the formal elements (colour, line, shape, texture, perspective, and facture), not a specific statement about these literary works or their value. It is only through the title and location of the work that these chronicles become increasingly cherished. *Les quatre cròniques* memorializes medieval works written in Catalan in an entirely political fashion. The art works to remind beholders of the historicity and importance of a language that was neither legally recognized nor valued in Franco's Spain.

The fact that the Generalitat confided in Tàpies to carry out this commission is interesting. Since 1980, Pujol and CiU had maintained the power of the autonomous government and would continue to do so until 2003. The CiU was formed in 1978 as a Catalan nationalist coalition uniting CDC and Unió Democràtica de Catalunya (UDC). Throughout the 1980s, as Andrew Dowling reported, 'the Pujolist discourse equated any attack on, or even lack of support for, Pujol or CiU with an attack on Catalonia and the identification of Catalanism with Pujolism became increasingly common'.[6] However, Pujol proved purposefully ambiguous in his political strategy concerning Catalan nationalism, taking care to maintain a balance between proto state building discourse within Barcelona and a more moderate position in Madrid.[7]

Closely linked to Pujol and CiU's nationalist agenda was the emphasis on language and its importance in political and civil society. During the 1960s and 1970s Spanish-speaking immigrants flocked to Catalonia, and while first generation immigrants may not have learned Catalan, their children would under the public education system. Tàpies's mural for the Generalitat effectively aggrandizes medieval literature that links the language to the land. Beyond the emphasis on the Catalan language, the use of these particular manuscripts as subject matter works to perpetuate the idea of Catalonia as an imagined community with a tremendously long history. Using the past as a means to identify with centuries old civilizations is a common strategy of nationalization, as it creates a sense of belonging and continuity for individuals. Guibernau discussed Pujol's stance concerning the importance of language in *Catalan Nationalism: Francoism, Transition and Democracy* as 'crucial for Catalonia to maintain and develop its specific identity, which goes back to the Middle Ages'.[8] This sort of language is representative of a continually evoked strategy to justify the idea that Catalan identity is historical and, by extension, significant. It is fitting that the topic of *Les quatre cròniques* was in accordance with the coalition's nationalist aspirations and idealization of the Middle Ages as the foundational moment of the Catalan nation, while the same artist's works for the Ajuntament de Barcelona tend to engage less with *catalanisme* and more with innovation in contemporary artistic practices, as seen in *Monument homenatge a Picasso* and *Complement miraculós* (2000).

In addition to commissioning public and semi-public artworks (works that belong to public institutions but are not always accessible to the public), the Generalitat and the Ajuntament de Barcelona financially supported the Fundació Antoni Tàpies. These two entities, along with the Spanish Ministerio de Cultura, contributed significant funds to support the establishment of the 'private' foundation, and have done so on an annual basis since the year prior to its opening in 1990.[9] Furthermore, the Ajuntament de Barcelona played an even greater role in the years leading up to the inauguration. It seems there were some obstacles for the Fundació to purchase the Casa Montaner i Simón building, however it is unclear what the nature of this problem was, but it was most likely financial and/or legal in nature. As the artist's youngest son, Miquel, wrote in the introduction to the book *Fundació Antoni Tàpies*, the Ajuntament de Barcelona was interested in the project, and decided to 'acquire' the edifice, pay for the renovations, and grant it to the foundation. The Mayor of Barcelona Pasqual Maragall signed a contract with Tàpies in early 1987, which definitively established the old Casa Montaner i Simón as a new cultural space in the urban district of l'Eixample. Preparing the building to function as the site of the Fundació Antoni Tàpies began in the spring of 1987. The Ministerio de Cultura paid for interior museum installations after the major renovations, that the Ajuntament financed, were completed.

The foundation has not made information concerning annual contributions from the Generalitat, Ajuntament, and Ministerio readily available to the public and, since it is a private institution, is not legally responsible to do so. The Generalitat, however, has facilitated a record of the exact amounts that it paid to the foundation since 1989 (see below). Extrapolating from a 2015 report concerning the fragile financial situation of the foundation, the Generalitat has spent the most on a yearly basis, ranging from 150,000 to 839,869 euros per year, while the Ajuntament pays less per year (529,410 euros in 2015). However, it seems the Ajuntament took on greater initial investments in purchasing and renovating the building. Finally, the Ministerio de Cultura pays the least of the three supporting bodies, 48,740 euros in 2015, significantly less than the Tàpies family's donation of 100,000 euros in both 2014 and 2015.[10] These large sums of money are inextricably linked to political intentions and the propagation of identities.

Year		normal contribution	interest loan	amortized loan
1989	150.000,00 €			
1990	150.000,00 €			
1991	150.000,00 €			
1992	210.000,00 €			
1993	300.000,00 €			
1994	300.000,00 €			
1995	300.000,00 €			
1996	240.000,00 €			
1997	300.000,00 €			
1998	270.000,00 €			
1999	270.000,00 €			
2000	300.000,00 €			
2001	300.000,00 €			
2002	300.506,00 €			
2003	330.550,00 €			
2004	330.557,00 €			
2005	340.560,00 €			
2006	372.600,00 €			
2007	385.000,00 €			
2008	395.000,00 €			
2009[11]	376.520,00 €			
2010	535.550,00 €	380.000,00 €	155.550,00 €	
2011	478.550,00 €	323.425,00 €	155.125,00 €	
2012	839.869,94 €	323.000,00 €	155.550,00 €	361.318,94 €
2013	795.602,41 €	278.733,47 €	138.639,82 €	378.229,12 €
2014	795.602,41 €	278.733,47 €	121.383,12 €	395.485,82 €
2015	795.602,41 €	278.733,47 €	103.339,08 €	413.529,86 €

For the foundation's opening in 1990, Tàpies crowned the building with a curious sculpture made out of 2,750 meters of aluminium tubing. *Núvol i cadira* [Cloud and Chair] is a twelve by twenty-four-meter cluster of metal spiralling around the top of the building like an intimidating barbed wire fence. Rising from the cloud of chaos is a delicate outline of a chair, positioned like a lofty throne yet slanted so that it almost disappears when viewed from certain angles. Chairs are, like the pair of scissors, a recurring element in the body of the artist's work. Perhaps Tàpies admired Vincent Van Gogh's 1888 painting of his own chair and its portrait like quality, created during a time when portraits of anything other than human beings were practically non-existent. Tàpies was fond of the Dutch artist's work and on 4 June 1951 he sent a postcard from Amsterdam to his friend Joan Brossa, member of Dau al Set and avant-garde poet who wrote exclusively in Catalan, with a photograph of one of Van Gogh's paintings. It is also possible that Tàpies's use of this type of chair sought to nullify Henri Matisse's 1908 statement from 'Notes of a Painter'. The leader of Fauvism claimed his desires for an art without depressing subject matter, an art that would have 'an appeasing influence, like a mental soother, something like a good armchair in which to rest from physical fatigue'.[12] Chairs are commonplace objects that, for Tàpies and Brossa's generation, provide a place to think and have little to do with the lofty utopia that Matisse dreamed about decades before. Like a beacon marking the building as a sanctuary for thinking, *Núvol i cadira* is what distinguishes the old Casa Montaner i Simón from the new Fundació Antoni Tàpies, which opened its doors to the public on 5 June 1990.

ABC described the new space as 'brilliant', serving the purpose of the foundation's objectives, with a lovely facade that is topped with a chair for the thinker.[13] Guitart expressed his esteem for the institution, stating in an interview with me that the Fundació Antoni Tàpies is undoubtedly deserving of public support and collaboration.[14] The project would not have been possible without the aid of the Generalitat de Catalunya, the Ajuntament de Barcelona, the Ministerio de Cultura, or Antoni Tàpies's investments. The continued support of these three institutions, in addition to the evident donations from the Tàpies family, has enabled the continued success of the cultural endeavour for over thirty years.

One of the first artworks that Tàpies donated to the foundation was a Miró sculpture that he received when he won the Premio Príncipe de Asturias de las Artes in 1990. This prestigious annual prize has been awarded to musicians, artists, architects, cinematographers, and dancers since 1981. Tàpies was the first Catalan bestowed with this honour. *ABC's* account of the event emphasized the Spanish and European nature of the artist's work.[15] *La Vanguardia* published two articles on the same page about the award. The first talked about Tàpies's gratitude towards Prince Felipe's visit to the artist's studio. The second, at the bottom of the same page, referred to Tàpies as *barcelonés* [from Barcelona] and 'very European', stating that his new foundation will present his innovative works to the *'pueblo español'*.[16] In a statement about the award published in *El País*, Jordi Pujol defined Tàpies as 'an artist, Catalan, and patriot'.[17] In doing so, the President of the Generalitat signalled that Tàpies is one of 'us', a proud Catalan. However, Pujol and CiU shared what Dowling expressed as 'a limited and limiting conception of Catalan culture, one that was often mocked by metropolitan intellectuals as one of *cantaires* and *sardanas* [singing and folk dances]'.[18] Tàpies undoubtedly shared this sentiment. Pujol, in ignoring the difference between Tàpies's leftist political philosophy and his own allegiance to the conservative CiU, sought to focus on their shared Catalan identity and use that to bring Tàpies closer to himself, adding the artist to his ample collection of Catalan patriots. The artist humbly accepted the award, appreciative for the committee's recognition of his 'artistic and professional maturity', yet he told the press that he would have been more emotional to have had won something like this when he was twenty-five years old. He went on to explain that prizes help to encourage younger artists, both artistically and economically.[19] Nevertheless, he graciously received the recognition and set out to support future generations of artists in a different way.

In 1990, Gregory Rood directed a documentary about Tàpies. The film aired in Barcelona on TVE Catalunya in June and shortly after on the United Kingdom's BBC as part of the *Omnibus* series.[20] Tàpies spoke about his motivation as an artist and thinker in the film:

> What drives an artist is a desire to know the truth [...] to search for a true equilibrium, to find a perfect balance between what a man knows and what he does, seems to me to be one of the most beautiful ends to which an artist can direct himself, and not only an artist, it should be the ambition of anyone who thinks seriously about the world.[21]

The documentary's release coincided with the Fundació Antoni Tàpies opening to the public. The centre has worked to promote the work of contemporary artists in Barcelona through a variety of exhibitions, workshops, lectures, film screenings, family activities, and performances. Through extension, political establishments have made these programs possible and accessible to the public. Tàpies was able to stabilize his reputation as the top living artist in the region and encourage future generations of artists to follow in his footsteps through a great deal of financial and institutional support. During the final decade of the twentieth century, the socialist run Ajuntament and conservative Generalitat were led by competing power structures, however both sought to establish a closer relationship with Tàpies and his work, albeit with differing objectives, which we will see as this chapter unfolds.

3.2. 'Mr. Tàpies's Unmatched Sock' and Other Public Works

In 1992 Tàpies's painted a mural for the Catalan Pavilion at the Universal Exposition in Seville. The event was organized to commemorate the five hundredth anniversary of Christopher Columbus' first journey to the Americas. Over one hundred countries participated in the Expo, which ran from April to October. Most pavilions attracted visitors through showcasing their interesting architectural designs. For example, Japan boasted the construction of the largest wooden structure in the world and the popular pavilion of Kuwait showed off their segmented, movable roof. The Catalan building, however, employed Tàpies's artwork to captivate crowds. The composition of the wall adorning the outside of the building is tendentious, albeit not entirely representational. It combines letters, symbols, and markings to connote Catalan nationalistic sentiments while simultaneously serving as a signpost for the pavilion. The enormous work consists of four major elements: the handprint, a large quasi-fist, two of the artist's trademark '+' markings, and the word *Catalunya*. A sketched form that could represent the socialist fist splits through the middle of the letters. There are a pair of intersecting lines on each side of the painting, that curious cross-like symbol frequent in Tàpies's work. Finally, the 'C' that begins the word *Catalunya* in the mural is shaped like the *barretina* that Miró's representations of Catalan peasants each adorn in both *Cap de pagès català* paintings. The mural deliberately resonates with Miró's nationalist compositions and embraces an aesthetic of violence through the handprint and the dark red colour. Furthermore, it is consistent with the ideas that Tàpies expressed in 1977 concerning the connotations of walls. Its resemblance to cave paintings and its tactile quality suggests that it could be a 'testimonial to the passage of time'.[22] Time was an important theme for Tàpies, particularly in works that seek to evoke the idea that Catalonia is a historically cohesive unit, as opposed to a region composed of a variety of different landscapes, cultures, and histories. Both *Pintura romànica i barretina* and *Les quatre cròniques* are consistent with the mural's style and similarly aim to achieve this sense of Catalan unity.

One of the most striking aspects of the Expo '92 mural is that it repudiates the Spanish or Castilian spelling of his nation: *Cataluña*. In using *Catalunya*, Tàpies demonstrated his allegiance to his mother tongue and broadcast that this was the most appropriate name to designate the pavilion. While the official languages of the event were Spanish and English, it is clear that the artist decided to present the vernacular spelling, which highlights the historical importance of Catalan and the promotion of its revitalization. Article 3 of the 1978 Spanish Constitution recognizes Castilian as the nation's official language while granting power to the autonomous communities to determine co-official languages. For many Catalans, this is a fundamental freedom of supreme importance. The semantic aspect of this artwork is interesting because it expresses linguistic liberty to a geographically diverse audience that travelled to visit the exposition in Andalucía.

Furthermore, since 1983 Pujol and CiU had been working towards 'linguistic normalization', a strategy that went hand in hand with the coalition's nationalist aims. Legislative acts were passed in order to convert Catalan into the 'normal language of the public sphere', with the major focus being in the public education system.[23] As a result, the understanding of the Catalan language rose significantly from 81% of the population of Catalonia in 1981 to 94.5% in 2001.[24] In 1993, *ABC* published an article titled 'Like Franco, but the reverse', concerning Catalonia's attempt to supposedly wipe out the Spanish language from the region.[25] Despite criticism like *ABC*'s accusation, Pujol's project concerning language revival was not greatly contested in Spain during the 1980s and 1990s.

From the outset, this linguistic policy fit into the Catalan government's overarching plan that created a 'double narrative of resistance and loss' surrounding Catalan nationalization, as Alejandro Quiroga and Fernando Molina explained in

'National Deadlock. Hot Nationalism, Dual Identities and Catalan Independence (2008–2019)'.[26] Resistance, here, refers to the how the region of Catalonia had historically resisted the centralizing power of Spanish governments, while loss has to do with the loss of Catalan identity, in terms of both language and liberty. The actions of Pujol's government had a lasting effect on school-aged children. The degree to which these individuals came to identify themselves as Catalan, however, would depend on a variety of different factors.[27]

In the 2000s the conservative government of José María Aznar unsuccessfully tried to impose a Spanish history curriculum that, as a result, would have eliminated considerable teaching time in the Catalan language. Catalan nationalist's devotion to official language policies clashed with conservatives that backed a new wave of Spanish nationalism stemming from Madrid. Tàpies's mural for the Catalan pavilion was created at a time when the legal linguistic 'normalization' in Catalonia was on the threshold, about to become a more contentions topic of debate in Spain. The mural incorporates language as part of a greater visual manifestation of culture.

Spain hosted both the Universal Exposition and Olympic Games in 1992. For savvy individuals and businesses these enormous events provided an opportunity to make money, quickly and not necessarily in a legal manner (*pelotazo*). In his fictional novel published in 1993, *Sabotaje olímpico*, Manuel Vázquez Montalbán satirized the economic, cultural, and moral consequences of these two events, describing them as 'privileged dramatizations' of Spain's modernity.[28] He went on joking, 'if nobody checked themselves into a mental hospital for being against the Olympic Games, it was not due to tolerance, but the *exhibition* of tolerance. It [Spain] was surrounded by exhibitionists'.[29] Exhibiting Spain as both modern and European was one of the primary goals leading up to the Olympics; people in Spain even associated modernity with 'being European' at this time.[30] One of Tàpies's previous works for the cover of the 1985 Europalia International Arts Festival in Brussels linked Spain to European modernity. In 1986, Spain joined the European Economic Community, and would go on to spend an estimated three trillion euros on new construction in Catalonia prior to the commencement of the Olympic Games on July 25, 1992.[31] Both public and private funds were poured into the city of Barcelona in order to prepare for the international event. CiU made an outstanding effort to represent Catalan identity to the global community that would visit during the summer, this worked to solidify patriotism within the region but also to establish Barcelona as a tourist destination, with a rhythm and culture different from Madrid.[32]

The stadium that was built for the athletic competitions is located on Montjuïc hill, neighbouring MNAC, the region's most grandiose art museum formed in 1990 from the fusion of modern and historic public collections and housed in the Palau Nacional. The inauguration ceremony for the Games of the XXV Olympiad were held in the Sala Oval of the Palau Nacional, a stunning, classical hall with an elliptical cupola in the centre of the museum. The space, originally designed in 1924 and completed for the 1929 International Exposition, began renovations in 1990 in preparation for the upcoming Olympics. Tàpies was solicited to create an artwork for the Palau Nacional, the idea being that a contemporary piece

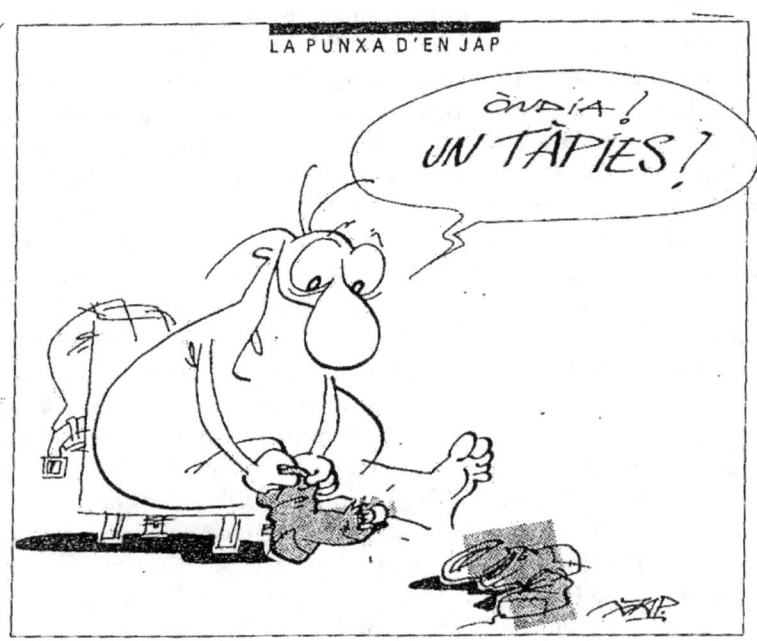

Fig. 3.3. Joan Antoni Poch, drawing published in *Punt Diari*, Girona, 26 January 1992

would complement the ornate decor of the room while simultaneously presenting Barcelona as a sophisticated centre of cultural production. The dynamic of this proposed project would have been different than Tàpies' work for the Universal Exposition in Seville. While both were oriented towards an international audience, the MNAC project would have had its home in Catalonia. This difference may seem subtle, but the idea of projecting outwards beyond one's territory is different from reflecting within. Still, what seemed like a straightforward commission on behalf of MNAC's directors, quickly snowballed into a media frenzy of critiques of Tàpies's proposal for the new work: an enormous sock, measuring eighteen meters in height. *Mitjó* [Sock] became notorious before it was ever made.

In the library of the Fundació Antoni Tàpies, there is a white cardboard box that contains a stack of approximately twenty centimetres of photocopied newspaper clippings. Each one is about *Mitjó*. The articles, published in the final months of 1991 and in 1992 (the majority between January and March), range from local daily papers in Spain to foreign periodicals like *The New York Times* and *The Wall Street Journal*. A few memorable titles include: 'Does Barcelona Really Want a Statue of a Sock, With a Hole?' in Marseille's *Herald Tribune*, 'Oda al calcetín' [Ode to the Sock] in Barcelona's *El Periódico*, and 'Poesia sobre el mitjó' [Poetry about the Sock] in Barcelona's *Avui*. The quantity of articles about the unmade sock is tremendous and newspapers from every one of Spain's seventeen autonomous communities all reported on the debate at least once.

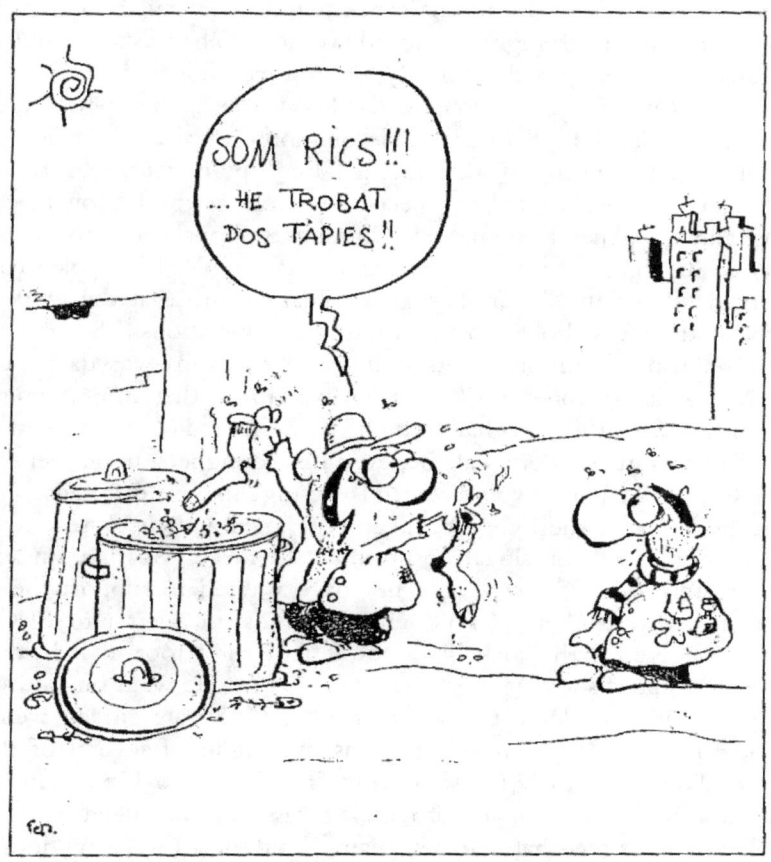

Fig. 3.4. Unknown, drawing published in *Avui*, Barcelona, 26 January 1992

Beyond opinion pieces and news concerning the status of the controversy, several cartoons poke fun at the idea of an old, tattered sock constituting a work of art. Girona's *Punt Diari* printed a picture of a nude bulb-shaped figure, with an enormous nose and bulging eyes, sitting on a chair while pulling up his sock; upon realizing that the sock has been worn through, leaving his toes exposed, the blob exclaims with excitement: 'Wow! A Tàpies!' (figure 3.3).[33] *Avui* printed a cartoon of two unshaven men standing next to a pair of garbage cans; while digging in the trash, holding up two dirty, smelly socks and looking back to his companion one announces: 'We're rich!!!... I found two Tàpies!!' (figure 3.4).[34] The Catalan nationalist papers *Punt Diari* and *Avui*'s drawings address the surface of an argument that an old sock could be found in the trash or even on your own foot; therefore, the sock cannot be considered a serious work of art. However, these laughable images ultimately reinforce the notion that art is supposed to be something else: beautiful, balanced, expensive, meticulous, etc. If all artists shared this conservative thought that art should possess particular qualities, Doménikos Theotokópoulos, also known as El Greco, would not have painted his spectacularly emotive figures, nor de Kooning his terrifyingly impactful women. When asked about the *Mitjó* project, Tàpies once responded comically 'do you wear socks?'[35]

In March of 1992, a journalist for *La Vanguardia*, Jaime Gustà Hernández, stated that the 'avalanche' of unfavourable opinions concerning Tàpies's proposed sock sculpture was causing panic amongst local politicians.[36] A three month long onslaught of criticism of the project came from art professionals, celebrities, politicians, and the general population. Comments about *Mitjó* ranged from mild statements of disapproval, such as the Partido Popular's (PP) spokesman in the Ajuntament de Barcelona Albert Fernández Díaz's claim that the work possesses a 'doubtful aesthetic', to bold and unforgiving denunciations.[37] Several Barcelona periodicals published opinion letters sent to them from everyday readers. For example, Maria Sala wrote to *El Periódico* explaining that *Mitjó* would remind Spaniards of the times that they had to mend sock, instead of buying new pairs, for the whole family. Furthermore, Sala believed that foreigners, upon seeing the sock during the Olympic Games, would return to saying 'Spain is different'.[38] This is an ironic interpretation of the hypothetical international audience's reaction because the Franco regime used this slogan to promote the idea of Spain as an 'exotic and passionate' country and Tàpies would not have wanted to support the dictator's ideological manoeuvres.[39] Abraham Méndez Ramos, in a letter to *El Observador*, mockingly wondered if the sock is for the left or right foot, if it belongs to an Olympic athlete and if so what sport they compete in. He went on to discuss how profoundly he had considered the work of art.[40] One irate citizen went beyond denouncing the commission and voiced his discontent of several of the artist's projects. Yves Rus wrote to *El Periódico* to say, 'The Fundació Tàpies, always empty, did not need a punk hairdo made of metal. Picasso did not need wet scraps of a container left on the street that marks his name. And the art museum does not need an old, white sock that would prove irresistible to our justified tomatoes'. In a mere few lines, Rus attacked the foundation itself, *Núvol i cadira*, *Monument Homenatge a Picasso*, and *Mitjó* and suggests that he is not alone in his desire to ridicule the sock, stating that others would also throw rotten tomatoes at it.

The restaurant Gran Colmado in Barcelona playfully included in their daily menu a raffle with a simple survey concerning the sculpture. Patrons were asked if they thought that *Mitjó* ought to be in the Salón Oval of MNAC (figure 3.5). The questionnaire included two boxes '*sí*' and '*no*' with space to leave your name, address, and phone number for the drawing of two gourmet meals. Gran Colmado reported to have collected over 1,000 responses, the majority voting against the artwork's installation in the Palau Nacional.[41]

Nevertheless, solid arguments were made in favor of continuing the project. *Diari de Barcelona* published an article titled '*Visca el mitjó!*' that reminded readers of the line of people waiting to see Picasso's first post-war exhibition in Spain at the Sala Gaspar in 1955 and confrontationally questioned if the citizens of 1950s Barcelona were more open to contemporary art than those of the 'city of miracles of '92'.[42] The article continued on to support Tàpies's work, claiming that the PP's opposition of *Mitjó* is in itself a reason to back the artwork.

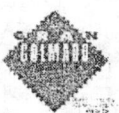

Fig. 3.5. Menú Diari Gran Colmado, Barcelona, 17 June 1992

In light of the wide range of public opinion concerning the commission, in January of 1992 MNAC's patrons under the leadership of Pere Duran i Farell, prudently decided not to make any official decisions until both the Ajuntament and the Generalitat submitted written documents in favour or in opposition of the artwork. MNAC's President of the board of trustees Duran i Farell stated that he should not make decisions about the sculpture 'because it has to do with Barcelona '92, and will end up being a political and societal act'.[43] The Vice President of MNAC's board, Ramon Guardans, had no problem stating his opposition, creating a schism within the museum's inner circle.[44] The Mayor of Barcelona, Pasqual Maragall, was in favour of the commission. He stated that adding a grand work of art by Tàpies to the empty hall seemed like a wonderful idea, and that he is the 'only indisputable artist that we have to do it'.[45] Oriol Bohigas i Guardiola, Councillor of Culture of the Ajuntament de Barcelona, architect, urban planner, and independent member of the PSC, agreed with Maragall's opinion concerning the sculpture yet refused to submit a written report for MNAC's board. Both Maragall and Bohigas positioned themselves in the debate affirming their support of the Tàpies project, but they decided to keep the Ajuntament officially neutral, advocating that the decision should be left solely to MNAC. Secretary of the PSC and candidate for the presidency of the Generalitat Raimon Obiols met with Maragall to discuss the artwork yet each maintained separate positions. Obiols stated that he was completely against the sculpture and joked that he himself was wearing two 'Tàpies', one on each foot.[46] Joan Guitart, the Generalitat's Councilor of Culture and member of the CDC, commented to *El País* (in reaction to Maragall's announcement of his support of *Mitjó*) that the Generalitat would seek the advice of professionals and that he would not base any political decision on his personal preferences.

On 6 February 1992 Guitart proposed finding another location 'more appropriate' to put Tàpies's creation, signifying the Generalitat's 'no' position in the debate.[47] The following day, *La Vanguardia* published a cartoon of a middle aged man with round glasses and a smug look on his face standing in front of the model of *Mitjó* and next to a grumpy representation of Tàpies with wiry, untamed hair. The man, a caricature of Guitart, tells the artist 'you are the best, your hairdo is wonderful, but we have to think of another place for your artwork'. Meanwhile, the sly, slender Guitart is thinking that the sock ought to be sent to the middle of snow-laden Siberia (figure 3.6).[48] Art historian and the first president of the Fundació Miró, Francesc Vicens, criticized Guitart's department for their disapproval of the project in an article published in *La Vanguardia*. He reminded readers that the decision was 'in theory' that of the museum, MNAC did not need to consult the Generalitat to install a new work of art, and Guitart could not veto *Mitjó*. Furthermore, Vicens stated that the artwork would 'help to dignify' the space, which had been neglected since 1929 and was finally under restoration, 'which ought to satisfy all Catalans'.[49] Jordi Solé Tura, Spanish Minister of Culture and member of the PSC, characterized the problem as a clash between creative liberty and public funding; adding that 'personally, Tàpies's sock doesn't particularly enthuse me'.[50] The heated debate concerning Tàpies's proposal continued through the first months of 1992.

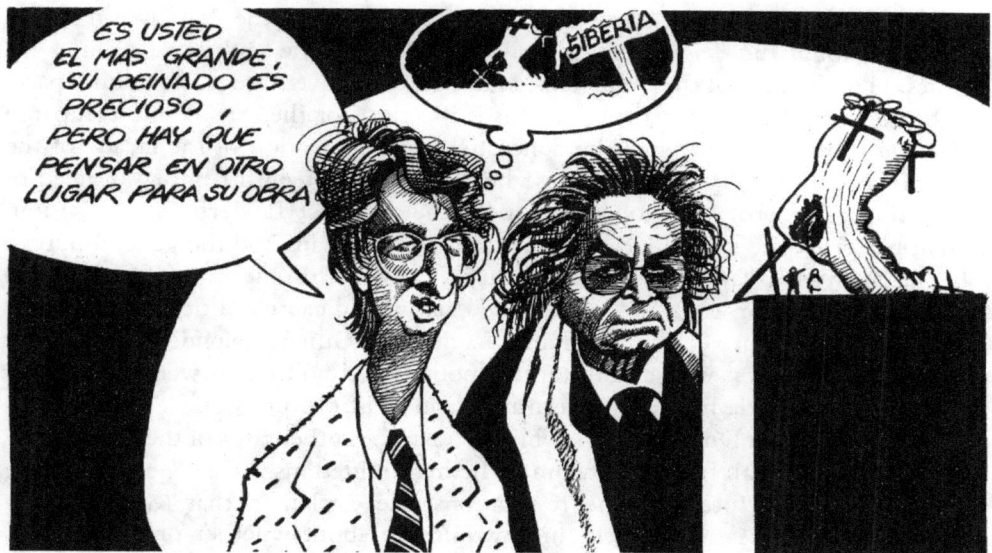

Fig. 3.6. Unknown, drawing published in *La Vanguardia*, Barcelona, 7 February 1992

On 26 February MNAC announced that they would not make any decisions until after the local elections, to be held on 15 March. Under normal circumstances, the board meetings were held on the first Tuesday of every month, however Duran i Farell did not want partisan interests to sway the decision about *Mitjó*.[51] While MNAC's board stalled the decision concerning the controversial commission as members of the board came from both the local and regional governing institutions and could not come to an agreement on the issues, the Ajuntament de Barcelona decided to award Tàpies with a gold medal of the city. On 29 February the press announced that Tàpies would be recognized the following Tuesday (3 March) for his dedication to art, his generosity in strengthening Barcelona's cultural activity, and his unwavering defence of democratic values and human rights.[52] While the Ajuntament did not submit an official report to MNAC in favour of or against the *Mitjó* project, honouring the artist at this moment in time is indicative of the city government's stance. Furthermore, the date in which the medal would be awarded is, coincidentally or not, the first Tuesday of the month. MNAC would have been meeting about *Mitjó* on this occasion, had Duran i Farell not decided to change the date due to upcoming elections.

Guitart recalled how the incident played out in a conversation with me. He remembered that with 'much' consensus between both MNAC's board and directors, that it was not the right moment to carry out the project, and that after construction was completed in the Sala Oval they could rethink it. He said that he had to communicate this decision to Tàpies, emphasizing that it was not a political choice but a circumstantial one. He expressed that 'some people and media sources did interpret it as a political decision', yet he did not see it as such.[53] Finally, he expressed that the work of politicians does not include the critiquing of art.

Pepe Serra, Director of MNCAC since 2011, recalled the 'totally ridiculous polemic', though he was in his mid-twenties at the time and just finishing his studies. He told me that the politicians, although they have to regulate public space, ought not to dictate over artistic style, as it is unjust for the artist.[54] He compared the *Mitjó* debate to a current issue concerning the renovation of the facade of the Gran Teatre del Liceu, an opera house built in the nineteenth century in need of restoration. The project's proposal includes the architect Frederic Amat's vision, which has provoked much debate both amongst politicians and the general public. One report went as far as calling the conflict a 'war' within the Ajuntament.[55] *Mitjó* was not the first, nor was it the last artwork that would cause politicians to become involved in artistic projects in Catalonia. As much as Guitart defended the fact that the MNAC's decision was circumstantial, politics and politicians were undeniably involved in this battle between government and artistic expression.

On April 23, 1992 Duran i Farell publicly spoke about the status of the renovations of the Palau Nacional. In a brief statement he highlighted his main concerns dealing with the financial future of the restorations. He explained that MNAC's first priority was to raise funds, then, they would see about whether or not Tàpies's *Mitjó* would fit into the plan. He addressed the overwhelming amount of attention the work was receiving and stated that debating about it is positive. However, he reiterated that the patrons of MNAC have more pressing priorities at the moment, like preparing for the opening ceremony of the Olympic Games.[56]

On 22 July 1992 *The Wall Street Journal* published an article titled 'Mr. Tàpies's Unmatched Sock'. Comically introducing the abundance of athletes in attendance of the international competition in Barcelona but the lack of one infamous athletic sock, reporter Lee Lescaze reviewed the history of the still unmade *Mitjó*. While the refurbishment of the Sala Oval was completed in time for the Summer Olympics, the hall was left void of any contrasting, contemporary work of art. For months, Tàpies and his sock were both attacked and defended in the local and international media without much official resolve. Lescaze's take on the controversy was positive. He praised the productivity of this sort of public discussion, characterizing it as 'stimulating' and a 'mark of civilization', concluding that in Barcelona 'a faith in the importance and power of art is alive and well'.[57]

After the conclusion of the Olympic Games, MNAC's Director, Xavier Barral, also spoke about the positive side of debating about art. Barral, speaking specifically about *Mitjó*, said 'it has been beneficial for MNAC, a lot of people did not even know we [the museum] existed [before]'.[58] The topic began to draw less media attention after the closing ceremony of the Olympics. Over a year went by before any substantial news concerning the project surfaced once again. In December 1993, the new President of MNAC's board, former Vice President Ramon Guardans, stated that Tàpies's sock 'will not be installed as long as I am president'.[59] Guardans spoke specifically about his opposition of the work that would take up much space in the Sala Oval. He did not address the prospect of locating the artwork in another part of the building.

Talk of *Mitjó* lasted two years, before Guardans seemed to bury the topic with his firm and patronizing statement. Politics, personal preferences, and financial shortcomings all played a part in the failure of MNAC's initiative to commission a contemporary artwork for the Palau Nacional in time for the Olympic Games. The museum's directors and board of trustees handled the situation in a way that benefitted their publicity. Drawing out the decision-making processes, stalling it during local elections, involving political institutions that did not need to be involved, and leaving the project unsolved for more than a year gained exposure for the museum, both positive and negative. Tàpies, likewise, became the focus of much attention due to the controversy. Some chose to publicly mock and denounce his art and others supported the sock and valued his professional career.

I asked Toni Tàpies if he remembered how his father felt concerning the whole *Mitjó* episode. Without hesitation, he recalled:

> The worst he felt since the moment that MNAC asked him to make a project for the Sala Oval, and when he presented his small model (which still exists, the sock) was when someone from MNAC said that they had not asked Tàpies to make anything, that he made the model because he wanted to, and the project ended there. If he made something it was because they asked him to make something, not because he had the idea of doing something there, it is absurd. He felt bad about this because it seemed like someone said that he was presenting a project that nobody sought him out to do, and that is not true. Later I think he became a little entertained reading the number of stories that were printed in newspapers, the majority were ridiculous, that in a way show the cultural and artistic level of this country, when in other countries this sort of project would be something normal that nobody would remark about to such an extent, here it turned into a hot topic of the press, the television, they made jokes and published caricatures.[60]

We continued discussing how public art is often controversial and the inevitability of its criticism. However, in this particular instance newspaper articles concerning the infamous sock reached a point of ludicrousness. He explained 'they ended up saying hurtful, atrocious things. Public sculptures are always going to be polemic, but the debate that occurred here with *Mitjó* was with extremely low levels of artistic analysis'.[61] The contents of that large box in the Fundació Antoni Tàpies filled with a giant stack of photocopied articles from the press includes innumerable opinions, however, the majority of which are satirical, only addressing the surface level aesthetic of Tàpies's sculptural proposal for MNAC.

The *Mitjó* debacle is an example of a direct relationship between art and politics, a theme this chapter will continue to elaborate on. What was initially a straightforward artistic commission turned into a media hyped debate spilling into the public sphere. Politicians, who held no credentials in aesthetics or art, made public statements that affected the project's outcome. It is not surprising that the Ajuntament supported the vanguard, non-traditional work while the Generalitat decided against it. The non-traditional sculpture would have fit with Pasqual Maragall and the PSC's narrative about Barcelona's modernity. Embracing the sock aligned with the sort of urban fabric that the Ajuntament was working to create, and *Mitjó* would have become a symbol of that era. On the other hand, the project clashed with the Generalitat and CiU's vision of Catalan culture. The plan was too transgressive, despite the regional government's endorsement of other works by

Tàpies, particularly those that reinforce Catalan nationalist narratives and myths. Comical drawings published in *Avui* and *Punt Diari* echoed the Generalitat's stance, poking fun at the artist, and ultimately disparaging *Mitjó*.

If the artist had proposed to create a giant *barretina* instead of a sock, would the Generalitat have approved of the commission for its nationalist representation?[62] It is both beneficial and productive to criticize and debate art. Unfortunately, politicians contributed to the prohibition of *Mitjó* and Tàpies never created the final version. The sculpture was never critiqued in its genuine form in its intended space. Furthermore, Tàpies's credibility as an artist was put under the microscope and local newspapers became active participants in the publicized debate, publishing not only news but opinion pieces from readers and comics. Although Guardans squashed the prospect of Tàpies creating the full-sized sculpture for the Sala Oval, the next chapter will reveal the final location of the mythical *Mitjó* and discuss the importance of location with respect to art and audiences. Despite the obstacles of the project from 1992 to 1993, it was never totally buried nor made and shipped to Siberia.

One of Tàpies' public works, housed in a different museum in Barcelona, is titled *Rinzen* (1993), which means 'a sudden awakening' in Japanese. Tàpies made this combination of sculpture and painting for the Spanish Pavilion at the 45th Venice Biennale and was presented, along with American artist Richard Hamilton, with the Golden Lion Award for painting. *Rinzen* is meant to condemn war, specifically the Bosnian War. However, the artwork is illegible without the artist's statement and the historical context in which it was first shown. None of the formal elements point out the horrors of the indiscriminate bombing, ethnic cleansing, and systematic raping of women in Bosnia during that period. However, Tàpies confirmed that *Rinzen* is meant to be an antiwar vision created in response to the first year of the Bosnian War, which began in April 1992. *ABC* published a brief interview with Tàpies just before the Biennale opened. Tàpies dramatically stated his distaste for realism, claiming that the style is shallow and glib. This may have been the reason that the Spanish government sought to appropriate the artist on this occasion, in order to highlight the nation's modernity. His intentions as an artist, as he sought to demonstrate with *Rinzen*, had to do with 'studying reality more profoundly, without dwelling on the surface of things'.[63] Not only did this interview seek to justify Tàpies's unique style, it simultaneously created friction between a handful of popular realist painters from Spain such as Antonio López, whose headshots were printed alongside that of Tàpies in the newspaper.

In 1998, Barcelona's contemporary art museum MACBA permanently installed the award-winning *Rinzen*. In the foyer of the entrance and rising up to the first floor, a large bed hangs diagonally below three numbers, '1 2 3', painted on the wall. Brown wood, rectangular frames, black netting, woollen blankets, and white pillows hang off the bed as gravity pulls them towards the floor. Opposite the iron bedframe, hanging on the wall of the first-floor gallery is a monochromatic painting, heavily textured and similar to Tàpies's Matter Paintings from the 1950s. A large glass window and door separates the two interior elements from the remainder of the work outside. From the inside, beholders can make out the title of the work painted on the adjacent wall of the exterior patio in black spray paint '*Rinzen*', which is emphasized with a rectangle around the letters and Tàpies's '+' marking boldly painted towards the upper left of the title. Two rows of five folding chairs are neatly organized as in a classroom. A metal strip snakes itself about the chairs, creating a physical connection between them. An eleventh chair sits away from the group, in the opposite direction, like an exile facing the wall. The artwork, modified in order to accommodate MACBA's space, is meant to lead viewers to a 'deeper understanding of reality'.[64] Does Tàpies's *Rinzen* accomplish this difficult task? The answer to this question is subjective and certainly depends on the emotions, memories, and experiences of the beholder.

After its exhibition at the Venice Biennale, Repsol purchased *Rinzen* for 70 million *pesetas*, more than 420,000 euros.[65] In 1997 the Spanish government sold their last ten percent of the partially privatized company, finalizing the privatization of Repsol. On 17 December the global energy company officially 'donated' the artwork to MACBA. Alfonso Cortina, the president of Repsol, attended the act along with the artist. Also present were: MACBA's Director Manuel Borja-Villel and President Leopoldo Rodés, the Mayor of Barcelona Joan Clos, and the Minister of Culture of the Generalitat Joan Maria Pujas.[66] Shortly after, the Seville edition of *ABC* published a full page with an image of the artwork, announcing Repsol's grand gesture.[67] The donation effectively relieved Repsol from paying a portion of their taxes, making *Rinzen* property of the state, not the museum. This is a popular model that large companies in the United States also use to 'support' the arts and lessen their tax burden.

After unveiling *Rinzen* at the Venice Biennale, and before its permanent installation in MACBA, Tàpies continued to work on large-scale public works. One example, which was not commissioned for any particular event, is in a suburb of Barcelona, Sabadell. In 1995, the artist presented a giant sculpture in the shape of a bell with a beam diagonally situated on top. Here, Tàpies reverses the relationship between the subject and strut of Classical sculptures, the latter serving as a means of physical support for the former. Ancient sculptors often added superfluous elements, such a tree trunk, to marble figures in order to reinforce the base. In the Sabadell sculpture, instead of the beam supporting the weight of the bell, the *bell* buttresses the more mundane element. Although the piece is similar to a church bell, Tàpies stated that his intentions were not religiously oriented, that the bell predates religion as a tool to warn communities of imminent danger.[68]

The sculpture is located outside of the Sabadell's municipal art museum and is the first public work Tàpies made in Spain outside of Barcelona. It also serves as a reminder that art is an extension of life, with its home just outside of the walls of the museum, and therefore not separate from politics. When the sculpture was first installed in Sabadell, local media highlighted that Tàpies had turned down an opportunity to make a mural for Madrid's airport.[69] The artist refused a commission from the Ayuntamiento de Madrid and donated a work to a community with far less international exposure in the same year. However, he made no comments concerning why he was uninterested in creating a mural for Barajas airport. On this occasion, Tàpies could have been asserting his nationalist politics, however without further documentation concerning the Madrid project, it is difficult to tell. In *Dictatorship, Workers, and the City: Labour in Greater Barcelona Since 1939* Sebastian Balfour wrote about a general workers' strike that took place in Sabadell in 1976. However, the act of resistance was about much more than concerns of working conditions and wages. A series of protests were sparked by the decision of the mayor, Josep Marcet, not to consider a petition for amnesty for political prisoners and ensuing acts of police brutality in Sabadell. The workers' strike advocated 'for union and political freedom as a form of struggle against repression', and they succeeded in taking down figures of power at the local level.[70] Perhaps the memory of these events, which Balfour characterized as a microcosm of what was going on at the state level, affected Tàpies's decision to give Sabadell one of his works of art.[71] There is no evidence that expresses a direct connection here on behalf of Tàpies, though, at the presentation of the artwork, Universitat de Barcelona Professor Antoni Marí made a statement that could allude to a correlation between the artwork and the workers strike. Marí stated that the bell is like a shelter, one that brings together spirits in harmony, with liberty, and justice.[72] At the very least, Tàpies would have known about the events that took place in the Barcelona suburb during the transition to democracy in Spain.

Although the bell was presented as a gift, an economic exchange did take place. Tàpies donated the sculpture to the Ajuntament de Sabadell. Shortly after, the Mayor of Sabadell Antoni Farrés, member of the environmentalist and post-communist party Iniciativa per Catalunya Verds (ICV), made a donation on behalf of the Ajuntament de Sabadell to the Fundació Antoni Tàpies of 9 million *pesetas*, around 54,000 euros.[73] While the sum did not amount to what private collectors may have paid for the work, it was still a substantial 'donation'.

The bell in Sabadell is mute, although looking at it suggests the sound it would make if it were hanging properly from the beam instead of supporting its weight. The absence of sound is also an important component in the artist's next major work, a meditation room for the Universitat Pompeu Fabra, a public university founded in 1990. In the centre of Barcelona, Tàpies created a space that prohibits noise, in order to encourage reflection, despite the hanging position of the painted bell. The *Sala de reflexió* combines painting, sculpture, and installation to mould the interior of a useful place (1996). A large mural with the symmetrical, curvy outline of a bell is centred on the back wall. To the left are five rows of five chairs, neatly hanging on the wall. Some of the chairs are moveable, although the third, fourth, and fifth rows are fixed to the wall and out of reach. To the right is a wooden cupboard, topped with an ordinary white plate and a coiled snake. The magazine *On* wrote that the snake has clear biblical references; however, as Tàpies was agnostic, the snake is more likely to reference a different sort of spiritual symbol.[74] In ancient Pompeii and Herculaneum, households of all social classes had shrine-like altars that functioned as part of ritual ceremonies to protect the domestic realm. These *lararia* were composed of architectural elements generally framing a painting.

The pictures often included snakes; a fine example exists in the ruins of the atrium of the *Casa dei Vettii* in Pompeii. Snakes were an important protective symbol in the home. While the best-preserved examples are in Italy, there is evidence of similar images in Northern Africa and the Iberian Peninsula, also predating biblical references to snakes.[75] The coiled snake in Tàpies's sculpture, in the context of a quiet retreat made for thinking, seems closely related to the safeguarding function of the snakes in ancient domestic *lararia*. Furthermore, the *Sala de reflexió* is purposefully non-denominational. It imitates the Rothko Chapel in Houston, Texas, designed in 1971 as a meditative space, an 'intimate sanctuary available to people of every belief'.[76] Lined with Mark Rothko's murals, the inviting interior provides an environment that is rarely found in the urban fabric. It is a quiet, calm sphere dedicated to the intellectual and emotional condition of the people who visit it. Similarly, Universitat Pompeu Fabra's *Sala de reflexió* aims to achieve a spiritual aura free from religious connotations.

Tàpies expressed his objectives of the project, highlighting the unnatural, accelerating rhythm and pace of life that he thought necessitated a counterbalance:

> Faced with the excesses of bustle, mental dispersion and the innumerable cults to false realities to which we are subjected in present-day societies, it seems to me very opportune to contribute to the creation of a space and images which favour seclusion, concentration and, in short, a closer approximation to our real nature.[77]

In the months following the completion of the work in September of 1996, the local media described it as a place to 'concentrate and meditate, in the midst of the distortion of the contemporary world'.[78] The artwork inside the *Sala de reflexió*, instead of taking on the role of a spectacle on view in a museum, is not the primary focus of the visitors. The art is meant to provide an environment conducive to the individual's needs for quiet contemplation. Tàpies thought that the space was ideal, as the overwhelming bustle of many museums has changed the way people experience works of art.[79] His project aimed for an emotive reaction that reverberates back to the people who visit, not the work of art itself. 'Tàpies's Chapel' was closed to the public shortly after its inauguration. As part of Pompeu Fabra's twenty-fifth anniversary celebration, the *Sala de reflexió* reopened to the public in 2016, with an entrance fee of five euros that includes admission into both Tàpies's room and another small gallery exhibiting additional artworks by Tàpies and Antonio Saura.[80]

As the art historian Xavier Barral wrote in *Avui* about the space, art is only valuable when it is integrated into life.[81] Art cannot be both valuable and detached from society. Tàpies was aware of this and sought to create involved works that have a real social function. He designed the *Sala de reflexió* for Pompeu Fabra, a public university that seeks to uphold 'the principles of freedom, democracy, justice, equality, independence, and plurality'.[82] The meditation room that he created for the newly established school did not include any overt references to one of his most commonly addressed themes: Catalan history and identity. Pompeu Fabra is not a historical institution and its aims are to embrace plurality, although

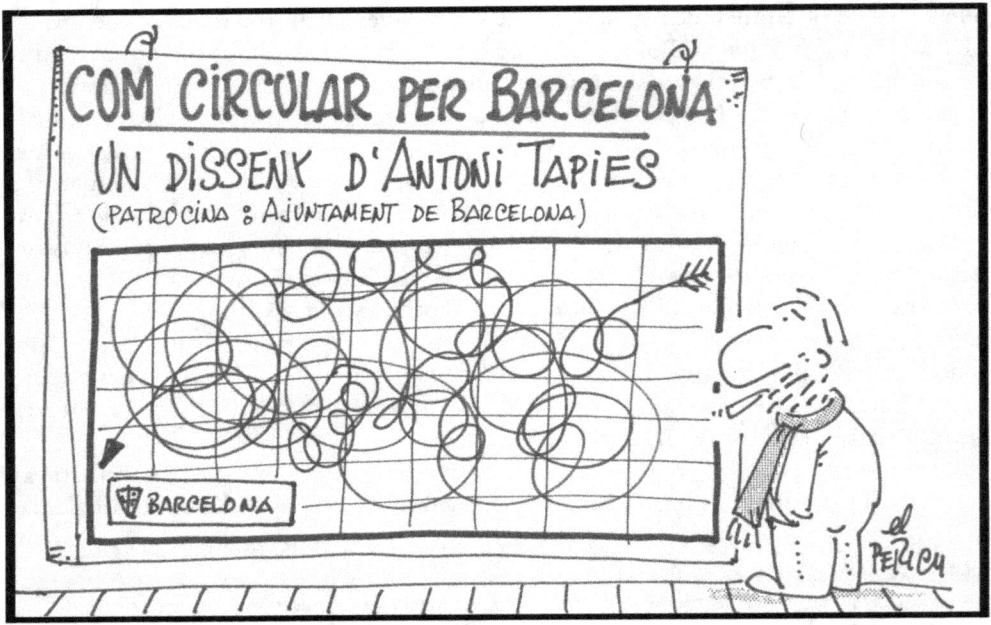

Fig. 3.7. Jaume Perich Escala, drawing with title 'Com circular per Barcelona', circa 1990–1995, Arxiu Municipal de Barcelona

the school is named after one of the most important figures in the history of the Catalan language, Pompeu Fabra i Poch.[83] Accordingly, Tàpies left out references to any one particular national identity. However, CiU created the school as an elite university, using a name that recapitulated a strategy of nationalization seeking to link the present with figures from the past. While the *Sala de reflexió* does not look much like Tàpies's works for the Generalitat, the project was tied to CiU. The following chapter will elaborate on works that do focus on the subject of Catalonia and Catalan identity, and it includes an analysis of the direct relationship between art and politics in both public and non-public works of art.

3.3. Concluding Remarks

A single, simple cartoon captures many of themes outlined in this chapter. Public funding, politics, time, and space are all addressed in this witty drawing (figure 3.7) by Jaume Perich Escala (known as 'El Perich').[84] A stout, dumfounded man stands in front of a map with the title 'How to Circulate Barcelona'. The chart is one ridiculous, squiggly line that transverses from the upper right to the lower left in an abundant series of loops. Below the title, it says that it is a design made by Antoni Tàpies and in parenthesis sponsored by the Ajuntament de Barcelona. This laughable image plays with a number of ideas starting with the practicality of the artist's work. The map recalls the metal coils of his *Núvol i cadira* sculpture that crowns the building of his foundation. It also suggests the artist's non-traditional or even non-practical tendency, as a normal map would show visitors a rational route through the city. The title and subtitles are written in Catalan and point out the Ajuntament's support of the artist. In a way, the cartoon is as ambiguous as some of Tàpies's Matter Paintings. Perich, in acknowledging Tàpies's idiosyncrasy and the local government's patronage of him, perpetuates his prominence while simultaneously poking fun at him. A more sardonic interpretation, on the other hand, could consider the cartoon as a critique of the Ajuntament's prudency, efficiency, and public spending. Although Tàpies's body of work engaged with international artistic tendencies and exhibited avant-garde techniques, it was also inextricably tied to the local institutions that supported him, critics that criticized him, cartoonists that poked fun at him, and Catalan compatriots that backed him.[85]

The Generalitat de Catalunya financially supported Tàpies throughout the 1990s and has continued to make annual contributions to the foundation well into the twenty-first century. While the institution did not back the installation of Mitjó in the Palau Nacional, it is the body that has provided the most financial aid for the Fundació Antoni Tàpies. The Ajuntament de Barcelona has also played a major role in funding the artist and his projects. Through extension, both CiU and PSC significantly bolstered Tàpies's professional career despite their ideological differences. Without the support of the most influential political institutions in Catalonia, Tàpies's exposure, repertoire, and legacy would have been reduced considerably.

Each of these two institutions maintained very different relationships with the artist. The Generalitat supported the Tàpies's nationalist representations, using some of these compositions to promote a Catalan nationalist narrative linked to historic civilizations. The Ajuntament, on the other hand, sought to present cutting-edge works in order to promote Barcelona's image as a cosmopolitan centre with a progressive cityscape. This distinction became most evident in the Ajuntament's approval of the proposed Mitjó project and the Generalitat's hesitation and final disapproval. This debate demonstrates much about the dynamic between art and politics. While a sizeable piece of red-and-yellow striped cloth is acceptable and appropriate in just about any corner of Catalonia, the Generalitat did not see that a work of contemporary art by an internationally acclaimed artist was fit for the centre of an art museum.

Whether or not he took up subjects that were Catalan or more instinctive and abstract, Tàpies continued to work the subversive style that he developed in the 1950s under the Franco regime. His decision to continue to create in this manner, decades after the dictator's death, is not particularly surprising. As journalist Luis Apostua pointed out in 1992, being an artist and anti-Francoist was a lucrative vocation. 'Why wouldn't Tàpies make a living off of *antifranquismo*? It is known to be a profitable enterprise'.[86] Still, both the Catalan and Spanish governments sought to project different parts of the same Tàpies, as seen in their public commissions. As a result, despite his style remaining astonishingly congruent, the circulation of the 'Tàpies' brand is somewhat *in*congruent. The following chapter will discuss in greater detail some of Tàpies's compositions that directly reference Catalonia, unlike the old sock, and the ways in which visual material can substantiate the idea that a nation is a natural, fixed entity.

Notes to Chapter 3

1. '¿Por qué no va a vivir Tàpies de antifranquismo? Es negocio de reconocida rentabilidad'. Luis Apostua, 'Calcetin con millones', *Navarra Hoy*, 9 February 1992.
2. For the contradictory nature of the 1992 celebrations in Spain see: Balfour and Quiroga, *The Reinvention of Spain*, 168–71.
3. Instituto Nacional de Estadística, Encuesta de empleo del tiempo 2002–2003, accessed 13 June 2016, http://www.ine.es/daco/daco42/empleo/dacoeet.htm.
4. Interview with Toni Tàpies, 4 February 2016.
5. Presumably the first autobiographical account of a medieval king in Europe, the original *Llibre dels fets* was lost. Jaume II commissioned a Latin translation of his father's work, although is the earliest surviving copy dates from 1343, after Jaume II's death. Scholars believe that Jaume I did not actually write out the work, instead he dictated to scribes, and there is even some speculation as to whether or not the king knew how to write himself. *The Book Of Deeds of James I of Aragon: A Translation of the Medieval Catalan Llibre dels fets*, trans. Damian Smith and Helen Buffery (Aldershot: Ashgate, 2003), p. 10.
6. Andrew Dowling, *Catalonia Since the Spanish Civil War: Reconstructing the Nation* (Portland, OR: Sussex Academic Press, 2013), p. 111.
7. Ibid., p. 123.
8. Guibernau, *Catalan Nationalism: Francoism, Transition and Democracy* (London: Routledge, 2004), p. 144. For more on language and identity in Catalonia see: Fernández, 'Becoming Normal: Cultural Production and Cultural Policy in Catalonia', 343; and Molinero and Ysàs, *La cuestión catalana*, pp. 250–59.
9. For an extensive examination of this sort of model see: Joaquim Rius Ulldemolins, 'Política cultural e hibridación de las instituciones culturales. El caso de Barcelona', *Revista Española de Ciencia Política*, 29 (July 2012).
10. 'La Fundació Tàpies, en la corda fluixa', *Ara*, 6 June 2015.
11. On 16 September 2009 the Generalitat signed a subsidy agreement, contributing 4,445,782.54 euros split between normal annual contributions, interest loans, and amortized loans to help pay for a renovation that kept the foundation closed to the public from January 2008 until March 2010.
12. Henri Matisse, 'Notes of a Painter', *Theories of Modern Art*, p. 135.
13. 'La Fundación Antoni Tàpies abre sus puertas', *ABC*, 7 June 1990, p. 146, accessed 13 June 2016, http://hemeroteca.abc.es/nav/Navigate.exe/hemeroteca/madrid/abc/1990/06/07/146.html.
14. Interview with Joan Guitart, 12 July 2016.
15. 'Antoni Tàpies galardonado con el Príncipe de Asturias'. *ABC* (Sevilla), 19 May 1990, p. 61.
16. Sergio Vila-San-Juan, 'Antoni Tàpies recibe el premio Príncipe de Asturias de las Artes', and Vicente González, 'El pintor barcelonés no figuraba en la lista de artistas preseleccionados', *La Vanguardia*, 19 May 1990, accessed 28 August 2016, http://hemeroteca.lavanguardia.com/preview/1990/05/19/pagina-37/33022907/pdf.html?search=Premio%20Pr%C3%ADncipe%20de%20Asturias%20Antoni%20T%C3%A0pies.
17. Catalina Serra, 'El Pintor Antoni Tàpies gana el Premio Príncipe de Asturias de las Artes', *El País*, 13 May 1990, accessed 19 June 2016, http://elpais.com/diario/1990/05/19/cultura/643068006_850215.html.
18. Dowling, *Catalonia Since the Spanish Civil War*, p. 131.
19. Serra, 'El Pintor Antoni Tàpies gana el Premio Príncipe de Asturias de las Artes'.
20. Catalina Serra, 'TVE- Cataluña y la BBC colaboran en un documental sobre Tàpies', *El País*, 28 June 1990, accessed 19 June 2016, http://elpais.com/diario/1990/06/28/radiotv/646524002_850215.html. Daniel Hernández also directed a documentary film on Tàpies titled *Alfabet Tàpies*, which aired in December of 2003 on Televisió de Catalunya.
21. *Tàpies*, Gregory Rood, dir., BBC and TVE Catalunya, 1990.
22. Tàpies, *Complete Writings Volume I. A Personal Memoir: Fragments for an Autobiography*, 290.
23. Dowling, *Catalonia Since the Spanish Civil War*, p. 127.
24. Daniel E. Jones, 'Pujol y la construcción de un espacio catalán de comunicación: Interacciones

entre instituciones políticas y empresas mediáticas (1980–2003)', *Ámbitos*, 16 (2007), 499–524 (p. 505–06).
25. Dowling, *Catalonia Since the Spanish Civil War*, p. 130.
26. Quiroga and Molina, 'National Deadlock', p. 3.
27. See also María José Hierro, 'Crafting Identities in a Multinational Context: Evidence from Catalonia', *Nations and Nationalism*, 21.3 (2015), 461–82).
28. Manuel Vázquez Montalbán, *Sabotaje olímpico* (Barcelona: Planeta, 1993), Kindle loc. 115.
29. Ibid., Kindle loc. 115.
30. Helen Graham and Antonio Sanchez, 'The Politics of 1992', *Spanish Cultural Studies*, p. 411.
31. Ferran Brunet i Cid, 'The Economic Impact of the Barcelona Olympics Games, 1986–2004', Centre d'Estudis Olímpics, 2002, accessed 1 September 2015, http://olympicstudies.uab.es/pdf/wp084_eng.pdf.
32. Dowling, *Catalonia Since the Spanish Civil War*, p. 138.
33. Joan Antoni Poch, *Punt Diari*, Girona, 26 January 1992. Signed 'JAP' on the lower right.
34. Unknown artist, *Avui*, Barcelona, 26 January 1992. Signed 'Fer' on lower left.
35. Antoni Tàpies, *El tatuaje y el cuerpo*.
36. Jaime Gustà Hernández, 'El calectín de Tàpies', *La Vanguardia*, 18 March 1992, p. 20.
37. 'El PP s'oposa a la instal·lació del mitjó de Tàpies al Palau Nacional', *Avui*, 28 January 1992.
38. Maria Sala, 'El calcetín de Tàpies', *El Periódico*, 18 February 1992.
39. Alejandro Quiroga, *Goles y banderas. Fútbol e identidades nacionales en España* (Madrid: Marcial Pons Historia, 2014), p. 71.
40. Abraham Méndez Ramos, 'En torno a un "calcetín"', *El Observador*, 7 March 1992.
41. 'Un restaurante crea una encuesta-sorteo sobre el "calcetín" de Antoni Tàpies', *El País*, 18 June 1992. See also: Ramon Alberch 'Un menú diario en el Archivo Histórico', *El Periódico*, 24 June 1992.
42. Àtremis, 'Visca el mitjó', *Diari de Barcelona*, 11 February 1992.
43. Rosario Fontova, 'La sala oval del Palau Nacional se abrirá en el 92', *El Periódico*, 17 December 1991.
44. Josep Massot, 'El vicepresidente del MNAC se opone a la escultura del calcetín', *La Vanguardia*, 23 January 1992. 'La Generalitat "pide" consejo sobe una obra de Tàpies', *Segre*, 25 January 1992.
45. 'Maragall no intervendrá en la decisión sobre el "calcetín" de Tàpies', *El País*, 8 February 1992.
46. 'A Obiols no le gusta el calectín', *Segre*, 8 February 1992.
47. 'La Generalitat se opone al calcetín de Tàpies', *La Vanguardia*, 6 February 1992. Guitart later became President of MNAC's board (1996–2004).
48. Unknown artist, *La Vanguardia*, Barcelona, 7 February 1992.
49. 'Vicens: Guitart no puede vetar el calcetín', *La Vanguardia*, 7 February 1992.
50. Rafael Villabona, 'Solé Tura: "El 'calcetín' de Tàpies no me entusiasma demasiado"', *El Observador*, 5 February1992.
51. 'El MNAC no decidirá sobre el "calcetín" de Tàpies hasta después de las elecciones', *El País*, 25 February 1992.
52. 'El Ayuntamiento de Barcelona concede a Antoni Tàpies la medalla de oro de la cuidad', *El País*, 29 February 1992.
53. Interview with Joan Guitart, 12 July 2016.
54. Interview with Pepe Serra, 27 June 2016.
55. María Jesús Cañizares, 'Guerra en el ayuntamiento por la nueva fachada del Liceu', *Crónica*, 31 March 2016, accessed 15 July 2016, http://www.cronicaglobal.com/es/notices/2016/03/guerra-en-el-ayuntamiento-por-la-nueva-fachada-del-liceu-35846.php.
56. 'Duran: "Que hi hagi mitjó no és decisiu pel museu,"' *Diari de Barcelona*, 23 April 1992.
57. Lee Lescaze, 'Mr. Tàpies's Unmatched Sock', *The Wall Street Journal*, 22 July 1992, A10.
58. 'Barral dice que la poémica del calcetín beneficia al MNAC', *La Vanguardia*, 10 September 1992. Over 142,000 people visited the Sala Oval of the museum that summer.
59. 'Tàpies, descalzo', *ABC de las artes*, December 1993 n. 90, accessed 9 September 2015, http://hemeroteca.abc.es/nav/Navigate.exe/hemeroteca/madrid/cultural/1994/02/04/024.html
60. Interview with Toni Tàpies, 4 February 2016.

61. Ibid.
62. For the arbitrary nature of national symbols, see Ozkirimli, *Contemporary Debates On Nationalism*, p. 188.
63. 'Antoni Tàpies abofeta al realismo: "Es pintura facilona para nuevos ricos,"' *ABC*, 11 June 1993, p. 12.
64. MACBA Collection, accessed 13 September 2015, http://www.macba.cat/en/rinzen-1461.
65. Catalina Serra, 'El MACBA instala la pieza que Tàpies presentó en la Bienal de Venecia', *El País*, 18 December 1998, accessed 14 September 2015, http://elpais.com/diario/1998/12/18/cultura/913935604_850215.html.
66. 'Repsol dona a la Fundació Museo d'Art Contemporani la obra Rinzen, de Antoni Tàpies', Repsol press release, 17 December 1998, accessed 14 September 2015, http://www.repsol.com/es_es/corporacion/prensa/notas-de-prensa/ultimas-notas/donacion_de_la_obra_rinzen_a_la_fundacio.aspx.
67. 'Tàpies: 75 años de creación', *ABC*, 20 December 1998, 83, accessed 13 June 2016, http://hemeroteca.abc.es/nav/Navigate.exe/hemeroteca/sevilla/abc.sevilla/1998/12/20/083.html.
68. Jordi Bordes, 'Sabadell, tercera cuitat d'Europa que té una escultura de Tàpies', *El 9 Nou*, 17 June 1995.
69. Jordi Bordes, 'Tàpies instal·la a Sabadell la seva primera obra fora de Barcelona', *El 9 Nou*, 13 June 1995; 'Sabadell, tercera cuitat d'Europa que té una escultura de Tàpies'.
70. Balfour, *Dictatorship, Workers, and the City*, pp. 224–25.
71. Ibid., p. 227.
72. Josep Ache, 'Tàpies dóna a Sabadell un símbol', *Diari de Sabadell*, 17 June 1995.
73. Ibid.
74. 'Sala de Reflexión en la Universidad Pompeu Fabra', *On* (Barcelona), 1997 num. 180, p. 95.
75. George K. Boyce, 'Significance of the Serpents on Pompeian House Shrines', *American Journal of Archaeology*, 46 (1942).
76. Rothko Chapel, accessed 18 September 2015, http://rothkochapel.org/index.php?option=com_content&view=article&id=3&Itemid=6.
77. 'Sala de Reflexión en la Universidad Pompeu Fabra', p. 95.
78. Pilar Parcerisas, 'Una cambra per al silenci', *Avui*, 6 February 1997.
79. Llàtzer Moix, 'Tàpies reinvindica el arte como vehículo de reflexión en su monumental obra para la UPF', *La Vanguardia*, 6 December 1996, accessed 9 June 2016, http://hemeroteca.lavanguardia.com/preview/1996/07/28/pagina-41/33957519/pdf.html?search=Sala%20de%20Reflexi%C3%B3n%20T%C3%A0pies.
80. David Palacios, 'En el interior de la capilla laica de Tàpies', *La Vanguardia*, 5 June 2016, accessed 9 June 2016, http://www.lavanguardia.com/local/barcelona/20160602/402225411601/capilla-laica-tapies-upf-reflexion.html.
81. Xavier Barral i Altet, 'Coherència tapiana', *Avui*, 7 January 1997.
82. 'A Brief History of a Young University', Universitat Pompeu Fabra, accessed 19 June 2016, https://www.upf.edu/universitat/en/presentacio/historia.html.
83. In 1904 he published *Tractat de ortografia catalana* which outlines the standards of modern Catalan orthography and in 1911 he wrote a book on Catalan grammar in Spanish titled *Qüestions de gramàtica catalana*.
84. This image, along with several thousand more of Perich's works, pertains to the Arxiu Municipal de Barcelona. It has no specified publication or date. However, considering its reference to Tàpies's 1990 spiral sculpture *Núvol i cadira* and Perich's 1995 death, the drawing must date to the early 1990s.
85. Quotation marks are used in respect to Billig's ideas concerning how politics often address the national audience as such, creating an us/them divide that becomes null once the topic jumps from the national to the global level. For more see: Michael Billig, *Banal Nationalism*.
86. Apostua, 'Calcetin con millones'.

CHAPTER 4

The Visualization of a Catalan Nation

This chapter considers how Tàpies represented the image of Catalonia up until 2006, which directly links some of his most visible works of art to the realm of politics. These images have contributed to the representation of the idea of Catalonia as a real and valuable place, not an imagined nation. 'The Visualization of a Catalan Nation' analyses compositions that deal with national identity, contemporary issues, and historical commemoration. The first section examines the ways in which politics has affected the work of the artist, paying particular attention to the topic of Catalan nationalism and the various times associated with the idea of the nation. The following section includes a discussion of the direct links between Tàpies's art and politics. The objective of this chapter is not to put forward an argument about Tàpies's own identity and politics, but rather to expose the ways in which he formulated his images, many of which are associated with Catalonia.

4.1. Art, Nationalism, and Identity

As argued in the previous chapters, Tàpies established a style that remained constant throughout his long career. However, the subject matter of his artworks is not equally consistent. Catalan culture is a recurring and politically charged theme that he tended to work with. Returning to a pair of examples introduced prior to this chapter, this time focusing on their nationalist content, allows for a more nuanced analysis of the political implications of the artist's work. The word 'visualize' can mean to form a mental image, to imagine, or to make something visible to the eye.[1] 'The Visualization of a Catalan Nation' has a double meaning. It is something that Tàpies created, making the idea of a national history and identity visible. It is simultaneously something that beholders imagine upon seeing some of his artworks. A closer look at artworks such as *Pintura romànica i barretina*, *Les quatre cròniques*, and the mural at the Universal Exposition in Sevilla illustrate the artist's role in presenting and perpetuating ideas concerning the legitimacy of Catalonia's nationhood and 'its' values and identity.

A nation is an abstract idea. Nations do not exist without humans conceptualizing their citizens, borders, and organization. When an artist makes an artwork, a single image cannot wholly capture the idea of a unified 'imagined' community.

However, they can represent concepts that perpetuate or transform the idea of the nation. A humorous example is Horatio Greenough's 1840 sculpture of the first President of the United States, George Washington, posed in the manner of an ancient Greek god. Seated in a chair, with a toga that only covers him from the waist down, Washington holds a sword in one hand and raises the other towards the sky. He is wearing sandals. Why did Greenough decide to depict the late president in this manner? He wanted to emphasize the importance of freedom and democracy, aligning his central figure with a god of one of the most cultured civilizations of the 'Western' world. What does this absurd (in that Washington is entirely idealized and wearing clothing that seems ridiculous for Philadelphian climate) statue say about the United States? It glorifies its past, as the statue was made over a century after Washington's birth, and it promotes the single most important 'American' value via a Latin inscription on the back that reads: 'Horatio Greenough made this image as a great example of freedom, and will not survive without freedom itself'. The sculpture alludes to the victory over the British Empire and establishment of a free country. However, the statue fails to address that while American Revolutionaries won liberty from foreign rule, during Washington's presidency Native Americans, slaves, and women were excluded from participating in the new 'free' state. Art, in this case, perpetuates the idea that the 'Founding Fathers' of the United States of America were the harbingers of freedom, giving them a heroic, divine status.

Art is also able to bring into question already established knowledge concerning the nation. For example, Peter Saul's 1967 painting *Saigon* is a fierce critique of US policy during the Vietnam War. Saul's representation of American G.I.s raping and torturing the family of the central figure, a Vietnamese female labelled 'innocent virgin', is both appealing in its bright colours and appalling in its content. Reiterating the action of the canvas is a phrase at the bottom, 'white boys torturing and raping the people of Saigon: high class version'. This artwork condemns the behaviours of American soldiers, undercutting the notion that the United States military is a protective and valiant organization. Greenough and Saul's works are two examples of how art participates in the conception of the nation, an idea that somehow manages to organize contemporary societies and individuals' identities.

How is Tàpies's artwork related to Catalan nationalism and identity? Remember that both nationalism and identity are not fixed terms, they can both change over time and through space. Furthermore, contrary to popular beliefs, nationalism is neither a natural phenomenon nor limited to extreme groups, such as fascists or separatists, as Michael Billig pointed out in *Banal Nationalism*.[2] Linking Tim Edensor's idea that sensuality plays a significant role in the construction of national identity and Alejandro Quiroga's elaboration on Fernando Molina's 'personalization' of the nation, it becomes clear that national identity and nationalism are bound to human emotion and personal experiences.[3] Tàpies addressed the Catalan nation in three ways: verbally, via artworks that employ obvious symbols, colours, words, and names of local 'heroes' associated with Catalonia, and through his stylistic embodiment of these elements. The *ways* in which Tàpies has presented symbols like the stripes of the *senyera* or the date 11 September contribute to the emotional charge that these works of art carry. Furthermore, they aggrandize the fabricated concept that nations are unchanging, definable, and historically justified entities.

Tàpies's artwork often takes up themes related to the Catalan nation, both expressing his own ideas concerning his national identity and representing nationalism visually, in space rather than time. The difference between Tàpies's work and bolder examples such as *Saigon* is remarkable. Saul's combination of flashy colours with shocking, cartoonish images makes the picture memorable. Once viewers allow their eyes to adjust to the shades of neon, they are left with a repulsive, disgraceful picture that remains imprinted in their memory. Tàpies's work, on the other hand, often employs a more subtle approach to the transmission of national ideas. For example, *Pintura romànica i barretina* does not leave beholders with such a fierce sensation directly linked to the idea of the nation. However, the image does reinforce the association between an everyday object, the red hat, and its iconographic significance in Catalonia. The international audience may not be aware that the representation of the *barretina* establishes two groups: 'us' and 'them'. That particular cap is linked to a host of meanings but is primarily associated with considering oneself a Catalan. The extraordinary aspect of this picture is its balance between the mundane and the revolutionary. Tàpies created *Pintura romànica i barretina* in 1971, during the late Franco dictatorship and during the same year as the first Assemblea de Catalunya. While the canvas does not depict a single, direct idea, Tàpies suggests themes that lead to a particular idea. The *barretina* is the most obvious symbol that deals with the concept of Catalan identity.[4] The rope alludes to violence and intolerable yet 'legal' acts that the dictatorial regime committed after the war. The combination of the rope and hat forms a pendulum, showing time standing still. An anti-Francoist artist's representation of Catalan identity, violence, and time during the early 1970s transmits a powerful message about the past and a hopeful one for the future. But Tàpies's work does not spell-out his ideas literally, as *Saigon* does.

Pintura romànica i barretina, particularly beyond the context of its 1970s debut, is closer to Billig's notion of a banal yet nationalist emblem.[5] In *Banal Nationalism*, Billig showed how language contributes to a more natural acceptance of the world as logically divided into nations, where linguistically similar populations become unified under a single state. Catalonia is a peculiar case, where the 'national' language differs from that of the Kingdom of Spain. Further complicating the study of nationalism in Catalonia is the great spectrum, both historically and contemporaneously, of patriotic feelings under consideration. In Franco's Spain Catalan nationalist groups were fragmented, differing in their political objectives but united in their opposition to the regime.[6] As Kathryn Crameri has expressed, 'fragmentation has been a perpetual characteristic of Catalan separatism up to the present day'.[7] In twenty-first century Catalonia there are a host of different ways in which individuals have considered their Catalan identities with respect to that of the Spain. Some citizens of the region have seen their Catalan national identity as compatible with a Spanish identity, while others have felt indivisibly Catalan.

Many individuals have felt more Catalan than Spanish and others more Spanish than Catalan, as has often been the case with immigrants living in Catalonia.[8] There are many intermediary points where people's individual identifications vary. However, each block has seemed to correlate with the population's desires for the future relation between Spain and Catalonia. For example, many of those who felt exclusively Catalan have advocated for an independent state whereas those who have opposed the independence movement often identified themselves, at least in part, as being Spanish. Nevertheless, the degree or nature of a citizen's national identification is unfixed and can sway under in time or under diverse circumstances. Factors that contribute to the moulding of national identities and therefore nationalism include, but are not limited to, the media, family life, experience abroad, education, and even sports.

Art, as a form of visual language, also shapes the way that national subjects conceive of themselves in respect to 'their' nation. This most often appears in Billig's realm of banal nationalism, a space where the very idea of the legitimacy of the national body goes unquestioned but is nevertheless constantly pulsating and structuring our notions of common knowledge.[9] However, as Quiroga has pointed out, Billig's work does not get into the process of reception on behalf of individuals and the application of this theory is Catalonia does not seem to work.[10] This may hold true in terms of overtly political signals like the *estelada*, which clearly clashes with Spanish nationalism. However, artworks that address the Catalan nation in a subtler format can be understood in Billig's terms as banal beacons of nationalism.

In 'Banal Catalanism?' Kathryn Crameri talked about Billig's theory, showing that through the 1979 acknowledgement of Catalonia's national status as a *nacionalidad histórica*, Catalan citizens stopped seeking to constantly justify the nation's existence, effectively shifting nationalism from 'hot' to 'banal'.[11] Currently, artworks such as *Pintura romànica i barretina* work within the boundaries of national ideology, recapitulating the power of nations to structure contemporary thinking and strengthening the binary of us/them. While Billig's thesis may have worked in Catalonia since the central Spanish government approved the recognition of Catalonia as a nation, in 1971 when Tàpies made *Pintura romànica i barretina* the national question was a more contentious, delicate matter. It did not work *within* the boundaries of a legally recognized nation, but it did work to promote a differentiation between two politically unified yet culturally different groups.

The 'us', in this case, is signified through the red hat, a symbol of Catalan identity employed as a marker to distinguish a difference from the 'them'. As the red hat is not an image with universal meaning, the 'them' that this canvas addresses signifies the rest of the Spanish population that does not consider themselves Catalan. The hanging position of the *barretina* victimizes the 'us' while simultaneously indicating the idea of time. In *Pintura romànica i barretina* time is static, frozen. The unmoving pendulum is awaiting a stimulus to begin anew. In the context of 1971, increased clandestine political activity and the desire for self-government in Catalonia could have been the spark that Tàpies saw that would instigate change. Meanwhile, he continued to work in his often discrete yet politically potent style, one that both demonstrated his anti-Francoist position *and* sought to glorify the history (including invented histories) of Catalonia.

Tàpies highlighted how important Catalonia was for him as an artist and intellectual in a 1990 BBC version of a documentary about him:

> I've been greatly affected by the geography of my personal circumstances, by my family life, and my life in the city of Barcelona, and by my life in my country: Catalonia. From an early age I developed the habit of probing beneath the surface, of looking always for a deeper reality. I couldn't stop thinking about the moral dilemmas involved in the pursuit of such things as truth, justice, and honesty.[12]

The way in which Tàpies referred to his 'country' is indicative of the emotional ties he had with the region. Here he voiced what some of his images point out: that he felt connected to Catalonia and that it formed part of his personal identity. While this identity is not always evident in every single work that he made, this statement demonstrates Tàpies's awareness that time and place were defining aspects of his life.

Some of the Tàpies's works fuse what Homi Bhabha coins as the 'pedagogical' and 'performative', strategic elements that ultimately enable the ability of national myths to flourish in the contemporary imagination.[13] In analysing Tàpies's pictures, it becomes clear that national tales concerning the past and future of Catalonia have impacted the artist a great deal. The way that he sought to recycle these tales is fascinating and Bhabha's concepts of the pedagogical and performative will help me to explain the visual language of art at work.

In his chapter 'DissemiNation: time, narrative, and the margins of the modern nation', Bhabha built a complex argument on the fundamental ambivalence that permeates national texts, which is also applicable to the plastic arts. This ambivalence affects both the concepts of time and cultural identity in the writing of the modern 'Western' nation. He characterizes a splitting that occurs between 'the continuist, accumulative temporality of the pedagogical, and the repetitious, recursive strategy of the performative'.[14] Bhabha deemed the pedagogical and the performative contrasting elements that contribute to the inherent confusion that national narratives create, or ambivalence. The pedagogical deals with the way that history is presented as a continuation of civilizations and the idea that the nation is a natural and unchanging entity. For example, Spanish history is not a neat tale of ancestral activity, but a messy story of the Iberian Peninsula, which has been dominated by a great number of people, ranging from Germanic tribes and Arab conquerors to Christian Kings and military officers from Andalucía and Galicia. What we call the Kingdom of Spain is an unnatural combination of communities based loosely on geographic location and historic allegiances that were constantly changing and will continue to change over time. Bhabha's pedagogical is the term that describes the over-simplification of historic societies, the conscious blindness to their complexity, and the preservation of the myth of the nation. The performative refers to the constant onslaught of national material used to evaluate and define national identities against others. This is magnified in capitalist economies where the nation is omnipresent in consumer culture. The nation and its virtues do not cease to enter our consciousness whether we are reading the newspaper or enjoying a holiday. The reinforcement of the pedagogical is thus left to the performative, the two are interdependent and they perpetuate the idea of the nation and national identities.[15]

National narratives have found a conventional niche in the friction between what Bhabha defined as the pedagogical and performative. The legitimization of the modern nation-state in the 'Western' world has ruptured old concepts of community, producing a new framework that defines and structures the portraits of modern civilizations. A dramatic change of perspective, Bhabha stated, 'emerges from an acknowledgement of the nation's interrupted address, articulated in the tension signifying the people as an *a priori* historical presence, a pedagogical object'.[16] Furthermore, the inhabitants of this political territory play a role in the 'performance of narrative, its enunciatory "present" marked in the repetition and pulsation of the national sign'.[17] This novel way of being, thinking, writing, and painting occupies an ambivalent place. The space between Bhabha's two poles is where both national narratives *and* art is negotiated.

Miró's *Cap de pagès català* provide a perfect example of this theory in practice. Both works show a vague form, aggrandized in its simplicity yet anonymous in identity. The label and red *barretina* make the images recognizable as the quintessential Catalan peasant. Miró preserved the memory of this figure while methodically presenting the image in an avant-garde fashion.[18] The beauty of these paintings lies in the tensions between the historic and novel, portraiture and abstraction, and the pedagogical and performative. It has become an iconic painting in Catalonia that fuses both archaic and modern modes of vision.[19]

In contrast to Miró's cheerful colours, Tàpies almost exclusively worked with a dull, sombre, even dirty palette. For the latter, modern art and *catalanisme* best coincided with the chromatic tones derived from the earth, dust, blood, sweat, stains, and filth. 'I'm positively allergic to colour', Tàpies proclaimed rather comically in an interview with Barbara Catoir.[20] The artist went on to discuss his aversion to primary colours, partially due to their overuse in advertisements. In creating his own visualization of a Catalan nation, Tàpies, like Miró, worked both sides of Bhabha's complex. This fusion of time resonates with Mihelj's concept of 'temporal orders and visions of modernity', which categorizes societies as oriented towards the past, present, or future.[21] Tàpies's mural could fit into all three, depending on the way viewers come to read it, which confuses the temporal dimension, similar to Bhabha's ambivalence.

In the Catalan Pavilion at the Universal Exposition in Sevilla, both Bhabha's pedagogical and performative elements communicated a political statement. Language in the Expo '92 sign simultaneously worked both of these concepts. The style (or visual language) and palette resonated with the celebrated prehistoric rock paintings found in Catalonia during the early twentieth century, which provokes reflection about the historicity of the region, its people, and their artistic endeavours. Tàpies encouraged the myth that the Catalan civilization has existed for centuries and shares a cohesive identity, rather than having portrayed the nation as a modern construction of society. Furthermore, the mural emphasized the historical and cultural value of the Catalan language instead of painting the region's name in Spanish or English, the official languages of the event. How would this mural's meaning change if it were publicly displayed in 2021? Time, and its flexibility, is a fundamental component in Tàpies's oeuvre, as the next chapter will further elaborate.

Les quatre cròniques, also made in the 1990s but still partially visible to the public, is a second example of Bhabha's theory at work. Remember that the mural is broken into four parts, each corresponding to an old manuscript originally written in Catalan. Symbols are mixed with phrases from the chronicles such as, 'what shall I tell you?' It is clear that the antiquity of these four texts corresponds with the pedagogical component of Bhabha's theory. The four works are glorified and united in order to demonstrate the similarity between them, the use of the Catalan language, and to point out their historical authenticity. Jumping from medieval themes to contemporary symbols, *Les quatre cròniques* boldly illustrates Tàpies's famous '+' mark in the first, second, and final panels. The third panel includes the four vertical stripes of the *senyera*. These symbols signify the performative aspect outlined in Bhabha's writing. The repetitive markings make the work 'authentic' on two levels. First, the work is stamped with Tàpies's ubiquitous sign. Second, the four bars of the Catalan flag suggest the continuity between the medieval and contemporary use of those simple lines to signify a group of people unified via a shared language and geographical region. The combination of the subject matter, the four chronicles, and the contemporary symbols compresses the time/space gap between medieval Catalonia and the current autonomous community. Linking the two through an artistic representation reinforces the notion that Catalonia is not a mere region of the Kingdom of Spain, but a historically legitimate nation with its own past, language, and culture. Furthermore, the combination of historic content and current location in the Sala Tarradellas, moved in 2006 from its 1990 original placement in the Sala Tàpies, where diplomatic meetings are held, also bridges the gap between the old and the new.

Les quatre cròniques is a nationalist work of art that is Janus-faced in its combination of the past with a desired future. Historic material is exalted in order to perpetuate the idea that Catalonia has been, and will continue to be, a unified, cultured community. However, the treatment of the chronicles masks a less venerated history. For example, although the *Llibre dels Fets* is ripe with religious 'justifications' concerning King Jaume's decisions to invade the territories of Mallorca and Valencia, it also includes passages of disgraceful violence. For example, during the conquest of Valencia, Jaume announced that if the *fenévol* (a type of catapult) missed the tower they were aiming for, it would at least hit the women and children below it. The mural aggrandizes four literary works for their use of Catalan, without delving deeply into the content of each story.

It is also worthwhile to point out that the contemporary conceptualization of language tends to blind understanding of historic forms of verbal communication. Billig pointed out that today we have to speak *'something'*, that something could be English, French, Spanish, or a host of other standardized forms of speech we call languages. However, the medieval peasant did not approach strangers asking which languages they were able to speak. They simply spoke and would or would not understand each other.[22] The concept is obvious, yet the current preoccupation with defining our 'mother tongue' and the rules of that language tend to mask the basic functions of any language: communication. Languages constantly change and transform to facilitate communication. Medieval Catalan was certainly quite different from the twenty-first century form spoken today in Northeast Spain. However, *Les quatre cròniques* looks to the medieval manuscripts as important sources, as origins of a celebrated culture. The artwork's historic content and current location in the government building epitomizes the Janus-faced rhetoric of Catalan nationalism in a visual format. It is a visualization of a Catalan nation.

Another example of Tàpies's commitment to illustrating ideas concerning Catalonia is his 1999 poster made for the centenary celebration of F.C. Barcelona. In 1974, Miró made a seventy-fifth anniversary picture for same team. Tàpies's image has a yellow field with four red stripes in the shape of arrows pointing upwards. In the centre is a large black 'B' starting the word *Barça* with an outline of a soccer cleat below. A rectangular colour sample of the team's uniform colours is at the bottom. Although Tàpies was not particularly fond of the sport, this poster showed his support for the local team, its legacy, and imagined future. This poster is more than just an image promoting a local club. Sebastian Balfour and Alejandro Quiroga explained in *The Reinvention of Spain: Nation and Identity Since Democracy*, people emotionally identify with unofficial national symbols like those of popular sports teams. Franco's 'appropriation' of the national soccer team and Real Madrid instigated some sports fans in Catalonia and the Basque Country to demonstrate their allegiance to F.C. Barcelona and Athletic de Bilbao as a means of positioning their stance against the dictator.[23] Symbols and emotions carry a significant weight in the production and perception of meaning within these types of unofficial spheres. Tàpies's poster was not meant to be a mere reproducible graphic (which can also connote important ideas), but an emotionally charged image that commemorates the history of an important club in Barcelona. Furthermore, this team has traditionally been linked to both Catalan identity and nationalism.[24]

Returning to Edensor's focus on the importance of sensuality and of feelings in relation to national identity, pictorial representations are a means of producing and reproducing sentimental responses concerning the iconography of the nation. Art, like music, has an extraordinary capacity to quickly trigger emotive responses. Reading the lyrics of the National Anthem of the United States of America is dramatically different from listening to someone sing it in front of thousands of spectators. Seeing *Les quatre cròniques* hanging on the wall in the Sala Tarradellas could elicit certain feelings that beholders would not achieve through reading the four texts that Tàpies decided to represent. Art is certainly not the only way to shape an individual's feelings concerning the nation and their own national identity. However, images are an important component contributing to the constantly transforming nature of national histories and origins, regardless of whether or not they only exist in the imagination of individuals.

4.2. Art and Politics, Direct Links

As discussed in the previous chapter, art with indirect links to politics can be subjective. Images may allude to political issues without explicitly expressing a particular position based on the visual evidence. This chapter has examined examples of artworks with direct links to politics. Some were commissions that political institutions solicited from the artist, while others were artworks made available to the public eye in various formats and locations. What they share in common is definitive political implications. It is not a coincidence that Tàpies's works for the Generalitat tend to take up themes that deal with Catalan identity but those for the Ajuntament de Barcelona and the Universitat Pompeu Fabra are more abstract, experimental, and cutting-edge. Any commissioned artwork automatically becomes political, as an exchange is dependent on certain criteria that the artist and patron establish. Alternative examples, such as *Rinzen* at MACBA or Sabadell's donated bell sculpture become political via their content and public installation. Tàpies's bed hanging on the wall is one of the first sights that visitors see upon entering Barcelona's contemporary art museum in the heart of the city. The work extends into an exterior patio, permanently occupying a considerable exhibition space within the museum. Furthermore, the work belongs to the State, however its display and care and has been left to the institution. Tàpies's gift to Sabadell could have been installed anywhere. However, the Ajuntament decided to place it in a central square and pay the artist back with a substantial donation for his foundation. Sometimes the direct links between art and politics are quite visible, as seen in the Expo'92 mural. Other examples, like *Rinzen*, require more thought and investigation in order to uncover the connections to politics, and by extension, power.

Another way that artworks are directly linked to politics is via their exhibition space. Rooms, entryways, businesses, parks, and streets are transformable spaces. The mere presence of art can alter the signals that individuals receive upon entering these places. Think about entering the lobby of a luxury hotel. The walls are often covered in artworks and mirrors with lavish frames and a colour palette that makes visitors feel calm and welcome. Now think about entering a dentist's office. There may be some art hanging on the wall, but the general impression is a lightly coloured space that seems clean. A certain ambiance is achieved in each of these private locations. Turning to public locations, think about the last time you considered how the architectural or artistic elements structured a particular place. Simply having art on the wall tends to dignify a space as important. It is not a coincidence that the western entrances of Madrid's Retiro Park are lined with marble statues and trimmed gardens, whereas the eastern entrances are nowhere near as extravagant, as they are closer to residential neighbourhoods. Entering the park from the city centre, on the western side, is an entirely different experience. Grandiose sculptures add an element of beauty but simultaneously impose structures of power. For example, there is a pathway lined on both sides with large marble statues of nine royal males and two queens, whose reign ranged from the seventh to the eighteenth century. The majority of the men are holding a scroll, dignifying their diplomatic skills in favour over violence. The women, however, are empty handed. They are idealized and elegantly dressed like the men, but they do not hold anything. The arrangement of the sculptures forms a path and visitors know where to walk because the figures form a lane that leads to the centre of the park. Why are these sculptures located in the western side of the park? They romanticize, memorialize, and commemorate historic leaders of Castile in an impressive fashion accessible to tourists. Public works of art structure the fabric of contemporary cities and parks. They create an ambiance that often conceals less obvious structures of power and social order. They are not merely decorative and ought to be analysed as objects that structure thought, movement, sentiments, and perception.[25]

Arjun Appadurai and Carol A. Breckenridge characterized the external factors that play a major role in museums in a chapter about experiencing exhibitions in India.[26] They argued that museums in the twenty-first century have 'internal and external logics [...] in which spectacle, discipline, and state power become interlinked with questions of entertainment, education, and control'.[27] Some of these 'external and internal logics' often remain unnoticed to visitors. Space is one of these elements.

Murray Edelman discussed this in his chapter 'Architecture, Space, and Social Order', to express how complex physical spaces are, despite how simple they may seem.[28] He was particularly concerned with public spaces, and articulated that their 'multiple realities' affect social order and the assertion of 'established hierarchies of status and power'.[29] Edelman went on to explain how public spaces can also provoke visitors 'to reconcile ambivalence in themselves and ambiguities regarding the social world, to turn from one meaning to another, or to defy logic by holding several incompatible cognitions at the same time'.[30] These ideas about spaces are also applicable to the structure of art museums, especially public ones. Individuals are often too preoccupied examining the objects that the institution presents to think critically about the form and structure within which museum professionals have situated those particular objects.

The arguments against installing Tàpies's *Mitjó* in the *Palau Nacional* addressed the way that the artwork would change the space. The presence of a large, wonky sculpture of a sock would deeply change the aura of the ornate and classically decorated hall. The juxtaposition of the old, traditional architectural style and the new contemporary style of the sculpture, albeit of an old article of clothing, would send contradictory signals of artistic value. The conservative, orderly decor won the battle, as *Mitjó* never found its home in MNAC. However, Tàpies's style has been valued in alternative locations such as the Universitat Pompeu Fabra's *Sala de reflexió*. He created a stark room with moveable chairs hanging from the wall and a symmetrical canvas at the line of sight to provide a meditative space that is meant to stimulate concentrated reflection. Here, the artwork structures the interior in its pairing down of excessive content. The canvas is a focal point, the chairs are functional yet optional. Distraction is not an option because the goal is that the artwork gives beholders an entry point to thinking without overwhelming or over-stimulating. The *Sala de reflexió* is a place specifically designed to transport beholders to an alternative, spiritual realm without religious connotations. The art creates the appropriate environment to achieve this goal, just as the art of a luxury hotel seeks to provide a sense of comfort, a home away from home. Art historians often focus on the content of individual works of art without acknowledging how that particular piece transforms particular spaces. A more nuanced approach to the study of art and its role in society is needed in order to better comprehend the relations between art, ideology, politics, and power. This is especially true for investigations concerning public works.

In 2006 Tàpies created a cover for the Estatut d'Autonomia de Catalunya, a document that sought to grant Catalonia greater political autonomy in amending the 1979 Statute of Autonomy. In 2004 the members of the Catalan parliament began to draft the work that would give the Generalitat more power and control. I have not been able to find any documentation regarding this work of art. Toni Tàpies was not certain about the conditions of the cover piece, but he assured me that it was a commission, supposedly on behalf of the Generalitat.[31] Pasqual Maragall and Artur Mas were photographed together on 29 September 2005 in front of one of Tàpies's paintings on the day before the Catalan parliament approved the statute. However, the picture that appeared in the *El País* photo was the painting titled *7 de novembre* (1971), a homage to the 1971 Assemblea de Catalunya, not the cover illustration that Tàpies made for the Estatut d'Autonomia.[32] *El País* did mention Tàpies's *7 de novembre* in the background, but did not say anything about his artwork for the newly approved statue.

The text of the Estatut d'Autonomia reflected Maragall's vision for the foundation of a multinational, federal Spain. Although he was the first to defeat Pujol's monopoly over the Generalitat, Maragall and the PSC failed to provide a successful alternative to CiU's conception of nationalism.[33] This later affected the party's voter allegiance. Nevertheless, all the major parties, save for the PP, supported the statute. The preamble expresses the historical authenticity of the community and their desire for sovereignty. 'The Catalan people have maintained a constant will to self-government over the course of centuries, embodied in such institutions as the Generalitat — created in 1359 by the Cervera Corts — and in its own specific legal system'. The introduction goes on to outline the major objectives while clearly stating that the proposed changes would be in solidarity with Spain and within the ambit of Europe.[34] On 18 June 2006 the new Estatut d'Autonomia de Catalunya passed and came into effect on 9 August of the same year. The passing of the new statue, and the Constitutional Court's 2010 ruling determining that fourteen articles were unconstitutional and twenty-seven needed to be modified, greatly impacted the trajectory of Catalan nationalism. The court's decision and its timing, two years after the onset of a global economic crisis, ultimately provoked a rapid shift away from the movement's dormant or banal form to a more active, hot topic.[35]

The cover design is the size of a normal piece of paper, with a cream-coloured background, black letters demarking the title 'Estatut de Catalunya' the year, three '+' marks arranged vertically, and Tàpies's signature. The most vivid aspect of the design is underneath the writing where there is a curved 'S' shape with five blobs to the right, in the same colour and texture as smeared blood. This work mimics the Expo'92 mural but its format is distinct. The small, intimate artwork is for private and up-close viewing, like Goya's *Disasters of War* etchings. It accompanies the text and is physically and directly related to politics. You cannot touch this cover without also touching the Statue. Part of this artwork's allure is its simultaneously visual and tactile stimulus and its approachable scale. The object is meant to be handled, instead of seen from afar with an imaginary boundary separating the work of art from the beholder.

However, not all works of art that are directly political are as recognizable as Tàpies's cover for the Estatut d'Autonomia de Catalunya. Abandoned projects like *Mitjó* also ought to be analysed in relation to government and political power. Even though the sculpture does not take up any flagrant or controversial content in its subject matter, its history includes intense partisan debates. In *From Art to Politics*, Edelman highlighted the need to further delve into these sort of nuanced relationships between art and the public sphere:

> Art ideally requires absolute freedom of imagination, thought, and expression, while governments inevitably try to restrict the exercise of these facilities and their consequences; and regimes like to define the restrains as freedom. Even in democratic states claiming to promote the arts, the link is always fragile and the arts are frequently obstructed. But that inevitable tension should not mean that awareness of the connections among art and politics is also obstructed.[36]

Whether or not the relationship between art and politics is hidden or simply unclear, it is important to understand that there is a connection between the two. Examining this relationship is a worthwhile exercise in that it can illuminate patterns of thought and emotions that are not always taken into consideration. Although we are saturated in a visual world, pictures and images tend to play a minor role in theories of identity and nationalism. A greater understanding of what Edelman deemed 'that inevitable tension' between art and politics will contribute to a more comprehensive perspective of the social history of art and the social history of imagined communities.

4.3. Concluding Remarks

Catalonia is a reoccurring subject in Tàpies's oeuvre. The cover illustration for the *Estatut d'Autonomia de Catalunya* epitomizes the artist's quest to balance his unique style of the past with an archetypal Catalan nationalist identity, not unlike Miró before him. Through works like this, Tàpies developed a visualization of Catalonia, one that is starkly different from the *noucentista* notion of a poised Mediterranean civilization.

Less than one hundred years separate Joaquim Sunyer's *Pastoral* (1910–1911) and Tàpies's mural for the 1992 Universal Exposition. Both images are nationalist in that they demonstrate their maker's privileging of a Catalan national identity, yet they look nothing alike. *Pastoral* is an idyllic scene that intends to align the Catalan landscape and its inhabitants with great historic societies. The Expo '92 artwork, on the other hand, is like an enormous cave painting made with blood. It employs letters, symbols, and fingerprints instead of carefully calculated brushstrokes. On the surface, these paintings have little in common. However, both pictures form part of the constantly transforming Catalan identity. They participate in the reconstruction of that identity. They are part of the visual language of a nation that inevitably changes over time, just as verbal communication changes. Billig did not address pictures in his discussion of how nationalism (similarly to racism, as Étienne Balibar previously posited) cannot exist without theory. Each of these images fit into his idea that 'nationalism involves assumptions about what a nation is'.[37] Sunyer's Catalan nation is sublime and tied to the land; it is imbued with a romantic idea of the pleasures of rural life. Tàpies's Catalonia is victimized yet victorious in its survival; the shared language is more important than the physical landscape. Nonverbal forms of communication certainly contribute to the 'assumptions' of what constitutes any particular nation, both from within and beyond its imaginary boarders. Understanding alternative forms of communication has not been a major focus of academic studies of nationalism and national identities. In the increasingly image-saturated world in which we live, where banal nationalism thrives in its inconspicuousness, it is wise to consider the ideological components of the visual. The analysis of pictures ought not to continue to be exclusive to a handful of disciplines, as the image has turned into an invasive part of our everyday experience since the invention of the digital photograph and the Internet.

'The Visualization of a Catalan Nation' points out a number of public projects that are directly related to politics although the connection is not always visible. The examples discussed in this chapter are not comprehensive; they are meant to demonstrate that there can be much more beyond the surface of any given work of art. Many of Tàpies's works address national issues, although he also made a number of works related to social issues, such as *Rinzen*; some include both national and social elements, as seen in his poster for the PSUC, in addition to countless works that are extremely ambiguous to read. A statistical analysis would provide evidence of the exact ratios of his artworks dedicated to each of these three categories, however the criteria would inevitably be subjective. What is certain is that the vast majority of his works show the artistic style that was unique in contemporary art. The subject matter of these images does not always directly reference national or social issues, but the form is a reminder of the sociopolitical conditions under which Tàpies first developed his artistic style in the 1950s and 1960s. There does seem to be a hierarchy of content, in that Tàpies's national subject matter was more prolific than his social subjects, while allegiance to his style (which is linked to both contemporary art and politics) trumps all.

Understanding the formal qualities of painting and sculpture is only part of the process. What happens to art once it leaves its maker's hands is equally important and requires attention. Much like national flags, which, as Billig pointed out are mere pieces of coloured cloth, art can contribute to the banal yet omnipresent flagging of the nation's presence in everyday life and thought. Centuries ago, when the concept of a nation was not a seemingly natural factor in human societies, pledging allegiance to scraps of bright fabric stitched together would have seemed to be a ridiculous act.[38] Flags and other visualizations of the nation are products of a particular historical moment and often go unquestioned. However, their broad acceptance and representation of nationalist philosophies is worth further investigation. It was not a coincidence that the Generalitat moved Tàpies's large mural named after four historic texts written in Catalan to a high-profile space but rejected his model *Mitjó*. The Catalan government openly embraced Tàpies's work when it corresponded with its agenda to promote a specific strain of Catalan nationalism. In our conversation concerning the relationship between politicians and art, Toni Tàpies expressed that politicians tend to use art for their own agenda; he stated, 'with some exceptions, generally politicians in this country do not understand very much about contemporary art'.[39] In a similar fashion, both public and private institutions are able to employ art in order to fit their various agendas. The following chapter will take an in-depth look at Tàpies's exhibitions from 2007 to 2015. They will consider how both national and international institutions have marketed the artist's work during the final years of his life and in the first post-mortem retrospectives organized in honour of Antoni Tàpies.

Notes to Chapter 4

1. Oxford Dictionaries, accessed 21 September 21 2015, http://www.oxforddictionaries.com/definition/english/visualize.
2. Billig, *Banal Nationalism*.
3. Edensor, *National Identity, Popular Culture and Everyday Life*, p. 140; Quiroga, 'The Three Spheres', p. 693; Fernando Molina Aparicio, *Mario Onaindia (1948–2003): Biografía patria* (Madrid: Biblioteca Nueva, 2012), p. 54.
4. The *barretina*, however, was also used under Francoism as a way of hailing regional traditions. See Núñez Seixas, 'La región y lo local en el primer franquismo', p. 137; and *ABC*, 23 March 1974, accessed 5 September 2016, http://hemeroteca.abc.es/nav/Navigate.exe/hemeroteca/madrid/abc/1974/04/23/001.html.
5. Billig, *Banal Nationalism*, pp. 40–43.
6. Guibernau, *Catalan Nationalism*, pp. 50–69.
7. Kathryn Crameri, *Goodbye Spain?: The Question of Independence for Catalonia* (East Sussex: Sussex Academic Press, 2014), Kindle loc. 525.
8. For more on these categories: Ivan Serrano, 'Just a Matter of Identity? Support for Independence in Catalonia', *Regional & Federal Studies*, 23.5 (2013), 523–45.
9. Billig, *Banal Nationalism*, 8.
10. Alejandro Quiroga 'Michael Billig en España. Sobre la recepción de Banal Nationalism', Pensar con la Historia desde el siglo XXI (Madrid: Universidad Autónoma de Madrid, 2015), p. 4195.
11. Kathryn Crameri, 'Banal Catalanism?' *National Identities*, 2 (2000), 145–57 (p. 154–55).
12. *Tàpies*, Gregory Rood, dir., BBC and TVE Catalunya, 1990.
13. Bhabha, *Nation and Narration*.
14. Ibid., p. 297.
15. Ibid., p. 298.
16. Ibid., p 298.
17. Ibid., p. 298.
18. Miró's mythic paintings break away from the nineteenth century regionalist and early nationalist imagery that aggrandizes historical material in uninventive styles. Borja de Riquer and Enric Ucelay Da Cal explain how late nineteenth century nationalists sought to recover 'popular memories of medieval Christian kingdoms through the romantic screen of folklore'. 'An

Analysis of Nationalism in Spain: A proposal for an integrated historical model' in *Nationalism in Europe: Past and Present*, Justo G. Beramendi, Ramón Maiz, Xosé Manoel Núñez Seixas, eds, (Santiago de Compostela: Xunta de Galicia and Universidad de Santiago, 1994), p. 23.
19. Krauss and Rowell, *Joan Miró: The Magnetic Fields*, p. 84.
20. Catoir, *Conversations with Antoni Tàpies*, p. 95.
21. Mihelj, *Media Nations*, p. 149.
22. Billig, *Banal Nationalism*, p. 31.
23. Balfour and Quiroga, *The Reinvention of Spain*, pp. 144–45. See also Quiroga, *Goles y banderas*.
24. Quiroga, *Goles y banderas*, pp. 134–35; p. 244. See also Guibernau, *Catalan Nationalism*, pp. 31–32.
25. For more on the relations between space, setting, structure, and power see Edelman, *From Art to Politics*; David Boswell and Jessica Evans, eds, *Representing the Nation: A Reader. Histories, Heritage and Museums* (London: Routledge, 1999); and Doina Petrescu, ed., *Altering Practices: Feminist Politics and Poetics of Space* (London: Routledge, 2007).
26. Arjun Appadurai and Carol A. Breckenridge, 'Museums are Good to Think: Heritage on View in India', *Representing the Nation*, p. 404.
27. Ibid., p. 418.
28. Edelman, *From Art to Politics*, p. 90.
29. Ibid., p. 90.
30. Ibid., p. 90.
31. Interview with Toni Tàpies, 4 February 2016.
32. 'El tripartito y CiU dan luz verde al Estatut tras un acuerdo sobre financiación y enseñanza pública', *El País*, 29 September 2005, accessed 29 August 2016, http://elpais.com/elpais/2005/09/29/actualidad/1127981820_850215.html. See also 'El parlamento de Cataluña aprueba el nuevo Estatuto', *El País*, 30 September 2005, accessed 29 August 2016, http://elpais.com/elpais/2005/09/30/actualidad/1128068217_850215.html.
33. Dowling, *Catalonia Since the Spanish Civil War*, p. 141.
34. Generalitat de Catalunya, Preámbulo, accessed 9 October 2015, http://web.gencat.cat/es/generalitat/estatut/estatut2006/preambul/index.html.
35. Crameri, *Goodbye Spain?: The Question of Independence for Catalonia*, Kindle loc. 1077–90.
36. Edelman, *From Art to Politics*, p. 146.
37. Billig, *Banal Nationalism*, p. 63.
38. Billig, *Banal Nationalism*, p. 50.
39. Interview with Toni Tàpies, 4 February 2016.

CHAPTER 5

❖

The Context of Artistic Content

This chapter focuses on how different historical contexts can affect the presentation of Tàpies's art. Taking a critical look at exhibition practices of the final years of the artist's career and the first post-mortem retrospectives demonstrates the political power of art. Centres like the Museu Nacional d'Art de Catalunya (MNAC) and Guggenheim Bilbao have presented the artist differently, creating narratives that could affect the conception of a contemporary Catalan identity both for 'insiders' and 'outsiders'. Cultural institutions participate in the negotiation of identity as transmitters of knowledge. That knowledge, however, is inevitably tied to the politics of the host institution that is showing works of art and educating visitors about those works. The first section discusses the spaces, times, and places that shape the way we experience art. Space here is in reference to the physical and architectural atmosphere in which art is exhibited, while place has to do with the geographic location. The following reviews three major shows organized in homage to Tàpies after his death on 6 February 2012. The concluding remarks deal with a general model to best understand the important role of cultural centres in the shaping of knowledge acquisition.

Framing 'The Context of Artistic Content' is a travelling exhibition *The Posters of Antoni Tàpies and the Public Sphere* (December 2006–2008) and a small 2015 show in Madrid *#DalíEnMalasaña*. During the eight years that separate these two exhibitions, several factors have caused major transformations within Spain. The European sovereign debt crisis, the 2012 bailout of the banking system, and the extravagant unemployment rate have all played a role in the direction of Spanish politics and civil society. Numerous cases of corruption investigations between 2008 and 2015 have demoralized citizens in and beyond Catalonia, some of the most outrageous examples concerned: high-profile members of the PP, Jordi Pujol's family, the PSOE in Andalucía and Santa Cruz de Paniagua, and CiU, PSC, and ERC in the Catalan health system. Mass demonstrations that began on 15 May 15 2011 imitated protests in Northern Africa while calling for radical political changes. In June 2014 King Juan Carlos I abdicated the throne and his son Felipe VI was crowned King of Spain. In November of the same year, Artur Mas led an unofficial referendum concerning the future of Catalonia's relationship with Spain. In 2015 around 22% of the Spanish population was unemployed, compared to a mere 8%

in 2007. In less than a decade the Kingdom of Spain underwent a number of great changes. Sociopolitical changes affect the ways in which individuals experience art and how art, in turn, affects the realm of politics, as this chapter will discuss in greater detail.

5.1 Exhibiting Tàpies

In the final month of 2006 Fundació Antoni Tàpies opened a travelling exhibition titled *The Posters of Antoni Tàpies and the Public Sphere*. In 2007 the show was brought to Madrid's Instituto Cervantes and the Museu Valencià de la Il·lustració i de la Modernitat. In 2008, it continued to the Instituto Cervantes in Toulouse, Prague, and finally Berlin. Unlike ordinary collections of paintings and sculptures, *The Posters of Antoni Tàpies and the Public Sphere* presented the artist's creations in conjunction with the various causes and groups that he supported. The works spanned from 1950 to 2006 and were made to announce Tàpies's own exhibitions and other occasions that he found important. As the foundation expressed, the aims of displaying these posters together were to present Tàpies's development of a visual language and the 'commitment of the artist to political and social events'.[1] For example, they included the fortieth anniversary poster that he made in 1976 for the PSUC dedicated to Catalonia, democracy, and socialism via the text below the image.[2] Other posters in the show included pictures for: a cycling competition, a festival for popular Catalan songs, an international music festival, the denunciation of the death penalty, the 1976 Liberty March, and the 1977 Congress of Catalan Culture.

The exhibition, beginning in Barcelona and later travelling to other European cities, highlighted Tàpies's commitment to social issues via the content of the artworks. In the accompanying publication the curator Nuria Enguita Mayo emphasized his posters that deal with Catalan themes:

> above all his posters are connected to events in the social, cultural and political history of Catalonia, both during the last years of the Franco regime and during the period from the restoration of democracy to the present, with posters dedicated to the Assembly of Catalonia, commemorating the Catalan national day on September eleventh and the fifth centenary of the first book printed in Catalan.[3]

Not all of the posters had to do with Catalonia. For example, Tàpies created images in favour of human rights (1981), to promote philosophy debates at the Centre Georges Pompidou in Paris (1983), and against apartheid in South Africa (1983). However, the book that was written to go with the exhibition emphasized the artist's special attention to the presentation and representation of topics dealing with Catalonia, Catalan culture, identity, and history.[4]

The content of the travelling exhibition *The Posters of Antoni Tàpies and the Public Sphere* is linked to the historical context in which it was developed. In September 2005, the Catalan parliament approved the use of the word 'nation' in the preamble of the Statue of Autonomy. In June 2006 the Spanish Parliament approved the statue and six months later the Fundació Antoni Tàpies inaugurated this politically charged exhibition, as if to show that the artist had been working for decades to support Catalonia's autonomy and cultural identity. Furthermore, exhibiting the posters in Madrid, Valencia, Toulouse, Prague, and Berlin served to expose both Tàpies's artworks and his participation as a Catalan activist. In addition to exhibiting the posters, the foundation also organized a series of lectures with the titles 'The Civil Weaponry of Art', 'Art and Message in Civil Posters in Catalonia', and 'Designing for the Utopia: Design and Social Engagement in Catalonia'. These talks worked to situate Tàpies's posters in a particular genus of art that fervently addressed social issues.

At the same time, *The Posters of Antoni Tàpies and the Public Sphere* needed to fit with the mission of Instituto Cervantes. One of the state funded institution's main pillars is the promotion and study of the Spanish language. For this reason, it seems fitting that the exhibition needed to include works that not only addressed topics dealing with Catalonia and the Catalan language. The foundation designed lectures that would delve into the topic of art in Catalonia, while the exhibition itself presented a less specific sample of posters that would resonate with the Instituto Cervantes's aim to present 'Hispanic cultures' abroad.[5] In the context of this particular exhibition, both Catalan *and* Spanish nationalists organizations presented the works of Tàpies to the public, in a project that represented the artist, Catalonia, and Spain as democratic, civilized, tolerant, modern, and diverse. When presented at the different Instituto Cervantes locations, Tàpies took on the persona of one of Spain's many great artists. This is not necessarily a false representation of the artist, but it does leave out an important part of his identity as a Catalan nationalist. Exhibiting the artist's creations in this way, worked to advertise Spain as the home of this internationally recognized visual artist that could be added to the list of other great Spanish artists: Miró, Picasso, Velázquez, Goya, etc., not unlike nation branding, which 'enhances methodological nationalism and connects notional image with stereotypes'.[6] Exhibitions organized by Spain's Ministry of Culture have demonstrated comparable strategies to present Tàpies in a similar way.[7] The following chapter will discuss, in greater detail, this concept of nation branding and how it relates to Tàpies the Catalan and Tàpies the Spaniard.

In 2009, on the other side of the Atlantic Ocean, the New York gallery Dia:Beacon held a distinct exhibition titled *Antoni Tàpies: The Resources of Rhetoric*. The content and objectives of this show greatly differed from those of the posters. *The Resources of Rhetoric* sought to carve out a niche for Tàpies within the construction of the history of Modernism, as well as position him amongst the most important painters from Spain. Instead of focusing on the artist as an individual engaging with social and political issues, Dia:Beacon's emphasis dealt with the difficulty of defining Tàpies's work and its place in the history of art:

> It has been lodged between two worlds, that of the modern [...] and that of the postmodern, which had yet to manifest itself. Tàpies's painting is perhaps too object-based for critics who sought an essential Greenbergian purity and too gestural, expressionist, and constrained by the restrictions of the frame for those who focused on the aesthetic of the expanded field [...]. Heir to Spain's brilliant

early avant-garde, whose most celebrated members include Pablo Picasso, Joan Miró, and Salvador Dalí, Tàpies is unquestionably the leading figure in the country's art world of the second half of the twentieth century and has remained an influential presence in Spain for over sixty years.[8]

In *The Resources of Rhetoric* Dia:Beacon sought to show how Tàpies's work is not easily defined nor is it similar to one particular artistic movement. Instead, his work is better conceived of as existing on the 'fringes of the modernist legacy'.[9]

Manuel Borja-Villel curated Dia:Beacon's exhibition, which was co-organized by the State Corporation for Spanish Cultural Action Abroad and began a series of collaborative shows between Dia Art Foundation and Madrid's Museo Nacional Centro de Arte Reina Sofia. Approximately 44,500 people visited the space between May and October 2009 while the show was on display.[10] Borja-Villel selected nearly twenty large-scale works to present Tàpies in New York. Spain's *El País* quoted the curator, who explained that 'Tàpies is in the market, what is needed is a return to history'.[11] What he wanted to get at was that in 2009 Tàpies was already a well-established and highly prized artist within the international art market, however, he saw it necessary to look back to understand how and why Tàpies occupied such an important position in the history of art and how other artists have learned from his technique and perspective. Borja-Villel stated that understanding Tàpies is 'fundamental in order to comprehend art of the second half of the twentieth century'.[12]

Although the medium of the different artworks shown in *The Posters of Antoni Tàpies and the Public Sphere* and the *Antoni Tàpies: The Resources of Rhetoric* exhibitions differed, the style of the artworks were similar. However, the content and context were unalike, which affects the way beholders understand and conceptualize artworks. *The Posters of Antoni Tàpies and the Public Sphere* was only shown in European countries (Spain, France, Czech Republic, and Germany). The pictures included accompanying texts, announcing (or flagging) and calling attention to viewers. The press release for the show and the exhibition book focused on Tàpies as an individual artist actively engaged in local, national, and international issues. The presentation of the posters worked as a historical collection of artworks that would give insight into the artist's personal values and ideological views. On the other hand, *Antoni Tàpies: The Resources of Rhetoric* embraced the artist's affinity for ambiguity. In New York, the exhibition sought to make sense of the artworks within a greater historical scope, without losing sight of the importance of process during the act of creating.

Comparing a pair of images, one from each exhibition, shows that the pictures themselves were not entirely dissimilar. For example, the 1973 poster for Tàpies's retrospective exhibition at the Musée d'art Moderne de la Ville de Paris shares fundamental characteristics with *L'escala* from *The Resources of Rhetoric* show (1974). Both artworks use a monochromatic palette with recognizable figures although their significance is unclear. The poster consists of a red footprint superimposed over what seems to be a pair of mathematical equations jotted down on a scrap piece of paper. Above the footprint is a group of painterly, diagonal streaks of red. The large swipe looks like a smear of blood or the tail of a shooting star hovering over the footprint; the pigments of the swipe fade away as the length of the brushstrokes elongate. *L'escala* also consists of identifiable figures, a ladder climbing vertically towards a floating snakelike form. The ladder and snake are not painted, but scratched into the thick, lightly coloured surface of the wood panel. Both works are gestural and include representations of familiar things. However, what those things signify is less apparent than *how* they create meaning. The crimson colour of the poster, together with the smoothness of the brushstrokes above the footprint, trigger particular sensations that would be entirely different if the colour were green. Similarly, the residue left from the scratched surface of the ladder and snake evokes a feeling that would be different had Tàpies painted those same figures on a smooth canvas. Both artworks, through their style more than their subject matter, *suggest* instead of dictate meaning.

Beholders would likely experience and comprehend these two artworks differently if they had been included together in the same show, because the context of the exhibition would have been different. The situation or circumstances of experiencing art is almost as important as the image itself. Location, time, space, sounds, accompanying texts, atmosphere, etc. all play a role in the way we experience art. Think about having to take the same fifty-question exam in an isolated, soundproof room or in the same room at zero degrees. Modifying just one factor (in this case temperature) will alter the examination process and most likely the results as a consequence. Experiencing art functions in a similar fashion in that the context of the event of viewing can fluctuate and change the ways we behave, think, or act in the presence of a work of art.[13] The circumstances (physical, historical, geographical, ideological, etc.) surrounding the European tour of *The Posters of Antoni Tàpies and the Public Sphere* and Dia:Beacon's *Antoni Tàpies: The Resources of Rhetoric* affected the content of each exhibition.

As part of their profession, curators make certain decisions that impact the reception of artworks such as the way the works are organized and grouped (thematically, chronologically, or otherwise). The title, overarching theme, and explanatory texts of an exhibition also play a part in the public's understanding of objects.[14] Furthermore, the political nature of the space where a work of art is exhibited affects the ways in which individuals perceive the visual arts. In the 1980s, the artist Hans Haacke drew much attention to this, forming an 'institutional critique' to call attention upon the ways in which museums collect and display works of art.[15]

The posters exhibition, because artworks often included some text as part of the work, gave viewers a concrete focal point that signified a shared meaning as long as they could have read that particular language. The point of insertion in *The Resources of Rhetoric* show, on the other hand, was more sensational and emotional because of the lack of text and the way that the exhibition embraced the intentional ambiguity of the artworks.

Context affects the ways in which beholders perceive, conceptualize, and understand works of art. This is important to keep in mind when thinking critically about works of art and the types of visual languages they create. Activation of the imagination occurs differently under varying circumstances. Even though we cannot travel through time, we can be aware that what we see and think is directly related to when and where we see things. Time conditions reality. Recall how different readers have come to understand Hugo's *Les Misérables*, turning the story into something relevant for a specific place and moment in time.[16] In order to analyse how works of art are presented to the public, the circumstance of its exhibition is tremendously important.

Tàpies's *Mitjó* initiative was highly criticized in the early 1990s, yet when he installed a similar version in a different place at a different time, it drew little critical attention. As previously discussed, the debate is an example of the tangled relation between art and politics. Although the project for MNAC's Sala Oval came to a halt in 1993, in 2010 Tàpies installed a smaller version of the infamous sock on the rooftop of the foundation. The institution had been closed for two years prior to the *Mitjó* installation. The site was under renovation, with an eight-million-euro budget, and when it reopened on 3 March 2010 the President of the Generalitat José Montilla and the Mayor of Barcelona Jordi Hereu i Boher attended the inauguration. In addition to modifying the structure of the building and its accessibility, the foundation topped the roof with the new version of *Mitjó* to reveal during the reopening. It measures a mere 2.75 meters in comparison to the eighteen meters that Tàpies had imagined for the original for MNAC. The two versions of *Mitjó* differed greatly in their scale, location, and date. When the actual sculpture was finally situated on the terrace of the Fundació Tàpies, it did not cause a scandal in the media, as was the case with the first one planned in the early 1990s. A month before its unveiling, *El País* published an article titled 'El "calcetín" de Tàpies existe' [Tàpies's Sock Exists] that covered the controversial history of the rejected original and featured the new one as the 'star' of the upcoming inauguration.[17]

In a different place and time, *Mitjó* did not become the focus of intense debate nor ridicule. Both MNAC and the Fundació Tàpies have received continual annual financial support from the Catalan and Spanish governments. However, the sculpture's new location was less visible to large audiences, and thus caused less outrage over how these governing bodies spend public funds. Furthermore, the new work fits with the foundation's other prominent sculpture, *Núvol i cadira*, instead of contrasting (or clashing) with the Classical architecture of the Sala Oval. Finally, the 1992 CiU-led Generalitat opposed the installation of the original *Mitjó* in the Palau Nacional, but in 2010 the PSC led both regional and local governing bodies. Just as *Les Misérables* has triggered different reactions depending on the *Weltanschauung* of its readers, Tàpies's *Mitjó*, in the imaginations of its beholders, will never be static. What it represents has changed, and will continue to change, depending on various circumstances. One of the most important factors was (and is) its physical location and surrounding environment. The sock sculpture finally found a home at the foundation of its creator; it is in harmony with the objectives of that particular institution. Had the original *Mitjó* been installed in the Sala Oval, it would, in turn, have affected the way visitors viewed the impressive space and MNAC's permanent collection of artworks in its adjacent rooms. The context of artistic creations depends on a multitude of elements that shift the way that we view, perceive, understand, and relate to art. The following section focuses on the organization of exhibitions and their impact on the experiencing of art after Antoni Tàpies passed away in 2012.

5.2 Exhibition Practices, Ideology, and Identity

In 'The Question of Cultural Identity', Stuart Hall defined ideology as 'mental frameworks — the languages, categories, imagery of thought, and the systems of representation — which different classes and social groups deploy in order to make sense of, define, figure out and render intelligible the way society works'.[18] Hall included both language and imagery in his description of the ingredients that ideology is composed of. Similarly, these two factors play a role in the formation of identity and the development of what Sebastian Balfour and Alejandro Quiroga have expressed as 'new layers of identity'.[19] Visual languages and 'imagery of thought' can create meaning, which contributes to the constant negotiation of the self. Both ideology and identity are complex, dynamic, and unfixed. The changing nature of these concepts makes it difficult to pin down particular elements that instigate their transformations. However, this section will examine how art, within different contexts, can play a role in the processes of the development and reconstruction of identity and ideology.

Before delving into specific examples, it is helpful to recall the ways in which Ferran Archilés and Miguel Ángel del Arco Blanco have discussed how to best study culture. Archilés explained the importance of a historical perspective that focuses on the cultural arena as a key component in understanding the national experience. Culture is what determines how we make sense of the world around us and it structures our ability to organize, categorize, and comprehend. Culture also establishes what we consider to be 'normal,' appropriate, new, or useful.[20] Furthermore, Archilés has outlined how narratives of belonging and identity (to which images should also be added) interact with personal 'experiences of the nation'.[21] He emphasized the plurality of experiences, because different classes, genders, and ethnicities under fluctuating historical circumstances and 'rotating hierarchies' do not always perceive things analogously.[22] Art exhibitions, coupled with the public's participation, can contribute to these personal 'experiences of the nation'. Del Arco highlighted how both real and fictional concepts are needed in order to fully make sense of history.[23] While empirical data is important for any historical investigation, what has happened in the imaginations of individuals and societies is also worth consideration. We can approach the study of works of art as static historical objects, but also as dynamic transmitters of information and knowledge, which is linked to power, as well as the imagination. Combining the realm of the real with that of the imaginary, especially when dealing with culture, is necessary to make sense of the past.

Antoni Tàpies died on 6 February 2012. The following day, the Catalan version of *La Vanguardia* reported the story with a heading 'Tàpies: The Ethics of Painting, the Catalan Artist Died at the Age of 88 in his Home in Barcelona'.[24] The article was prefaced with the phrase 'on the death of a Catalan and universal artist' and included an image of Tàpies in his studio that was taken in 2003. *Ara* published a farewell article titled 'Tàpies, Immortal' with a subtitle referring to him as a Catalan artist; the story opened with two short sentences, 'Tàpies has died. It is a sad day', and closed with a comment about *Mitjó*.[25] *El Punt Avui* titled their obituary 'The Great Artist and Thinker', and stated that Tàpies was the most internationally renowned Catalan artist.[26] *El Periódico* called Tàpies Catalan and also referred to him as '*barcelonés*'.[27] Finally, *El País* remembered Tàpies as 'dazzling', Catalan, and *barcelonés*.[28] The journalist Jacinto Antón wrote a remarkable text about the late Tàpies, providing more than the essential details. For example, Antón discussed that MNAC halted the *Mitjó* project, fearing ridicule, a stance that 'would have also have left us without the Sistine Chapel'.[29]

ABC's newspaper in Sevilla dedicated the full front page to reprint of one of Tàpies's works that made for one of the periodical's special editions in 1998. In the centre of the artist's crimson and gold composition, *ABC* printed their own title: 'Tàpies, goodbye to the great renovator of Spanish art'.[30] *The New York Times* also dedicated a piece to remember the life and works of the artist, calling Tàpies a 'Spanish Abstract Painter' in the headline.[31] *El Mundo* did not use the word Catalan, Catalonia, Spanish, or Spain in their announcement of the artist's death.[32] Each newspaper used different adjectives and ways of bidding farewell to the artist. The variety of ways Tàpies's identity has been categorized is indicative of the struggle for different nationalist groups to appropriate the artistic figure as one of their own, or of the avoidance of taking sides. *El Mundo* was the only periodical that seemed to leave out any words that could have caused tension in terms of identity. This is surprising coming from a right-wing newspaper. *The New York Times* may have been theoretically correct in calling Tàpies Spanish, but they missed the mark in referring to him as just a painter. Even after the artist's death, Tàpies's images and legacy are far from fixed, as the remainder of this chapter will explore in detail.

On 21 June 21, 2013 MNAC and Fundació Tàpies opened a bipartite exhibition *Tàpies. From Within* in Barcelona. It was the first major retrospective since the artist had passed away. One of the most peculiar and fascinating works shown at MNAC was a large mural from 1992 titled *Parla, parla*. The expansive brown background is pocked with red, orange, black, white, and grey markings. Eight strips of white, six of which are oriented horizontally, resemble words or phrases that have been erased in censored material or documents. In the centre, amongst the random markings and white strips are two heads sketched in profile in black. The large hand of one person is choking the other around its neck. The victim's head is tilted up with its mouth open shouting or gasping for air. This image is remarkably similar to Picasso's 1937 studies for what became his 'weeping' woman, first appearing in *Sueño y mentira de Franco II* [Dream and Lie of Franco II].[33] Hastily written over the two heads in Tàpies's mural are the Catalan words 'parla, parla'. Ironically the white words appear backwards, just like Picasso's first weeping woman, which was sketched as mirror image on a plate later used to print multiple copies of the same image. *Parla, parla*, complete with its allusions to Picasso and political corruption, is an archetypal Tàpies artwork. Violence is not absent from the picture, but upon first glance the image seems quite tame.

In MNAC's presentation of the exhibition *Tàpies. From Within* the artworks were organized chronologically. Visitors entered viewing Tàpies's early surrealist compositions and weaved their way through several rooms, each containing works from later dates. Time was compressed into a relatively small space, as viewers could walk from Tàpies's paintings of the late 1940s to his murals from the 1990s in a few moments. This proximity of space and organizational method yields to a natural desire to experience these works as a progression. Beholders saw the career of a recently deceased artist unfolding as they moved through the museum. However, the order of the show negates the title. *Tàpies. From Within* was created using many works from the late artist's personal collection. The idea was that the show would provide both a general and intimate experience of his long career. Reflecting on the organization of the show, Toni Tàpies thought showing fewer artworks would have improved the experience. Giving space for the works to breathe, in his opinion, would have facilitated a more adequate environment for visitors to calmly contemplate the works of his father.[34] Furthermore, the strict order of the exhibition automatically negated its intimacy. Moments in life, events, and experiences generally trump numerical dates in human memory. Only when people remember particular sights, sounds, smells, emotions etc., do they begin to situate those memories as moments in time. *Tàpies. From Within* is a reconstruction that ultimately echoes the exhibition model of MNAC's permanent collection. Sketching a brief history of the museum is useful in order to fully understand the institution's capacity to structure knowledge and learning via its content and presentation.

The museum is housed in the Palau Nacional, formerly titled the Palacio Nacional, which was constructed for the 1929 International Exposition in Barcelona. Its initial use was to showcase an exhibition of Spanish art, including thousands of works from various areas of the country to celebrate Spain. The building served as the primary focal point of the event. Originally, Josep Puig i Cadafalch was commissioned to design the building and urban planning of the site for the Exposition. However, Primo de Rivera's regime removed Puig from the project, due to his overtly Catalan nationalist agenda exemplified in his previous architectural projects such as *Les Quatre Columnes*. Puig i Cadafalch's columns represented the four stripes of the Catalan flag, positioned vertically on the slope of Montjuïc hill. The classical design fit with the *noucentista* agenda to present Catalonia as the inheritors of a sophisticated Mediterranean, as opposed to Castilian, cultural tradition. Primo de Rivera's regime ordered the *Les Quatre Columnes* to be destroyed in 1928 in order to present Barcelona as a Spanish city at the International Exposition and new architects were appointed to do the job after winning a design contest. Eugenio P. Cendoya, Enric Catá, and Pere Domènch i Roura were responsible for the final plan of the entire Exposition complex. Some years later, in 1934, the museum opened to the public as the Museu d'Art de Catalunya. However, just a couple years later the collections were moved to Olot and Darnius, northern Catalan towns bordering France, to safeguard the works during the Civil War.[35] The onset of war interrupted the progress of the museum's early development and the reinstallation of the collection was not immediate, the entire body of works was not fully replaced in the Palau Nacional until 1943. In 1990, after Catalan parliament passed the Museums Act, the Museu d'Art de Catalunya was re-titled Museu *Nacional* d'Art de Catalunya. This law essentially worked as 'a metaphor, an institutional illusion of a nation-state'.[36] In 2010, two decades after the renaming of the museum, just below MNAC's entrance and close to their original site, Puig i Cadafalch's *Les Quatre Columnes* were reconstructed as a symbol of Catalan national pride and at the same time linking Spain to authoritarianism.

MNAC is an art museum committed to the collection, protection, and presentation of Catalan culture. The museum boasts an impressive Romanesque collection, which consists of panel paintings, woodcarvings, metalwork, and stone sculptures ranging from the eleventh to thirteenth centuries. These works came primarily from churches of the Pyrenees Mountains, and were brought to the museum in order to ensure that they would be preserved and that they would never leave the region. The Gothic collection consists of a range of similar media, but the works come from different locations, from the Països Catalans. Dating from the end of the thirteenth through the fifteenth century, the Gothic works were collected from Catalonia, as well as former regions of the Kingdom of Aragon that encompassed the coastal city of Valencia, the island of Majorca, and Aragón, territories that many Catalan nationalists consider as irredentas.[37] The Romanesque and Gothic works were the original core of MNAC's collection. They constituted the former Museu de Belles Arts, situated in Barcelona's city centre, until the founding of the Museu d'Art de Catalunya in 1934, at which point the collections were relocated to the Palau Nacional.[38] As mentioned in the 1990 Museums act, the national art museum is dedicated to the permanent exhibition of the 'artistic expression of Catalonia and the territories most culturally related to Catalonia, during the distinct historical periods, until the present day'.[39] Beyond the scope of the museum, the idea that the representation of Catalan culture should not be restricted within the borders of the autonomous community was part of a strategic manoeuvre between CiU and the local academic community to develop a framework of institutions dedicated to media in Catalan during the first years of the new democracy in Spain.[40] The goals of establishing new media sources for the Països Catalans, which includes the medieval Kingdom of Aragon and extends into Southern France (also irredenta), were to 'construct means of socialization for a 'new Catalonia', strengthen the Catalan forms of communication, and produce new agencies of practical action for intellectuals'.[41] The extension of these objectives beyond the borders of the Autonomous Community of Catalonia mirrors MNAC's intentions of embracing a broader community and harking on their 'historic' belonging to a Catalan, albeit imagined, community.

The museum also has an extensive Renaissance and Baroque collection. Catalan artists created the majority of these works, although a number of foreign masters have been displayed as well, such as Peter Paul Rubens and El Greco. These artworks came largely from donations made to the museum, such as Francesc Cambó's opulent bequest. The museum's collection from the Middle Ages and the way it is presented to the public mirrors nationalist narratives that seek to romanticize regional culture during this period. Politicians and public figures have echoed this idea, claiming that Catalan culture has its origins in the medieval era.[42]

The museum's Modern collection assembles works from the early nineteenth to the mid-twentieth century and illustrates a number of different stylistic approaches that these artists were working with, ranging from Neoclassicism to the avant-garde movements like Art Nouveau and *Noucentisme*. There is also a small but growing photography collection, an area that the museum has been working to develop in order to diversify its displays.[43]

Paintings and sculptures are not the only means that the museum has used to feature the distinctive qualities of Catalan art. MNAC also houses the Numismatic Cabinet of Catalonia, which includes an incredible 134,000 pieces. The coins range from the sixth century BCE to the twenty-first century and include 'examples that illustrate, step by step, the historic and economic evolution of these lands'.[44] Highlights of the collection are the coins that were minted in Catalonia during the Reapers' War (1640), the War of Spanish Succession (1701–1714), and the French Occupation (1805–1813). In May 1640, Catalan peasants banded together in a violent strike against the Spanish Empire in protest of having to house and support the Spanish army, the onset of what would later be remembered as the Reapers' War. On 17 January 1641 a group of Catalan aristocrats declared a Republic of Catalonia, effectively joining the Kingdom of France. The Catalans won a major battle against the Spanish troops at Montjuïc, the location of the museum, that year, but were eventually unable to defeat the Empire after a decade of conflict. The French crown relinquished Catalonia in 1652 but held control of the northern province of Roussillon. MNAC displays a coin issued during the short-lived Catalan Republic, explaining that the previous image of the late Spanish King Felipe IV's name was replaced with *Principatus Cataloniae*. Exhibiting historic currency in the museum context draws attention to the economic, social, and political history of Catalonia as well as its relationship to the Spanish State.

Unlike traditional 'universal' museums such as The Louvre Museum in Paris or The National Gallery in London, MNAC positions its regional art as the centre of its scope. The institution's mission statement emphasized that 'Spanish and foreign works are shown either individually or in groups as specific points of reference or background material to the exhibition of Catalan art'.[45] This fits with the overarching goals of the institution invested in enabling art historians and the public to 'appreciate the differences between Catalan art from the rest of Spain and abroad'.[46] Both MNAC's collection and display demonstrate a complex political agenda: to characterize Catalan art as distinct from Spanish works. However, these objectives do not classify Spain as being foreign. Instead, Spain occupies an in-between space, neither grouping it with foreign cultures nor considering it as being abroad. While the Spanish government helps to fund MNAC, the installation strategy seeks to identify Catalan culture as fundamentally different from the rest of the Iberian Peninsula, in an effort to highlight and celebrate that difference. Furthermore, MNAC's institutional project has gone beyond simply displaying Catalan art. As outlined in part of their mission statement, another aim of the museum is to dramatically alter the perception of the history of Catalan art. Instead of understanding artistic production in Catalonia as an echo of other European centres, or an addendum of 'Western' art, MNAC has called attention to the need for an objective history of Catalan art, with the desire that this history acknowledges that Catalan artistic production is an arena interrelated with European and Spanish artistic traditions, but one that nevertheless has its own, unique narrative.[47] Other museums in stateless nations, such as National Museum Wales, have sought to achieve similar ends both through the presentation of culture and official language policies.

MNAC's development of their Department of Restoration and Preventative Conservation indicates the early impulse to protect their collection. This facility has existed since the museum's initial installation in the Palau Nacional. Its longevity demonstrates MNAC's conscious commitment to the careful preservation and conservation of their artworks. This department is crucial in maintaining the condition of the objects and it takes on the difficult initiative to preserve works, a process that then becomes part of a greater cultural history. The importance that MNAC has placed on this department, in conjunction with the goals of the museum, makes manifest a clear plan, as stated on MNAC's website: 'restoration is not carried out in the hope of returning works to their original state; but rather, to take into account the passing of time and any work that has already been carried out on the piece, and which now forms part of the history of restoration in Catalonia in general'.[48] The early establishment of the museum's Department of Restoration indicates that one of the institution's principle goals has been to preserve and represent Catalan culture as a whole.

MNAC seeks to show its collection as unique yet simultaneously universal. It is an institution that has tried to find a balance between its twofold task: to present Catalan cultural heritage to both local and foreign patrons and to share information about its rich collection. One of the institution's main challenges has been to find a way to present Catalan culture in a manner that is oriented both inward and outward, in a way that demonstrates its differences from other regions but also its relationship to a more universal history of artistic production. The Museu Nacional d'Art de Catalunya is not simply a collection of Catalan art, but also an active institution devoted to the past, present, and future of Catalan culture. However, that future is far from predictable or static. Just as Daniel E. Jones outlined in his article on Pujol and the construction of a 'Catalan space for communication' between political institutions and businesses, as a result of globalization, the different spaces and scopes of communication are creating societies and cultures that are ever more complex and varied; a rereading of the interconnectedness between communication, political, and cultural life is needed, one that takes on a 'much more open and ample vision, one that does not exclusively focus on the territorial, ethnic, or linguistic'.[49] In viewing the museum as a communicative place with a critical perspective, it becomes clear that art is inseparable from politics in the time and space of the museum.

Tàpies. From Within was organized in a chronological format paralleling MNAC's narrative of the history of Catalan art. Another exhibition, scheduled just a couple of months later, reaffirmed this strategy. On 31 August 2013, MNAC inaugurated *A Visit to the Romanesque: In Company of Antoni Tàpies*. The objective of this exhibition, as the museum described, was twofold: 'to offer a contemporary look at medieval art, and at the same time to enrich Tàpies's universe with elements linking it to the art of our past'.[50] The Director of MNAC, Pepe Serra told me about the conception of the exhibition.[51] The museum's professionals were looking to give life to the static and difficult to move Romanesque collection and they saw an opportunity to simultaneously increase the exposure and value of Tàpies within the institution. With the collaboration of Fundació Antoni Tàpies and private collectors, MNAC was able to put together a show that would fuse a connection between the centuries-old works and the recently deceased Tàpies. Serra stated that there was a 'natural connection' between Tàpies's oeuvre, in addition to medieval works from the region that the artist once owned, and those on display in the museum. Serra told me that Tàpies knew these pieces very well, and that in the 1950s he was part of El grup de Taüll. There is a photograph of the seven members in MNAC, then called Museo de Arte de Cataluña, standing below the Romanesque apse painting extracted from the Church of Sant Climent in the village of Taüll (1955). Tàpies is third from the right in the photo, standing together with Jordi Mercadé, Modest Cuixart, Marc Aleu, Joan Josep Tharrats, Josep Guinovart, and Jaume Muxart. El grup de Taüll recognized the space of the museum, and its rich Romanesque collection from Catalonia, as a space of liberty. They saw its works as distinctly Catalan, and positioned themselves as inheritors of them, which implied 'obvious political connotations', as Serra explained to me.[52] El grup de Taüll was basically just this photograph, but their shared thoughts on the museum's collection and space illustrates their personalization of the artworks and how they related themselves to previous artists of the region. *A Visit to the Romanesque: In Company of Antoni Tàpies* was, in Serra's opinion, a great success and many people visited the exhibition.

Pintura romànica i barretina served as the publicizing image (1971). The work posits themes concerning Catalan identity, medieval art, time, and violence. Meaning in this particular work of art, however, is neither fixed nor stable. For example, the sociopolitical circumstances and an individual's ideas concerning Catalan identity or violence in 2013 were naturally different from the early 1970s when Tàpies created this artwork, which in turn affect the way individuals perceive *Pintura romànica i barretina*. In 1971, Franco's regime would not have tolerated open protests against the idea of Spain as '*Una, Grande y Libre*'. In 2013, however, peaceful forms of civilian protest would have been considered commonplace and part of the democratic process. Shifting historical circumstances have altered the shock value, or lack thereof, of this work of art. As part of the *A Visit to the Romanesque: In Company of Antoni Tàpies* show, MNAC emphasized the similarity between *Pintura romànica i barretina* and the older artworks in their collection, as opposed to the different ways in which interpretation is unquestionably dependent upon historical circumstances. MNAC positioned Tàpies alongside Catalan artists of the past, in attempt to create a more cohesive, progressive, or 'sanitized' narrative about the most celebrated Catalan artists (the overwhelming majority being white males) in history.[53]

Both *Tàpies. From Within* and *A Visit to the Romanesque: In Company of Antoni Tàpies* were intended to honour the late artist. The way that MNAC conceived of the shows (including their titles, selected artworks, accompanying texts, promotional material, etc.) had less to do with the pictorial language of Tàpies and more to do with his legacy as one of the most illustrious Catalan artists of the modern era. Furthermore, both exhibitions used artworks that portrayed Tàpies's commitment to Catalan culture while downplaying his commitment to leftist politics. The agenda of MNAC is clearly different from other institutions showing Tàpies's work in the twenty-first century such as Dia:Beacon. The New York gallery's exhibition *Antoni Tàpies: The Resources of Rhetoric* sought to express the artist's value as a pioneer and non-conformist, as were the most renowned avant-garde artists of previous generations, working at a time when the centre of the so-called art world had shifted away from Europe to the United States. Will Tàpies's legacy be that of an inventive Spanish painter within the international art scene or, as MNAC suggests, a renowned artist in the long history of Catalan art? The place and time of these types of exhibitions ultimately contributes to the public's understanding of the 'truth.' For each show, there are multiple interpretations that have become available. Media reports and published interpretations about the artist surrounding his shows further complicate the matter. However, depending on the goals of each organization, it is clear that certain factors have taken precedent over others. These nuances require attention in order to avoid oversimplification and the acceptance of neatly designed histories with restricted perspectives. Temporary exhibitions do not determine the definitive legacy of any specific artist, but they do contribute to the remembrance, or purposeful forgetting, of particular attributes. Toni Tàpies explained to me that the Fundació Tàpies is the primary institution that will encourage future generations to come to learn and understand his father's work.[54] Meanwhile, museums will continue to show their various versions of what is most important concerning the artist's life and works.

On 4 October 2013 Guggenheim Bilbao opened *Antoni Tàpies: From Object to Sculpture (1964–2009)*. As explained on the museum's webpage, which is available in English, French, Spanish, and Basque, the sculptural show that demonstrated a span of over five decades of the artist's work was organized both chronologically and thematically in order to best demonstrate Tàpies's 'evolution as an artist'.[55] The text immediately recognized the artist as Catalan, which is interesting considering the website is accessible in both Spanish and Basque, but not Catalan, and it concluded with this curious statement: 'this exhibition unveils Tàpies's constant preoccupation with the sculptural problem and, for the first time, brings his sculpture face-to-face with itself'.[56] *Antoni Tàpies: From Object to Sculpture* was one of the first retrospectives organized after the artist's death and the very first exclusively dedicated to his sculptures. Its purported inward perspective worked to orient viewers to consider the processes of the artist at work and the materials he employed using a particular sensibility. The museum, which belongs to the non-profit organization Solomon R. Guggenheim Foundation, offered an alternative approach to Tàpies's work, differing from that of MNAC. The general objective of all the Guggenheim institutions is to sponsor various forms of modern and contemporary art while collecting, preserving, and encouraging its investigation. This exhibition sought not to construct a cohesive narrative but to demonstrate a personal 'evolution' of the artist's three-dimensional works.

Why did Guggenheim decide on showing these works in Bilbao instead of New York? During his lifetime, Tàpies had many more exhibitions in New York City than he did in the Basque Country. One reason could have concerned the logistics of the works that were loaned to the museum for the show. Another could have been that the sculptural quality of the Bilbao location, both the building itself as well as Richard Serra's massive installations inside could have inspired the museum's directors to select Bilbao to host Tàpies's sculpture show. Finally, perhaps another possible conclusion could have to do with the similar political philosophies that exist amongst Basque and Catalan nationalist groups concerning their relations to the Spanish State. In *El peso de la identidad: Mitos y ritos de la historia vasca*, Félix Luengo Teixidor examined the way that symbols are conceptualized, specifically looking for the distinction between icons of the Basque Country and those of Basque nationalism.[57] The line that separates the two becomes blurred at times, making the meaning of images difficult to pin down. The same can be said of symbols associated with Catalonia and/or Catalan nationalism such as the *senyera*, *barretina*, or an artwork by Miró or Tàpies. Hosting *Antoni Tàpies. From Object to Sculpture* in Bilbao does not mean that the Guggenheim Museum is a radical nor partial institution, but that the local audience could have been a factor in the decision to hold a the retrospective in the Basque Country, as opposed to the Guggenheim in New York City or an alternative location, because of the demographics of the potential visitors. Toni Tàpies said that museum's representatives never articulated to him the option of showing the exhibition in The Big Apple.[58]

This section has covered three different presentations of Tàpies's works, all of which opened in 2013, approximately a year and a half after the artist's death. Both MNAC and Guggenheim Bilbao created exhibitions that ultimately celebrated the life and work of the artist. However, the objectives of their exhibitions were distinct. The curators formed their own representations of Tàpies's work and highlighted what they thought was most significant. *Tàpies. From Within* was curated by Vicente Todolí, former director of London's Tate Modern. He was selected specifically for his non-expertise concerning Tàpies, as the organizing committee sought a fresh perspective to construct the show. MNAC's Assistant Curator Gemma Ylla-Català, specialized in medieval art and restoration, curated *A Visit to the Romanesque: In Company of Antoni Tàpies*. Finally, Guggenheim's curator of contemporary art, film, and video Álvaro Rodríguez Fominaya organized *Antoni Tàpies: From Object to Sculpture*. What Todolí, Ylla-Català, and Rodríguez Fominaya have in common is that they were trained in areas other than Tàpies. What they managed to do, as curators of their respective exhibitions, was to bridge their area of expertise with the world of Tàpies. Visitors, having moved through these spaces, experienced both the artist and the curator's visual languages.

Some 85,000 people saw the exhibition *Tàpies. From Within* during the summer and fall of 2013.[59] Between October of the same year and January 2014, Guggenheim Bilbao hosted more than 200,000 people while *Antoni Tàpies: From Object to Sculpture* was on display. The show ran for a total of ninety-one days, during this period the museum averaged 2,376 visitors per day, of which 18% hailed from the Basque Country, 24% from the rest of Spain, and 58% from foreign countries, with the highest figures from France, the United States, Great Britain, and Germany.[60] These figures may seem high in terms of people who have spent time looking at works of art by a single artist, but when compared to the attendance of other events the statistics are quite low. The soccer stadium of F.C. Barcelona has a capacity of 99,000. In a single evening, the number of soccer spectators, in conjunction with viewers who watch on television or online, can easily surpass the total number of those who attended one of these Tàpies shows which lasted several months. Nevertheless, the art exhibitions did receive a significant range of people, especially the Guggenheim's *Antoni Tàpies: From Object to Sculpture*.

Returning to Hall's definition of ideology, language and representation are contributing factors to our 'mental frameworks' that establish how we understand society and its norms. Regardless of the beholder's personal artistic taste or preference, the act of going to these exhibitions ultimately has had an impact on how and what they think. Their thoughts could have ranged from ideas that have been changed (or slightly altered) to affirmed ideas. It is a process that is not immediate but accumulative. If a visitor felt indifferent after going to a particular exhibition, they probably saw things that were already within their developed vocabulary of images and visual stimuli. The artworks and their presentation did not excite, provoke, or challenge them. Their ideas remained the same. On the other hand, if a visitor was awestruck after seeing a show, that curiosity and wonder transformed their previous conceptions about the visual realm.[61] These thoughts that contribute to greater structures concerning ideology and society, in turn, affect how individuals conceive of themselves. Their relationship with those around them, and those understood to be different from them, become susceptible to modification.

For example, between 2012 and 2013 Paris's Centre Georges Pompidou and Madrid's Reina Sofía hosted an exhibition dedicated to Salvador Dalí. The show, which included over two hundred of the artist's works, sought to present a 'reappraisal of Dalí as a thinker, a writer and the creator of a very particular vision of the world'.[62] Promotional material for the enormously popular exhibition, the second most visited show of all time in the Centre Pompidou, said nothing about Dalí's connection to Franco's regime. In concentrating on other aspects of the artist's eccentric character, curators conveniently decided not to mention that the artist 'lived like an genuine king in Franco's Spain' for his savvy political connections.[63] A previous exhibition that detailed works of art that stemmed from

Dalí's sphere of influence was organized in 2004 at the Reina Sofía. As journalist Benjamín Prado pointed out, Dalí's relationship with the Franco regime was left out because the curators chose to only show artworks ranging from 1927 to 1939, 'solving the ideological problem by omission'.[64] This pattern of purposefully ignoring Dalí's political stance is problematic because it creates a false representation of the artist's political position in society. Viewers marvel at his works, often times without knowing the intolerable benefits that Dalí reaped from supporting the Franco dictatorship.[65] Does this make his artwork any less valuable technically or aesthetically? No. However, being aware of this information may change the monetary value of the artworks and the way that individuals conceive of themselves in relation to Dalí.

In 2015, a small gallery in one of Madrid's trendy neighbourhoods opened the exhibition *#DalíEnMalasaña*. Galería de Arte Rodrigo Juarranz organized the show that included over forty of Dalí's works from private collections. The promotional text for *#DalíEnMalasaña* is dumbfounding, opening with the following question: 'Would Dalí have been a hipster from Malasaña?' While hipster is an elusive term, the twenty-first century version of this label is different from that of Dalí's lifetime (1904–1989). In fact, as Víctor Lenore explained in *Indies, Hipsters y gafapastas: Crónica de una dominación cultural*, what used to be labelled a 'hipster' in the late twentieth century is now better described as '*friki*.'[66] According to Lenore, the term in 2014 was married to capitalism and accumulation.[67] So-called hipsters may still listen to alternative or Indie music, but large companies have stripped the underground music scene of its allure in appropriating songs and beats to advertise their products. Lenore explained, 'the 'independent' scene is the culture industry's favourite: an attractive mixture of reasonable inversions, artistic reputation and opportunities for economic *pelotazo*'.[68] There is a simple response to the gallery's headlining question; Dalí would absolutely not have been a hipster of Malasaña. The artist may have shared the non-conformist attitude of the twenty-first century hipster stereotype, but his work had little to do with his own consumption of 'culture'. He and his peers were more interested in undoing already-established cultural norms, as evident in his film *Un chien andalou* (1929, directed by Luis Buñuel) that was, at the time, a shocking and graphic silent, surrealist composition. Finally, if Dalí was living 'like a king' during the Franco dictatorship, the gallery's question could turn into an offensive, as opposed to an enticing, one. What the exhibition text does, beyond avoiding an explanation of Dalí's sympathies with Francoism, is to connect the artist with the public. The opening question essentially links Dalí to a 2015 social group tied to a particular location. Ignoring the historical circumstances that the artist lived and worked under, readers are led to imagine Dalí as one of themselves or as one of 'them' (the hipsters of Malasaña). Art and the way it is curated may not always make someone change the way they think about certain ideologies and of themselves, but it does play a role in a greater chain of thoughts that have a transformative nature.

5.3 Concluding Remarks

Art museums, galleries, and curators shape knowledge via the preparation and exhibition of visual art. As seen in the previous chapters, often times this process is directly linked to political groups with varying degrees of power. Nevertheless, the act of exhibiting art publicly is always political and always a product of inescapable sociopolitical circumstances. For example, in January 2003 the United Nations covered up a replication of Picasso's *Guernica* outside the Security Council's chamber room during press coverage concerning the United States' War with Iraq. Laurie Brereton, an Australian delegate, criticized the act of censoring the image, reminding viewers that just like the bombing of innocent civilians in the Basque town of Gernika, the horrors caused by war are not something that we can simply 'pull a curtain over'.[69] Picasso's shrieking mother and mutilated soldier were reminders, at that moment in time, of the terrors of experiencing war. In a different time and place, the same image may not resonate so close to home. Viewers often marvel at the original mural as a relic of cubist excellence or a historical object brought to Spain for the first time in 1981, but when a tapestry version of the image was lingering in the background of new reports concerning war in New York, the aura of the image was undoubtedly altered.

Time and space are major factors that condition the ways in which we see and come to understand visual languages. Through the comparison of different exhibitions that have focused on Tàpies, it has become clear that his legacy is, and will continue to be, constructed. In the first decades of the twenty-first century, Tàpies has not been memorialized as a supporter of the PSUC nor the Catalan left, but as a Catalan nationalist. He did collaborate with Pujol's Generalitat and the two men shared similar sentiments concerning the importance of Catalan culture. However, Tàpies was also actively engaged with the PSUC in the 1970s. Recent retrospective exhibitions at MNAC and Guggenheim Bilbao have not provided visual evidence that is indicative of the artist's relationship to the political party, however, they have embraced Tàpies's construction as a Catalan nationalist. Furthermore, the Spanish government has appropriated Tàpies as an important cultural figure to exhibit abroad via Instituto Cervantes. *The Posters of Antoni Tàpies and the Public Sphere* toned down the artist's role as an activist in 1970s Catalonia, and emphasized other initiatives that Tàpies created images for, in order to satisfy the different standpoints of the host institutions of the travelling exhibition. The following chapter will focus more acutely on the ways in which we comprehend art in correlation to national identity.

Notes to Chapter 5

1. 'Tàpies's Posters and the Public Sphere', Fundació Antoni Tàpies, accessed 4 November 2015, http://www.fundaciotapies.org/site/spip.php?rubrique632.
2. The anniversary poster for F. C. Barcelona was not included in the exhibition although it would have fit with the theme.
3. Mayo, Nuria Enguita, Sandra Fortó, Núria Homs, and Pilar Parcerisas, *Los carteles de Tàpies y la esfera pública* (Barcelona: Fundació Antoni Tàpies, 2006).

4. Ibid.
5. 'La institución', Instituto Cervantes, accessed 29 August 2016, http://www.cervantes.es/sobre_instituto_cervantes/informacion.htm.
6. Katja Valaskivi, *Cool Nations: Media and the Social Imaginary of the Branded Country* (London and New York: Routelage, 2016), Kindle loc. 752.
7. For example, the exhibition *Antoni Tàpies: Exposición retrospectiva*, Ministerio de Cultura. Dirección General de Patramonio Artístico, Archivos y Bibliotecas, Museo Español de Arte Contemporáneo, Madrid, May–August 1980. Giulia Quaggio, *La cultura en transición*, pp. 226–27.
8. 'Antoni Tàpies: The Resources of Rhetoric', Dia Art Foundation, accessed 4 November 2015, http://www.diaart.org/exhibitions/introduction/9.
9. Ibid.
10. Statistic provided by Dia Art Foundation. For press related to the exhibition see also Nicole Berry, 'Antoni Tàpies at Dia:Beacon', *AccessibleArt*, 24 June 2009; Ceus, 'Tàpies, más allá de la pintura'; Jentleson, 'Antoni Tàpies'; and Colin Lang, 'Antoni Tàpies: The Resources of Rhetoric', *Art Forum*, May 2009.
11. Ceus, 'Tàpies, más allá de la pintura'.
12. Ibid.
13. Edelman, *From Art to Politics*, p. 73.
14. D. Preziosi and C. Farago, eds., *Grasping the World: The Idea of the Museum* (Aldershot: Ashgate, 2004). See also Petrescu, *Altering Practices: Feminist Politics and Poetics of Space*; Peter Weibel, Andrea Buddensieg, and Rasheed Araeen, *Contemporary Art and the Museum: A Global Perspective* (Ostfildern: Hatje Cantz, 2007); and Robert Williams, *Art Theory: An Historical Introduction* (Malden, MA: Wiley-Blackwell, 2009).
15. Williams, *Art Theory: An Historical Introduction*, p. 269.
16. Rancière, *The Politics of Aesthetics*, p. 62.
17. Catalina Serra, 'El "calcetín" de Tàpies existe', *El País*, 17 February 2010, accessed 14 November 2015, http://elpais.com/diario/2010/02/17/catalunya/1266372439_850215.html.
18. Hall, 'The Question of Cultural Identity', p. 26.
19. Balfour and Quiroga, *The Reinvention of Spain*, p. 204.
20. Archilés, 'Lenguajes de nación', p. 100.
21. Ibid., p. 104.
22. Ibid., p. 105.
23. Del Arco Blanco, 'Un paso más allá de la historia cultural', p. 13.
24. Josep Massot, 'Tàpies: l'ética de la pintura, L'artista catalá mor als 88 anys al seu domicili de Barcelona', *La Vanguardia*, 7 February 2012, p .28.
25. Catalina Serra, 'Tàpies, immortal', *Ara*, 7 February 2012, accessed 29 August 2016, http://www.ara.cat/cultura/Tapies-immortal_0_641935882.html.
26. Maria Palau, 'El gran artista i pensador', *El Punt Avui*, 7 February 2012, accessed 29 August 2016, http://www.elpuntavui.cat/cultura/article/19-cultura/504330-el-gran-artista-i-pensador.html.
27. 'Muere en Barcelona el artista Antoni Tàpies', *El Periódico*, 6 February 2012, accessed 29 August 2016, http://www.elperiodico.com/es/noticias/ocio-y-cultura/muere-genio-del-informalismo-antoni-tapies-1393283.
28. Jacinto Antón, 'Antoni Tàpies, un artista deslumbrante', *El País*, 6 February 2012, accessed 29 August 2016, http://cultura.elpais.com/cultura/2012/02/06/actualidad/1328557005_302756.html.
29. Ibid.
30. 'Tàpies, adiós al gran renovador del arte español', *ABC Sevilla*, 7 February 2012, 1.
31. William Grimes, 'Antoni Tàpies, Spanish Abstract Painter, Dies at 88', *The New York Times*, 6 February 2012, accessed 13 January 2016, http://www.nytimes.com/2012/02/07/arts/design/antoni-tapies-spanish-abstract-painter-dies-at-88.html?_r=0.
32. Vanessa Graell, 'Muere Tàpies a los 88 años', *El Mundo*, 7 February 2012, accessed 29 August 2016, http://www.elmundo.es/elmundo/2012/02/06/cultura/1328557633.html.
33. While Picasso's image of the weeping woman first appeared in *Sueño y mentira de Franco II*, he painted and sketched, almost obsessively, many versions of the suffering female during the

summer and fall of 1937. The crying figure even appeared in *Guernica* (phase 4–7) until Picasso decided to paint over the teardrops that sliced through the woman's face late in the process. For more see Judi Freeman, *Picasso and the Weeping Women* (Los Angeles: Los Angeles County Museum of Art, 1994) and van Hensbergen, *Guernica: The Biography of a Twentieth-Century Icon*.
34. Interview with Toni Tàpies, 4 February 2016.
35. 'MNAC, Museu Nacional d'Art de Catalunya', Mission statement, renovation plans, and year 2000 goals, Metropolitan Museum of Art, Thomas J. Watson Library, 5.1.3. A copy of a document is available at the University of Connecticut library (Storrs campus). The Prado collection was also relocated to Valencia and later Geneva during the Civil War.
36. As quoted by Ricard Vinyes (2000) in Martín Alonso, *El Catalanismo, del Éxito al Éxtasis* (Barcelona: El Viejo Topo, 2014), p. 166.
37. It is fitting that works completed outside the boundaries of contemporary Catalonia are displayed in this context, as it exemplifies the interrelated nature of the Catalan region with the rest of the historic Kingdom of Aragon (stretching along the East Coast of the Iberian Peninsula from the Pyrenees to Granada under Jaume I, before Aragon and Catalonia were politically united with Castile in 1469) and its independence from Castile. The museum prominently positions a wall painting of Jaume's Conquest of Majorica in this section. See Borja de Riquer, dir., *Història, política, societat i cultura dels Països Catalans* (Barcelona: Enciclopèdia Catalana, 1996–1999).
38. *Museu Nacional d'Art de Catalunya* (Barcelona: Generalitat de Catalunya, 2005).
39. Ley 17/1990, 2 de noviembre, de museos. Generalitat de Catalunya, accessed 22 January 2016, http://dogc.gencat.cat/es/pdogc_canals_interns/pdogc_resultats_fitxa/?action=fitxa&documentId=59538&language=es_ES.
40. Pablo Giori, 'Cataluña, nación y medios: La construcción del espacio nacional de comunicación (1978–2014)', *Revista internacional de Historia de la Comunicación* (3.1, 2014: 119–39), p. 120.
41. Ibid., p. 120–21.
42. Guibernau, *Catalan Nationalism: Francoism, Transition and Democracy*, p. 144.
43. 'The Museum', Museu Nacional d'Art de Catalunya, accessed 20 January 2016, http://www.museunacional.cat/en/museum.
44. *Museu Nacional d'Art de Catalunya*, p. 122.
45. 'MNAC, Museu Nacional d'Art de Catalunya', Mission statement, renovation plans, and year 2000 goals, 5.1.5.
46. Ibid., 5.1.2.
47. Ibid., 5.1.2.
48. Museu Nacional d'Art de Catalunya, 'The Department of Restoration and Preventative Conservation', accessed 1 April 2011, http://www.mnac.cat/serveis/ser_tec_restauracio.jsp?lan=003.
49. Jones, 'Pujol y la construcción de un espacio catalán de comunicación', p. 502.
50. 'A Visit to the Romanesque: In company of Antoni Tàpies', MNAC, accessed 13 November 2015, http://www.museunacional.cat/en/visit-romanesque-company-antoni-tapies.
51. Interview with Pepe Serra, 27 June 2016.
52. Ibid.
53. The general idea of a sanitized narrative in the museum setting comes from Boswell and Evans, *Representing the Nation*, p. 5–6.
54. Interview with Antoni Tàpies, 4 February 2016.
55. 'Antoni Tàpies. From Object to Sculpture (1964–2009)', Guggenheim Bilbao, accessed 18 November 2015, http://tapies.guggenheim-bilbao.es/en/exhibitions/introduction/.
56. Ibid.
57. Fernando Molina and José Antonio Pérez, eds., *El peso de la identidad: mitos y ritos de la historia vasca* (Madrid: Marcial Pons, 2015), p. 57.
58. Interview with Toni Tàpies, 4 February 2016.
59. MNAC reported having 61,506 total visitors and Fundació Antoni Tàpies reported 24,480, there is undoubtedly an overlap as some visitors would have been counted at both of the locations. Statistics provided by MNAC and Fundació Antoni Tàpies.
60. 216,227 visitors total. Statistics provided by Guggenheim Bilbao.

61. Edelman, *From Art to Politics*, p. 143. See also Howard Zinn, *Artists in Times of War* (New York: Seven Stories Press, 2003).
62. 'Dalí: All of the poetic suggestions and all of the plastic possibilities', Museo Nacional Centro de Arte Reina Sofía, accessed 21 November 2015, http://www.museoreinasofia.es/en/exhibitions/dali-all-poetic-suggestions-and-all-plastic-possibilities.
63. Benjamín Prado, 'Dalí el fascista', El País, 8 July 2004, accessed 21 November 2015, http://elpais.com/diario/2004/07/08/madrid/1089285859_850215.html.
64. Ibid.
65. Ibid.
66. Víctor Lenore, *Indies, Hipsters y gafapastas: Crónica de una dominación cultural* (Madrid: Capitán Swing, 2014), 148.
67. Ibid., p. 27.
68. Ibid., p. 28.
69. Van Hensbergen, *Guernica: The Biography of a Twentieth-Century Icon*, pp. 1–3.

CHAPTER 6

Art as a Nationalizing Tool

> All memory is individual, unreproducible — it dies with each person. What is called collective memory is not a remembering but a stipulating that this is important, and this is the story about how it happened with the pictures that lock the story in our minds.
> SUSAN SONTAG[1]

This chapter revisits the theme of Catalan nationalism and art, this time considering the exhibition of visual material as opposed to its creation. While I highlighted a number of the artist's works that deal with the idea of Catalonia in previous chapters, 'Art as a Nationalizing Tool' assesses the ways in which artworks with content concerning the nation have been exhibited publicly. The first section begins with a discussion about national identity in Catalonia and is followed by an examination of how art is involved in the shaping of different identities. The next section is an examination of how art affects politics and includes an analysis of the twenty-first century separatist movements in Catalonia. Using survey data from Catalonia's Centre d'Estudis d'Opinió, this section outlines different models of self-identification and analyses how emotions and art partake in the conception of oneself and the social world. The concluding remarks address what Tàpies's work has to do with Catalan independence and how art is an invaluable tool to instigate thought.

6.1. Marketing National Identity

In 'The Three Spheres: A Theoretical Model of Mass Nnationalization: The Case of Spain' Alejandro Quiroga theorized three areas where nationalist messages are transmitted and how those messages are personalized and rationalized as a component of an individual's identity.[2] The three spheres refer to the public 'official' and 'non-official' realms and the 'private' one. The official public sphere consists of the space where public organizations, such as the police force or the public education system, act. Museums like MNAC fit into this category for its organization and state patronage. The non-official public sphere is made up of 'private institutions [that] act in public spaces'.[3] An example of this category is the Fundació Antoni Tàpies for its officially private status yet public accessibility. Finally, the private sphere is composed of the interactions between an individual and their family and friends. Mass nationalization occurs within each of these three categories; however, the messages and modes of transmission differ depending on the origin. Complicating the matter, sometimes varying signals may act within the same sphere simultaneously. Consider, for example, two public high schools in the United States; one is located in Weston, Connecticut and the other in rural Mississippi. The idea of the nation and what it means to be 'American' is not likely to be consistent in each of the schools due to their stark socio-economic contrasts. Quiroga focused less on the 'official' narratives that come from the state level and more on the ways in which individuals come to associate those ideas with themselves. As previously explained, he understood the individual as an 'active subject who "personalizes the nation."'[4] Nationalism and national identity are connected via this personalization. And, as Quiroga concluded, historians cannot wholly rationalize the phenomenon of nationalism and the fact that humans are willing to 'sacrifice their lives for such an artificial and abstract entity as the nation', however, they are able to 'elucidate the creation, transmission and transformation of national identities…'.[5] This section focuses on the transmission of a Catalan national identity within Quiroga's official and non-official spheres.

On 12 December 2013 Artur Mas publicly announced that he would hold a controversial referendum. The President of the Generalitat de Catalunya declared that on 9 November 2014 Catalan citizens would have the opportunity to submit a ballot responding to the following: 'Do you want Catalonia to become a State?' Those responding affirmatively would also be asked if they believe that the state should be independent. While the Spanish Constitutional Court made it clear that this type of ballot was not constitutional, Mas led his region in an unofficial vote as promised, without the central government's approval. *The New York Times* reported on the event in an article titled 'Catalonia Overwhelmingly Votes for Independence From Spain in Straw Poll'.[6] A straw poll is synonymous with an impromptu or off-the-record vote; the name comes from the action of holding a piece of straw in the air to see which way the wind is blowing. Catalans living abroad were allowed to vote, but not those living in other regions of Spain.[7]

The results of Mas's popular consultation favoured the yes-yes option (those that want Catalonia to become an independent state), as approximately 80% of the more than 2 million voters opted for separation from Spain. Note that this figure reflects a percentage of voters, not the entire population nor a sample. The Generalitat de Catalunya published statistics and graphs of the votes online. The high percentage of the yes-yes response is represented as part of a bar graph (with the alternative bars representing yes-no, yes-blank, no, blank, and others), while the breakdown of the two questions is separated into two pie charts. The first chart that shows 92% of the voters wished Catalonia to be a state and the second shows that, out of those voters, 88% of them wished for that state to be independent.[8] The most significant data for Mas and CiU (the 80% yes-yes column and the 88% yes to an independent state section) stand out due to their bright orange colour, whereas the section with the highest percentage (92% responding that they want Catalonia to be a state) is a much more bland, phthalo green shade. The data nonetheless showed some 2 million opinions concerning the political future of Catalonia, marking a measurable shift in the Spanish winds.

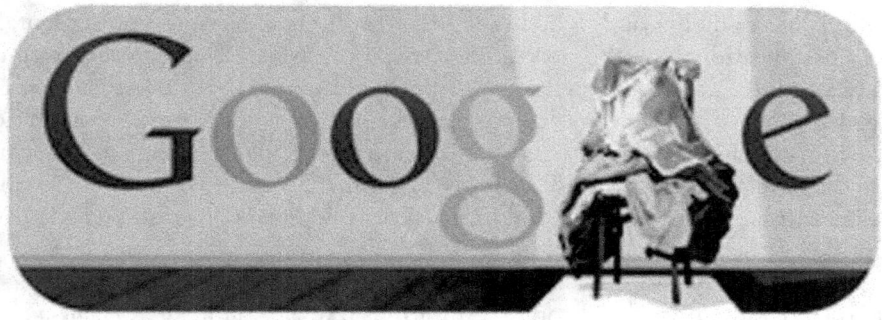

Fig. 6.1. Google, Google Doodle, 13 December 2013

On the day following Mas's 2013 announcement about the referendum, the Google doodle was a tribute to the life and work of Tàpies (figure 6.1). The artist would have been celebrating his ninetieth birthday if he had not passed away at the age of eighty-eight the previous year in Barcelona. The homepage of the search engine replaced the penultimate letter of their logo with an assemblage that the artist made in 1970, a work titled *Cadira i roba*. It looks like a heap of filthy laundry piled on top of an everyday chair; to the average viewer, this work seems like nothing more than a bunch of soiled fabric slovenly tossed on an old wooden chair. *Cadira i roba* deals with the notion of time and accumulation. It echoes Robert Rauschenberg's 1955 *Bed* in the way that it uses ordinary textiles to instigate reflections about the physical and mental layers that incessantly accumulate with the passing of time.

Art, among the plethora of omnipresent images, signs, and symbols in 'Western' culture, is able to selectively aggrandize national, historical memory. In 'The Role of Commemorations in (Ethno)Nation-Building. The Case of Catalonia' Josep Llobera examined the topic of historical memory in the '(re)making of Catalan national identity after Franco's death'.[9] He discussed the sociocultural importance of the *Diada* (September 11) and Saint Jordi's Day (April 23). These two holidays have a symbolic significance where voluntary 'collective' or historical memory shapes the modern Catalan identity. As Susan Sontag pointed out, the concept of collective memory is imaginary. Memory is individual and irreproducible. She explained, 'what is called collective memory is not a remembering but a stipulating: that this is important, and this is the story about how it happened, with the pictures that lock the story in our minds'.[10] Both the 'real' history and the imagined myths and traditions associated with these two holidays do not stem from collective memory, rather a communal will to accept similar narratives as valid and to perform similar rituals in the name of tradition.

Similarly, selective historical memory effectively reinforces a continuous national narrative in the athletic arena. Quiroga addressed the connection between historic figures and contemporary professional soccer players in *Goles y banderas: Fútbol e identidades nacionales en España*. As in the art world, athletes were constantly compared to idols from previous generations of prominent figures of the nation's history. Twentieth century media outlets facilitated that millions of citizens could mentally connect current athletes with patriotic heroes of the past.[11] Popular celebrations, official holidays, athletics, and art all contribute to a national culture that fosters a sense of shared identity. Quiroga has examined this tactic of creating a connection to the past through comparison in his investigation of national soccer teams in Spain. There are a number of places also working to connect a cohesive national history such as the Museu d'Història de Catalunya, El Born Centre Cultural, and MNAC. The subtitle of the Museu d'Història de Catalunya's webpage is 'The memory of a country'[12] and the website for El Born Centre Cultural describes the space as 'a core of collective memory'.[13] Through exhibitions like *A Visit to the Romanesque: In Company of Antoni Tàpies*, MNAC has sought to tie together the past and the present via works of art. All three institutions combine together Uhl Heidemarie's concept of solid and liquid memory, as outlined in 'From Discourse to Representation: "Austrian Memory" in Public Space'.[14] Solid sites of stipulated historical memory include monuments, commemorative plaques, museums, etc., while liquid memory deals with discursive narratives and temporal media. Exhibitions unite both solid and liquid memory via real objects and transient explanations that justify or express the reasons for presenting those particular objects.

This idea of liquid memory is also related to emotions and personal identity. As Ludger Mees explained, cognition and emotion are *not* mutually exclusive. 'Emotions cannot exist without a cognitive process, and cognition never develops in a supposedly "neutral" terrain or one that is free from emotional processes and memories'.[15] Extrapolating on this argument that cognition and emotion are directly related, making sense of a work of art must also be related to feelings and emotions.

Returning to the Google doodle, the face value of *Cadira i roba* has little to do with Catalan nationalism or identity. There are no stripes or colours of the *senyera*, nor letters hailing the Catalan nation. However, the search engine's inclusion of this piece on that particular day contributes to the remembering of Tàpies, whose art has been turned into a symbol of Catalan identity. In her 2003 paper 'Nationalism and Intellectuals in Nations without States: The Catalan Case', Montserrat Guibernau explained how the internationally acclaimed Catalan artists Miró, Gaudí, Dalí, Tàpies, and Casals have been converted into icons that play a role in the emotional arguments linked to Catalan nationalism.[16] Toni Tàpies commented on this sort of appropriation and marketing on behalf of both political and cultural institutions:

> this tends to happen, and more so in a small country like Catalonia that is still fighting to affirm its identity. When figures emerge like Miró, my father, like Casals, like Gaudí, there is a tendency to use them a bit as a projection of our culture. This has been done, and I suppose it will continue to be done, they are taken as models, to make a statement about having a powerful culture. They have used the name of Tàpies, of Gaudí, and a series of other figures to project this image of Catalonia.[17]

This is also a frequently employed tactic of both nationalization and nation branding, the projection of public figures such as actors, athletes, musicians, writers, etc. as emblematic characters inseparably associated with one particular nation. Katja Valaskivi explained this in *Cool Nations: Media and the Social Imaginary of the Branded Country*, 'successful musicians and artists are used in nation states for nationalistic and nation branding purposes, but the field in which they play is not primarily based on the global system of nations'.[18] Even though artists may like to consider their work as somehow detached from this global system, technology and globalization have made that increasingly difficult to evade. Many nations create a halo effect around prosperous artists from their region, instrumentalizing their creative capacity as something that belongs to the nation. For the sake of nation branding, the difference between selecting artists and musicians, as opposed to admirable public figures such as human rights activists or politicians, is that their work is more easily converted into marketable goods. Valaskivi reminded readers that the 'branded country is interwoven with capitalism and consumer culture'.[19]

In reproducing Tàpies's art online in 2013, Google, one of the world's most valuable companies, stipulated (using Sontag's concept) Tàpies's Catalan identity, indicating: 'this is important'. However, it is doubtful that Spain's Google users considered whether or not Tàpies's would-be ninetieth birthday had been something to celebrate. Will Google repeat a similar homage in 2023 in order to memorialize (and once again remind us that 'this is important') the one hundredth anniversary of the artist's birth? Or was it only significant to commemorate Tàpies's date of birth in 2013 because of the previous day's events concerning Mas's new objectives for Catalonia? Toni Tàpies said that he himself was surprised to see the doodle on his late father's birthday. He had no prior knowledge of the gesture nor was he aware of any previous requests for permissions to use the image on behalf of the search engine. Google is a company that controls an unthinkable amount of data on a daily basis and undoubtedly had statistics concerning the number of people that searched for news about the significant political announcement in Catalonia the previous day. It seems probable that Google made the tribute in response to user activity in Spain, in order to complement the political news in Catalonia with an element of culture that is associated with the same region. It seems doubtful that the company had planned beforehand on acknowledging the would-be ninetieth birthday. Culture, in this case art, played a role in linking people to the idea of the nation and it did so in a way that seems 'normal,' as Archilés has expressed.[20]

In *Banal Nationalism*, Billig discussed the signs and symbols that remind us of the nation without necessarily taking centre stage. He used the ubiquity of national flags as an example. Google's tribute to Tàpies worked in a similar fashion in the non-official sphere as the image is not tied to anything concretely Catalan, yet the artist's background and the day in which it was posted is inseparable from Catalan politics and society. Billig rightly claimed that the conglomeration of this sort of flagging does not create Anderson's imagined community; instead, the signs, symbols, mediatization, and rhetoric of national communities have become so embedded into contemporary thinking that their *absence* is unimaginable.[21] Pictures from other famous artists such as Miró or Dalí have become part of Catalonia's visual vocabulary throughout all three of Quiroga's spheres. According to Billig's theory, their works may contribute to what the Catalan community considers to be normal, but their absence would have more of an impact because these figures have become banal hailers of Catalan identity.

Catalan institutions in the official and non-official spheres act as transmitters of these pictures, turning them into 'normal' images that constitute part of the greater Catalan culture. Part of this phenomenon comes from the media; recall the avalanche of press surrounding Tàpies's *Mitjó* during the early 1990s. Even those uninterested in art or sculpture probably saw, at least a handful of times, something in the newspaper related to Tàpies and his work. Other factors include the interest of nationalist groups and nation branders. Nationalists have appropriated and commissioned artists and works of art in Catalonia in order to bolster their claims of harbouring an authentic, unique culture. Both Pujol and the Generalitat used Tàpies to these ends. Nation branders, on the other hand, may be less interested in presenting culture as genuine and more interested in representing it as 'cool' and competitive in a global market, prioritizing industrial interests over citizens' interests.[22]

The problem with this is that the 'normal' is rarely contested because MNAC is a professional institution and its visitors may not think of it as a particularly politicized space. However, it is impossible to separate the practice of artistic exhibition from politics. Art, depending on the context of its exhibition, is able to support both prosaic and radical political ideologies.[23] Further complicating the marketing of a specific Catalan national identity is its changing nature. Catalan nationalism and the desire for Catalan independence are not co-dependent. During the twentieth century many Catalan nationalist groups did not consider secession a necessary nor beneficial step. However, during the early twenty-first century the two have become more closely related; not all Catalan nationalists have opted for independence, but the correlation has been strengthened in the wake of both social and political crises in Spain.[24] Nationalism in Catalonia in 2015 had a greater association with the independence movement than it did during the previous century.

Joan M. Minguet Batllori, contemporary art history Professor at the Universitat Autònoma de Barcelona, asked what the future of the arts in Catalonia would be like in his 2015 *Contra la Cooltura; Art i Política a Catalunya*.[25] As president of l'Associació Catalana de Critics d'Art, an organization established in 1978 that links together professionals with various roles in the arts (critics, curators, docents, etc.), his response was optimistic yet critical of the institutionalization of the arts; he stated that the future could be how *we* want it to be, and offered the first proposition: to convince *ourselves* that *we* do not need the arts under the direction of public (official) administration, which is so often 'surrounded by mediocrity and cowardice'.[26] Communication theory Professor at the Universitat Pompeu Fabra Josep Gifreu shared an analogous opinion years before in his 2005 *La Pell de la diferència: Comunicació, llengua i cultura dels de l'espai català*. In a similar fashion, he discussed that culture has come to be understood in Catalonia as an administrative question of the management of patrimony.[27] Minguet, calling for a dramatic change, proposed major transformations that he would like to see in the future, beginning with 'vindicating the dignity of creation',[28] pointing out that the government ought to dedicate much more financial support to the cultural sector, which could be read as contradictory to his previous affirmations. Nostalgically recalling the close relationship between the Mancomunitat de Catalunya and *Noucentisme* during the early twentieth century, he also reminded readers of the historicity of the social function of art.[29] Finally, he concluded with the following statement: 'long live the arts in liberty, there must always be liberty and equality for anyone practicing art. And for those who view and, above all, think'.[30] Are liberty and equality feasible in the future for Catalan artists and thinkers? Minguet himself suggested otherwise, implying that freedom is only achievable to a certain degree in the world of nations; he discussed how the Generalitat has emphasized culture and art as signs and markers of Catalan identity, yet the governing parties have proved to be useless in establishing ideas about what the history of Catalan art was, what the image of Catalan art is in 2015, and how to make Catalan art for the future without sufficient funding.[31]

In 2010 the Generalitat's spending allocation for culture was 458.4 million euros and in 2015 it was less than half that amount, 192.09 million euros.[32] Similarly, Spain's spending on culture in 2010 was 1.199 trillion euros and by 2015 had been reduced to 749 million euros.[33] The Generalitat's spending on the visual arts dropped from 21,572,600 euros in 2010 to 9,182,000 euros in 2013, however the budget for linguistic normalization (similarly grouped with culture) increased during the same period from 34,788,100 euros to 38,008,900 euros, peaking at 45,026,400 euros in 2011.[34] The downward spiral of public spending allowance for the visual arts and culture in general, compared to the increase in linguistic normalization, reflects the Generalitat's priorities concerning the national language and the aspired benefits of increasing the number of people who would be able to speak and understand Catalan. Furthermore, with less financial support from the government, both official and non-official cultural institutions have often been pressured to seek funding from private entities. This further complicates the politics surrounding the exhibition of cultural objects. For example, the second largest energy company in Spain, Iberdrola, sponsored Guggenheim's 2013 *Antoni Tàpies: From Object to Sculpture* exhibition. The income of the company's CEO José Ignacio Sánchez Galán in the same year was 7.4 million euros and Iberdrola's board of directors earned 14.53 million euros, exceeding what the Generalitat spent on the visual arts in the same year.[35]

Beyond the issue of funding is the problem that, once government or private institutions finance works of art and artistic exhibitions, artists and curators lose that very liberty that Minguet claimed they needed. The unrealized *Mitjó* exemplifies how politics can interfere with artistic liberty. The future of art in Catalonia, as Minguet expressed, can be how they (or we) want it to be. However, that would involve more autonomy for living artists and artistic institutions to operate freely with substantial funding from the government. He formed a useful analogy for those politicians that act in the cultural realm: that they should be more like excellent soccer officials, that when they do their job correctly you hardly notice their presence.³⁶ Instead of posing for photographs at openings or speaking to the media about their personal tastes, they should work more humbly and discretely, giving professionals in the field the resources and responsibility to do their work. Finally, Minguet mentioned three artists whose works represent the epitome of socially engaged (and 'good') art. Interestingly, they are all women artists: Núria Güell, Mireia Sallarés, and Mireia C. Saladrigues.³⁷ In doing so, he highlighted both the need for a greater focus on artists whose work deals with sociopolitical tensions and the desperate need to incorporate women into what could become the future history of art in Catalonia.

In *From Art to Politics* Edelman gave voice to the relationship between art and the official sphere, which Minguet's sentiments echo:

> Although it is a central theme of this book that art is a major influence on government, the two institutions are bound to remain at odds with each other. Art ideally requires absolute freedom of imagination, thought, and expression, while governments inevitably try to restrict the exercise of these faculties and their consequences; and regimes like to define the restraints as freedom. Even in democratic states claiming to promote the arts, the link is always fragile and the arts are frequently obstructed. But that inevitable tension should not mean that awareness of the connections among art and politics is also obstructed.³⁸

Edelman sought to expose the very real links that exist between art and politics, not in hopes of separating one from the other, but in order to be able to better comprehend their relationship.

The purpose of this chapter is not to propose a model that liberates art from political ties. All works of art, once they are shown to the public, become political. However, the ability to manipulate, bend, or twist the perceived meaning of an image is too easy a task to ignore. MNAC is an official institution that partakes in the negotiation, or marketing, of a national identity via works of art.³⁹ The museum simultaneously educates foreign visitors about the history of Catalan art and aims to show locals to relate and personalize those images as part of their own cultural heritage. Complicating the situation is the fact that MNAC is a consortium 'independent' from its three members (the Generalitat de Catalunya, Ajuntament de Barcelona, and Spanish State) with the possibility of adding private entities if unanimously agreed upon. It has an official status, but one that is neither fully part of the State Administration nor truly independent from it. The museum presents the idea that Catalonia has been, is, and will be a unified social group, one that is distinct from the rest of Spain.⁴⁰ Visitors have naturally identified themselves as belonging to this group, viewing the works of art as belonging to their own culture, or as outsiders eager to discover what makes Catalan art unique. However, just because an artwork was made in Catalonia, does not necessarily make that work essentially Catalan. It is true that we can identify particular tendencies and trends in the historical practice of art, but the creators of those characteristics historically had little regards for the contemporary imagining of clearly defined state and sub-state boarders that we use as an unquestioned device to distinguish one area from another. As Billig explained in *Banal Nationalism*, the concept of naming a language in the medieval era was unusual; people spoke and others understood, or not; the ability for the listener to understand diminished as the speaker travelled further away from their home.[41] MNAC's medieval collection is linked to the territory in which it was created (present day Catalonia), but the individual artworks themselves are products of specific locations that were not ideologically nor politically unified in the same manner as today's Autonomous Community of Catalonia. *A Visit to the Romanesque: In Company of Antoni Tàpies* drew attention to the 'Catalan' characteristics of Tàpies's works,[42] the same characteristics that were downplayed in Guggenheim Bilbao and Dia:Beacon's exhibitions. Comparing these three institutions and their presentation of Tàpies's artwork shows just how malleable, flexible, or arbitrary the organization and contextualization of artworks can be both in official and non-official spheres. This comparison is not meant to generate a right verses wrong binary, rather, it is meant to show that the content and context of artistic exhibitions are delicate and can entail politically charged initiatives.

Similarly, educational resources are able to point students to certain facts, while purposefully ignoring others. For example, in a history textbook written in Catalan for the final year of compulsory secondary education, there is a section devoted to post-1945 avant-garde art. The text, published in 2008 by the Barcelona editorial Teide, used both 'Europe' and 'Catalan' while introducing Tàpies, disregarding the fact that he was also a Spaniard and lived his entire life in Spain.[43] Despite the nationalist overtones, amplified by the fact that there was an image of one of Antonio López's canvases yet no mention of the Spaniard under the hyperrealist section, Teide's explanation of Tàpies's contribution to avant-garde art was significantly more credible than other art history textbooks. In Albert Domènech's 2009 textbook for second-year baccalaureate art history students, also published in Catalan by Teide, Tàpies was briefly mentioned in relation to the group Dau al Set.[44] However, the group ceased publishing in 1956 and the text is not representative of the long, successful career that Tàpies experienced after the 1950s. A different textbook, designed for the same course and published in Spanish in the same year by Santillana in Madrid, merely listed Tàpies's name with a string of other 'Spaniards'. In this book, Tàpies was grouped with the most prominent Spanish '*informalistas*': Manolo Millares, Martín Chirino, and Antonio Saura.[45] These three very different ways to introduce the same artist are demonstrative of the flexibility of learning and knowledge within public education in Spain. While the 2013 Ley Orgánica de Mejora de la Calidad Educativa established core subjects, in addition to their standards and evaluation criteria for the official sphere, the law did not create a strict standard as to *how* those subjects would then be presented to the students via non-official textbooks.[46] Publishing companies have had room to shape the ways in which students are able to access knowledge concerning different topics. While Tàpies's identity and legacy may seem trivial, it is part of a greater body of knowledge that is presented to young students in a factual manner. This knowledge, or absence of knowledge, is subject to the various political, social, or economic agendas of the publishing companies, much like the different programs of cultural institutions.[47] Through official curricula and narratives, schools work to construct normalities, closely related to Stuart Hall's 'mental frameworks'.[48]

6.2. How Art Affects Politics

The realm of politics plays a role in the imagination, creation, and exhibition of visual art. The inverse of this statement is also true: the imagination, creation, and exhibition of visual art plays a role in the realm of politics. Previous chapters have considered the indirect and direct relationship between Tàpies's art and politics in Catalonia. But how does his art affect politics? Tàpies's work engenders thought and reflection. Sometimes his works are even illegible without taking the time to think about them. Depending on the ways in which his works are presented, the focus of his art can differ. Tàpies's place in the constructed history of art, as was the focus of Dia:Beacon's 2009 exhibition, is not a highly contested terrain. However, the artist's Catalan identity and his connection to medieval art and literature, as seen in MNAC's 2013 exhibition or the Generalitat's 1990 commission of *Les quatre cròniques*, deal with a more sensitive subject. His work is part of the many signs, symbols, and narratives associated with Catalan identity. However, as seen in the different obituaries published in various periodicals, Tàpies's legacy is not fixed. Furthermore, what used to be a perfectly compatible dual identity, both Catalan and Spanish, has been destabilizing since the 2010 protests against modifying the 2006 Statue of Autonomy. The ensuing rise in support for an independent Catalan State has affected the ways in which individuals conceive of their identities and allegiances in the private sphere, although some variation of a dual Spanish and Catalan identity has remained the most common throughout the first two decades of the twenty-first century. As Daniele Conversi explained in *The Basques, the Catalans, and Spain: Alternative Routes to Nationalist Mobilisation*, once national conflicts break out, 'people are helplessly drawn into it on each side [...they] are compelled to take sides'.[49] While Conversi spoke about violent acts of nationalist expression, the idea of taking sides also works in non-violent yet heavily debated conflicts.

In 2000 in 'Banal Catalanism?' Kathryn Crameri stated that the social and legal acceptance of Catalonia's status as a nation, in addition to the institutions that mimic those of a state, has engendered banal forms of Catalan nationalism despite its lack of statehood.[50] In recognizing Catalonia as a nation, Crameri showed that the community no longer needed to justify its own existence as a nation, effectively shifting national ideas and symbols along a spectrum that ranges from contentious to mundane.[51] Crameri stated that banal nationalism 'is indeed becoming the more dominant form in Catalonia: the types of symbols and media which are necessary for this are in place and functioning more or less as they would in an established nation, despite the overlapping existence of the Spanish State and its symbols'.[52] She concluded suggesting that the Catalan nationalists who fear that the region's autonomy may revert to a more restricted form in the future ought to understand how Billig's theory of banal nationalism works before taking action. Since the transition to democracy and before the 2010 protests, groups seeking to increase the nationalization of Catalans and Catalanist values were disjoined. Individuals who considered that Catalonia's inclusion as an autonomous community in the democratic Kingdom of Spain was acceptable largely outnumbered pro-independence nationalists. Historically, a number of both civil and political groups have sought to encourage the idea that Catalonia is remarkably distinct from the rest of Spain, however popular support for secession has been a more recent development.

About a decade after Crameri published her article, a resurgence of media attention concerning Catalan nationalism weakened her theory that nationalism was on the wane and institutions of the official sphere have been supporting art exhibitions such as *A Visit to the Romanesque: In Company of Antoni Tàpies* and *Tàpies. From Within*. National identity, the individual's personalization of nationalist concepts, has been a major factor with real political consequences in Catalonia during the twenty-first century and its importance does not seem to be diminishing. The population of supporters in favour of Catalan secession reached a peak in 2012 around 57%, as compared to about 43% in 2011 and 55% in 2013.[53] Although the more than 2 million citizens who showed up to vote on 9 November 2014 may conceive of their individual national identities as fixed, statistical data has shown that self-identification concerning national identity in Catalonia is fluctuating and variable.[54]

Data from the Centre d'Estudis d'Opinió showed that in 2012, 35% of questionnaire participants indicated that they felt as much Spanish as Catalan, while 29.6% felt only Catalan.[55] In November 2016 almost half (44.1%) responded that they are Catalan and live in Catalonia, as opposed to Catalan living in Spain or Spanish living in Catalonia or Spain; when asked to locate themselves on a scale from zero to ten (zero corresponding to '*màxim espanyolisme*' and ten '*màxim catalanisme*') 36.7% situated themselves in the middle of the two poles while 4.5% placed themselves at zero, 14.6% at ten, and 11.1% at eight.[56] In the same survey, in a question that asked about the current political situation in Spain 39.4% responded that it was bad and 47.6% very bad. Dissatisfaction with Spanish politics, concerns with the economic situation of the autonomous community and the Spanish State, high unemployment rates, low job security, and the polarization of political parties in Catalonia are contributing factors that have caused shifts in public opinions and feelings.

In 'Secessionism in Catalonia: After Democracy' Guibernau outlined three main issues that caused the independence movement to accelerate to unprecedented levels. First, she highlighted the inability of José María Aznar's government (1996–2004) to address increasing demands for further autonomy in Catalonia. Second, she outlined how the Constitutional Court's 2010 ruling for modifications to the already-sanctioned 2006 Statute of Autonomy in Catalonia caused tension between the regional and central governments. Finally, Guibernau addressed how the public's understanding of the repercussions of accumulating annual deficits in Catalonia affected how individuals felt towards government spending.[57] Although Guibernau defined these as the leading causes, she also acknowledged how personal sentiments have played a part in the rapid development of the independence movement: 'the emotions they [the factors outlined above] have triggered are closely connected with the rise of secessionism in Catalonia'.[58] Feelings and emotions also impact the ways in which individuals determine the weight of their Spanish and/or Catalan identities.

As Guibernau discussed in 'Catalan Secessionism: Young People's expectations and Political Change', modern nationalism in Catalonia did not develop as a 'unified phenomenon'.[59] Similarly, Crameri stated in 2014 in *Goodbye Spain?: The Question of Independence for Catalonia*, 'fragmentation has been a perpetual characteristic of Catalan separatism up to the present day'.[60] Part of this disjointed nature stems from the various ways in which individual's conceive of their identity, in turn having an effect on what they believe about the relationship between the nation of Catalonia and the nation of Spain. However, what was a minority and fragmented movement before the global financial crisis of 2008 and the 2010 Constitutional Court rulings concerning the legality of the 2006 Autonomy Statue snowballed into a much more powerful push towards sovereignty in the ensuing years, with the 'most significant leaps in support' occurring just after Tàpies's death, between March and November of 2012.[61]

The great leap in support from what was historically a fragmented, disjoined movement could fit into Ian Shapiro's theory concerning human action and the resistance of domination outlined in *Politics Against Domination*. In a discussion of the term 'non-dominance', Shapiro stated, 'political philosophers pay too little attention to the reality that people know a lot more about what they are against than what they favour, and that one of the things they resist is domination or the prospect of it'.[62] The tremendous increase in support for independence did not occur in 2006 parallel to a push for further autonomy within Spain, but as a reaction to circumstances that Catalan citizens did *not* want: such as reforming the Autonomy Statue and to continue financing less wealthy regions of Spain via tax payments to the central government. Perhaps the increase in support for independence has more to do with what individuals *do not* want, than the objective of becoming a nation separate from the Kingdom of Spain.

Although popular support of the separatist movement started to decline around 2012, the movement's organization and paralleled political power has not diminished. The pro-independence Candidatura d'Unitat Popular (CUP, established in 1986) increased from three seats in 2012, the party's first year running in the elections for the Catalan parliament, to ten seats in 2015, and dropped to four in 2018. At the same time, as Astrid Barrio and Juan Rodríguez Teruel explained in a 2013 article concerning the radicalization of political parties in Catalonia, the spectrum of *'españolismo/catalanismo'* became increasingly important along with the emergence of new parties during the first years of the twenty-first century, convoluting the traditional model based on a liberal/conservative spectrum. In 2012 CiU and ERC were hedging one another to compete for Catalan nationalist voters, resulting in the polarization of political parties to 'levels without precedent'.[63] Barrio and Rodríguez Teruel interestingly pointed out that while great shifts that occurred within the party system are related to changes in the electorate, their correlation is not exact.[64] In June 2015, the CiU coalition split. The CDC advocated for Catalan independence, to which UCD held a much milder stance. For the September elections of the same year, CDC allied with ERC as part of the coalition Junts pel sí, consolidating sixty-two of the 135 seats in the Catalan Parliament. Although voter support for independence may have fallen since 2012, political parties have set agendas to position themselves more favourably in relation to other parties, which does not necessarily reflect a perfect match with the opinions of the electorate.[65]

Enric Martínez-Herrera and Thomas Jeffery Miley emphasized a similar point in 'The constitution and the politics of national identity in Spain'. They pointed out that the 'preferences of the general public stand in sharp contrast with the preferences of influential sections of the Basque and Catalan regional political establishment [...] current challenges to the constitutional compromise are driven by political elite'.[66] This fits with Martínez-Herrera and Miley's understanding of the elite instigation of the nationalist movement in Catalonia, as opposed to bottom-up models that point to the number of citizens that attended massive demonstrations in 2010 and 2012.[67] Consequently, as Justo Beramendi has persuasively explained, in 2015 the independence movement was characterized as 'too strong to permit compromises and too weak for the secession to be indisputable'.[68] Too strong because in 2015 ERC and CDC had already set clear separatist agendas, contributing to the June dissolution of CiU, and too weak because the population was split concerning support for independence. At this point, almost a third of Catalan citizens considered themselves equally Spanish and Catalan, however it is important to remember that there is not an exact correlation between national identification and support for independence.

Those that conceive of themselves as partially or wholly Catalan have been faced with the dilemma of supporting or opposing the separatist movement. Here is where the concept of 'nested' vs. 'bi-cultural' identities comes into play.[69] In 'Against the Thesis of the Civic Nation', Miley argued that in contemporary Catalonia both of these models are in operation. Nested identities refer to those who consider that being Catalan is part of being Spanish. The visual representation of this would look like a small circle (Catalan) within a larger circle (Spanish), like an egg in a nest. An exemplary public figure that embodies this concept is the professional basketball player Pau Gasol, in a 2008 interview in the United States Gasol stated, 'I consider myself Catalan but I am also Spanish'.[70] In *Goles y banderas*, Quiroga showed the compatibility of these two identities, manifested in the streets of Barcelona in 2010.[71] Hundreds of thousands of people banned together on 19 July 2010 in protest of the Spanish Constitutional Court's decision to modify the 2006 Statute of Autonomy. Òmnium Cultural, an association fostering the spread of Catalan language and culture with clandestine origins under Franco's Spain, organized the protest using the slogan *'som una nació'*. The following day, Spain's national soccer team won the World Cup for the first time and thousands of supporters celebrated in the streets of Barcelona chanting *'yo soy español, español, español'*.[72] These events demonstrated the coexistence of both Catalan and Spanish identities via the physical and ideological participation of the crowds of people that took part in these acts. For many, being Catalan was not (and is not) incompatible with being Spanish nor was the population's diversity of identities problematic in this situation.

Miley proposed another model that he linked primarily to native Catalan speakers. The bi-cultural form also includes both Catalan and Spanish identities, yet they are conceived of as separate and distinct identifications. This would look like two circles floating in separate spaces. The decision to separate from Spain would seem more logical to those that consider themselves as foreigners, only Catalan, or bi-cultural. The ethno-linguistic characteristics of the population that has adopted the bi-cultural model has determined Miley's thesis against calling the Catalan nationalist movement 'civic.' Instead, he argued that the national project in Catalonia was broadly an elitist, top-down effort emphasizing ethnicity and language as markers of what it means to be Catalan.[73]

The balance between Miley's two categorical distinctions (nested/bi-cultural), that broadly encompass the majority of the population living in Catalonia, is not static. Identity is not a fixed property determined at birth. Future generations could include this disparity or yield and reflect other fusions, such as a more European orientation. Art and culture can be used as nationalizing tools in all three spheres as a means of changing the ways in which individuals understand the world. Hall's notion of 'mental frameworks', which allow people to make associations and comprehend the ways in which society works, is the primer for actions. Ideas are followed by thoughts about what individuals ought to do.[74]

Art and its contemporary exhibition is one of the many ways in which the Catalan nation has been presented as a legitimate political and historical entity. El Born Centre de Cultura i Memòria, formerly El Born Centre Cultural, is one example that has worked to solidify a single narrative concerning the history of Catalonia. Fundació Miró, nestled behind MNAC on Montjuïc, has also formed exhibitions directly related to the institution's vision of Catalan history in the semi-public sphere. For example, in 2001 and 2004 the Fundació Miró hosted the temporary exhibitions *Joan Brossa o la revolta poètica* and *Manifest groc: Dalí, Gasch, Montanyà i l'antiart*. The Generalitat sponsored both shows, which highlighted a number of Catalan artists without mentioning their Spanish identities.[75] Failing to point out Brossa, Dalí, and Gasch's Spanish identities is not a falsification. However, it would have guided visitors' 'mental frameworks'. Presenting these figures as admirable for their artistic constructions and political engagement, and leaving out the fact that they were both Catalan and Spanish, is significant. This seemingly small detail can have a more extensive impact when beholders come to reflect on their relationship to these figures and their works of art.

At different moments in time, in different spaces and spheres, Catalonia has been differentiated from Spain, while other times it has been projected as nested within Spain. Art has often played a key role in the Catalan nationalist narrative that presents Catalonia as a sophisticated and modern nation vis-à-vis the representation of Spain as backwards, old-fashioned, and unsophisticated. MNAC's use of Tàpies is an example of this at work within the official sphere. However, as we have seen with some alternative exhibitions in official and non-official cultural institutions, as well as in literature and press related to Tàpies, a bi-cultural model has also been employed, albeit less frequently, in order to assert and celebrate the artist's Spanish heritage. Each version is true, and this is why it is important to think when standing before, or reading about, a work of art.

In the final chapter of Edelman's *From Art to Politics*, the author spoke about the beneficial role of art in democratic societies:

> Although art is no more a bastion of democracy than elections and lobbying are, it does strengthen democracy in some respects. Because it excites minds and feelings as everyday experiences ordinarily do not, it is a provocation, an incentive to mental and emotional alertness. Its creation of new realities means that it can intrude upon passive acceptance of conventional ideas and banal responses to political clichés. For that reason art can help foster a reflective public that is less inclined to think and act in a herd spirit or according to the cues and dictates provided by a privileged oligarchy.[76]

This is exactly what Tàpies intended to accomplish with his artwork. He sought to engage viewers, compelling them to think through his compositions and not focus on the aesthetic surface value.

His art repeatedly referred directly to topics concerning Catalan history and identity, but he also addressed political topics not necessarily tied to Catalonia such as war in Bosnia or apartheid in South Africa. Still, a great deal of his work remained less focused and more meditative. What all his works had, and continue to have, in common is a link to the political world and their creator's insistence on their function as a starting point. That starting point serves as the building block for further thoughts, experiences, and actions. The starting point can shift, alter, or strengthen previous 'mental frameworks' and ways in which individuals come to understand the world. Tàpies's works were not necessarily meant to instigate political action. Instead, they were made to stimulate the thoughts that come before calculated actions.

Tàpies stated in 1969 that 'these images, as most works of art, have never been an end in and of themselves, they should rather be viewed as a springboard, as a means to reach farther ends'.[77] The farther ends that Tàpies spoke about are in essence the seeds of knowledge. Art may or may not teach us anything about what Michel Foucault called the 'regimes of truth'. However, good art makes us think and as Minguet rightly claimed: *'ens fa més savis'* [it makes us wiser].[78]

6.3. Concluding Remarks

What does the work of a modern artist have to do with Catalan independence? James C. Scott reminded us that behind social movements exist layers of hidden and disguised transcripts. In the Catalan case, different ideas concerning the nation and its relation to Spain have spanned more than a century. At times these ideas have been discussed openly and other times kept behind closed doors. Tàpies created a visual language in the 1950s that sought to undermine Francoism and uphold values of democracy and freedom. Via Tàpies, art has played a role in the imagination of a Catalan nation. His work helped to propel the visualization of a contemporary *Catalunya*. While his art does not always reveal his resolute commitment to Catalan nationalism, it composed part of the hidden and infrapolitical dialogue that has a long and rich visual history in Catalonia. The artist and his works of art, with the support of government and cultural institutions, have been turned into symbols of Catalan culture in all three of Quiroga's spheres. Similarly, Spanish agencies have done the same in the public sphere through exhibitions that highlight the artist as one of Spain's many extraordinary and internationally renowned visual artists. These two different classifications are not mutually exclusive but have framed the artist and his legacy in distinct formats. During his lifetime, Tàpies was most often portrayed as both ideologically progressive and a Catalan nationalist. However, independence was not one of his preoccupations. After the transition to democracy, the artist supported Catalonia's position as part of Spain. Toni Tàpies explained to me that we could certainly categorize his father as a Catalan nationalist, but for him that meant the reestablishment of Catalonia's autonomy after Franco's death in a democratic Spain similar to models in other European countries with federalist systems. According to his son, under Franco's regime Tàpies defended Catalan nationalism that (for him) corresponded to a historical model of government absent of absolute power. As Toni explained, 'Catalonia was one of the first countries to have a constitution, to defend this was to defend, at that time, something that did not yet exist in Spain, and in this sense my father was a Catalan nationalist'.[79] This tells us little about Tàpies's thoughts towards the independence movement, but it does highlight the fact that he was invested in more than a cultural form of Catalan nationalism.

In 1996 Stuart Hall hypothesized that the consequences of globalization would change the post-modern identity. He proposed three possible outcomes: national identities would become eroded and replaced with homogenized international identities, national identities would become strengthened in resisting globalization, or that national identities would disappear in favour of new hybrid identities.[80] In the case of Catalonia, national identity has become strengthened in the aftermath of the central government's intervention in the Statute of Autonomy's legality, a major economic crisis, and abundant cases of political corruption throughout Spain. Both those that have sought independence and those that have advocated for the right to vote concerning the issue (in a legal referendum similar to that of Scotland on 18 September 2014) do not seem to have been harking on their national identities in resistance to globalization; nor has there been any recent attempt on behalf of Madrid's government to convert or absorb Catalan identity, language, or culture into a greater Spanish one.

The shift from banal to hot nationalism that has taken place over the last decade in Catalonia has accelerated in response to socioeconomic circumstances rather than in resistance to a competing supranational or homogenized global identity.[81] Regardless of whether or not Catalonia becomes an independent state in the future, nationalism has emerged in both political and civic spheres as a heavily debated issue. For future generations, what it means to be or feel Catalan could become less compatible with being Spanish in a shared, nested identity. However, in 2015 the balanced coexistence of the two identities outweighed any other combination, demonstrating the gap that Barrio and Rodríguez Teruel explained between electorate opinion and the party system. Further complicating the situation is that some of those who felt both Catalan and Spanish may have thought that an independent Catalan State would be the best option. The change from a less evident to a more visible form of nationalism in Catalonia was not solely reflected in the official political sphere as a radicalization of parties, emphasizing not a spectrum of right/left but of national allegiance *'españolismo/catalanismo'*.[82] Official cultural institutions have also been actively participating in the contemporary construction or marketing of identity and the conception of how it relates to the past, as seen in MNAC's temporary exhibitions in addition to other museums and cultural centres. As demonstrated with different combinations of Tàpies's works, politics inevitably plays a role in the content, context, space, and time of displaying art. Think back to his work that looks like a noose with a hanging *barretina*, where Catalan identity is brought to the foreground with a solemn backdrop of violence and fear. Our perceptions of artistic exhibitions, in turn, can cause political ramifications in the future.

Is it a coincidence that Google decided to commemorate Antoni Tàpies on Friday 13 December 2013? As far as I have been able to tell, it was an improvised act directly related to Mas's announcement on the previous day. What message did the 400-billion-dollar company convey in celebrating the would-be birthday of a deceased Catalan artist the day after the President of the Generalitat made a controversial political announcement? It could have been an attempt to provide a less controversial accompaniment to the news, dealing with the same geographic region. In a society where visual culture is rapidly converting into an increasingly technological aggregation of digital applications and advertisements, does the death of Tàpies mark the end of an era or the beginning of a major secession in Spain? While the Centre d'Estudis d'Opinió data has shown that support for independence decreased between 2012 and 2016,[83] the party system has radicalized, and that system has not necessarily aligned perfectly with voter opinions. Further complicating the situation, another attempted referendum was held in Catalonia in 2017, resulting in political prisoners and lengthy trials held in Madrid concerning this event.

Finally, when Madrileños turn on the evening news and see the enormous *Les quatre cròniques* looming in the background of presidential meetings in Barcelona's government headquarters, will they notice the historic content and contemporary significance of Tàpies's visualization of a Catalan nation? Probably not, partially because Tàpies's style has remained as ambiguous as it was under Franco's regime, but also because it is a banal form of hailing Catalan nationalist narratives. Beyond Catalonia, it does not seem to be such a powerful image. The mural that he made in 1990 could have been much more open in terms of political expression, yet the artist chose to continue working in the style that he developed in the 1950s and 1960s, leaving much to the imagination. As Miguel Ángel del Arco Blanco stated, we ought to consider not only the so-called real history but also the history of the imagined.[84] One could also add the failed or unfinished. While it is possible to trace the making of a work of art such as *Les quatre cròniques*, it is much more difficult to explain what goes on in the imaginations of its many beholders. However, that difficulty ought not to be ignored. The study of art should also include the history of the imagined, whether those ideas concern that of a nation or of an old sock depend on the individual work of art, the context of its exhibition, and the viewer's act of thinking.

Notes to Chapter 6

1. Susan Sontag, *Regarding the Pain of Others* (New York: Farrar, Strass and Giroux, 2003), p. 86.
2. Quiroga, 'The Three Spheres'.
3. Ibid., p. 688.
4. Ibid., p. 693.
5. Ibid., p. 697.
6. Rafael Minder, 'Catalonia Overwhelmingly Votes for Independence From Spain in Straw Poll', *The New York Times*, 9 November 2014, accessed 25 January 2016, http://www.nytimes.com/2014/11/10/world/europe/catalans-vote-in-straw-poll-on-independence-from-spain.html.
7. Alonso, *El Catalanismo, del Éxito al Éxtasis*, p. 161.
8. '9N 2014', Generalitat de Catalunya, accessed 25 January, 2016, http://www.participa2014.cat/resultats/dades/ca/escr-tot.html.
9. Josep Llobera, 'The Role of Commemorations in (Ethno)Nation-Building. The Case of Catalonia', *Nationalism and the Nation in the Iberian Peninsula*, Clare Mar-Molinero and Angel Smith, eds., (Oxford: Berg, 1996), p. 196.
10. Sontag, *Regarding the Pain of Others*, p. 86.
11. Quiroga, *Goles y banderas*, 24. 'Como en el caso de los artistas, los deportistas fueron continuamente comparados con los ídolos del pasado, con figuras claves de la historia nacional. Esto hizo que millones de ciudadanos acabaran conectando mentalmente a los deportistas contemporáneos con los héroes patrios del pasado'.
12. Museu d'Historia de Catalunya, accessed 26 January 2016, http://www.en.mhcat.cat/.
13. 'El centre cultural', El Born Centre Cultural, accessed 26 January 2016, http://elborncentrecultural.barcelona.cat/el-centre/. The Ajuntament changed the name from El Born Centre Cultural to El Born Centre de Cultura i Memòria in 2016.
14. Berger et al., *Narrating the Nation*, p. 207.
15. Mees, 'Emociones en política. Conceptos, debates y perspectivas analíticas', p. 44.
16. Montserrat Guibernau, 'Nationalism and Intellectuals in Nations without States', p. 25.
17. Interview with Toni Tàpies, 4 February 2016. Not surprisingly, Toni did not mention Dalí's name when referring to Guibernau's list of artistic icons of Catalonia. It was not an oversight but an aknowledgment of Dalí's problematic (for Toni Tàpies and his father) relationship with Franco's regime.
18. Valaskivi, *Cool Nations: Media and the Social Imaginary of the Branded Country*, Kindle loc. 3230.
19. Ibid., Kindle loc. 3901.
20. Archilés, 'Lenguajes de nación', p. 100.
21. Billig, *Banal Nationalism*, p. 77.
22. Valaskivi, *Cool Nations: Media and the Social Imaginary of the Branded Country*, Kindle loc. 4224. See also: Simon Anholt, *Competitive Identity: The New Brand Management for Nations, Cities and Regions* (Basingstoke: Palgrave Macmillan, 2007); Melissa Aronczyk, *Branding the Nation: The Global Business of National Identity* (Oxford: Oxford University Press, 2013); and Charles Lindholm, *Culture and Authenticity* (Oxford: Oxford University Press, 2008).
23. Edelman, *From Art to Politics*, p. 7.
24. Montserrat Guibernau, 'Secessionism in Catalonia: After Democracy', *Ethnopolitics*, 12:4 (2013), 368–93; 380–81.
25. Joan M. Minguet Batllori, *Contra la Cooltura; Art i política a Catalunya* (Barcelona: Edicions Els Llums, 2015).
26. Ibid., p. 67.
27. Giori, 'Cataluña, nación y medios: La construcción del espacio nacional de comunicación', p. 131.
28. Minguet Batllori, *Contra la Cooltura; Art i política a Catalunya*, p. 68.
29. Ibid., p. 128.
30. Ibid., p. 70.
31. Ibid., pp. 67–70; pp. 132–33.

32. 'Generalitat public sector. Budget. 2010–2015', Official Statistics Website of Catalonia, accessed 27 January 2016, http://www.idescat.cat/pub/?id=aec&n=683&lang=en.
33. Estadísticas 2006–2015: Presupuestos Generales del Estado Consolidados 2015, Gobierno de España: Ministerio de Hacienda y Administraciones Públicas, accessed 30 January 2016, http://www.sepg.pap.minhap.gob.es/sitios/sepg/es-ES/Presupuestos/Estadisticas/Documents/2015/01%20Presupuestos%20Generales%20del%20Estado%20Consolidados.pdf.
34. Estadístiques Culturales de Catalunya, Generalitat de Catalunya, February 2015, accessed 27 January 2016, http://dadesculturals.gencat.cat/web/.content/sscc/gt/arxius_gt/Estad_culturals_Catalunya_2015.pdf, p. 12.
35. David Fernández, 'Galán gana 7,4 millones entre sueldo y acciones al frente de Iberdrola en 2013', *El País*, 21 February 2014, accessed 27 January 2016, http://economia.elpais.com/economia/2014/02/21/actualidad/1392991404_982190.html.
36. Ibid., p. 133.
37. Ibid., p. 110.
38. Edelman, *From Art to Politics*, p. 146.
39. Edensor discussed the marketing of national identities through landscapes and national parks in *National Identity, Popular Culture and Everyday Life*, p .40.
40. 'MNAC, Museu Nacional d'Art de Catalunya', Mission statement, 5.1.3.
41. Billig, *Banal Nationalism*, p. 30–31.
42. 'A Visit to the Romanesque: In Company of Antoni Tàpies'.
43. 'A Europa, el català Antoni Tàpies va desenvolupar la pintura matèrica: el pintor s'interessa per la superfíce del quadre, a la qual afegeix materials diversos i pobres, com ara terra, sorra, draps, etc.', A. Alcoberro, et al., *Història: Ciències Socials, 4 ESO (Barcelona: Teide, 2008)*, pp. 262–63.
44. A. Domènech, *Història de l'Art: Vitrall 2, Batxillerat (Barcelona: Teide, 2009)*, p. 354.
45. Carmen Aguilar Díaz, et al., *Historia del Arte 2, Bachillerato (Madrid: Santillana, 2009)*, p. 445.
46. Boletín Oficial del Estado, December 10, 2013, accessed 15 June 2016, https://www.boe.es/boe/dias/2013/12/10/pdfs/BOE-A-2013-12886.pdf.
47. See also Ken Montgomery 'Banal Race-thinking: Ties of Blood, Canadian History Textbooks and Ethnic Nationalism', *Paedagogica Historica*, 41.3 (2005), 313–36; and *(Re)Constructing Memory: School Textbooks and the Imagination of the Nation*, ed. by James H. Williams (Boston: Sense, 2014).
48. Williams, *(Re)Constructing Memory: School Textbooks and the Imagination of the Nation*, p. 321; Stuart Hall, 'The Question of Cultural Identity', 26.
49. Daniele Conversi, *The Basques, the Catalans, and Spain. Alternative Routes to Nationalist Mobilisiation* (Reno and Las Vegas: University of Nevada Press, 1997), 269.
50. Kathryn Crameri, 'Banal Catalanism?' *National Identities*, 2:2 (2000), 154.
51. Ibid., pp. 154–55.
52. Ibid., p. 154.
53. See Montserrat Guibernau, 'Catalan Secessionism: Young People's expectations and Political Change', *The International Spectator: Italian Journal of International Affairs*, 49:3 (July 2014: 106–17), p. 114 and Baròmetre d'Opinió Política (BOP). 3ª onada 2012- REO 705, Centre d'Estudis d'Opinió, Generalitat de Catalunya, accessed 7 March 2016, http://ceo.gencat.cat/ceop/AppJava/pages/estudis/categories/fitxaEstudi.html.
54. Thomas Jeffrey Miley, 'Against the Thesis of the "Civic Nation": The Case of Catalonia in Contemporary Spain', *Nationalism and Ethnic Politics*, 13:1 (2007), p. 10.
55. Baròmetre d'Opinió Política (BOP). 3ª onada 2012- REO 705, Centre d'Estudis d'Opinió.
56. Baròmetre d'Opinió Política (BOP). 3ª onada 2016- REO 835, Centre d'Estudis d'Opinió, Generalitat de Catalunya, accessed 25 January, 2017, http://ceo.gencat.cat/ceop/AppJava/pages/home/fitxaEstudi.html.
57. Guibernau, 'Secessionism in Catalonia: After Democracy', pp. 380–81.
58. Ibid., p .381.
59. Guibernau, 'Catalan Secessionism: Young People's expectations and Political Change', p. 109.
60. Crameri, *Goodbye Spain?: The Question of Independence for Catalonia*, Kindle loc. 525.
61. Ibid., Kindle loc. 551.
62. Ian Shapiro, *Politics Against Domination* (Cambridge, MA: The Belknap Press of Harvard University, 2016), Kindle loc. 53.

63. Astrid Barrio and Juan Rodríguez Teruel, 'Por qué se han radicalizado los partidos políticos en Cataluña? El sistema de partidos y el ague del soberanismo (1999–2012)', *Pôle Sud*, 38.2 (2014), 10–13.
64. Ibid., 5.
65. Ibid., 5.
66. Enric Martínez-Herrera and Thomas Jeffery Miley, 'The Constitution and the Politics of National Identity in Spain', *Nations and Nationalism*, 16 (2010), 6–30 (p. 6).
67. Ibid., p. 17. See also Miley, 'Against the Thesis of the "Civic Nation"'.
68. Justo Beramendi, 'Cataluña y el derecho a decidir', *Ayer*, 99 (2015), 280.
69. Miley, 'Against the Thesis of the "Civic Nation"'.
70. NBA Los Angeles Lakers, http://www.nba.com/lakers/multimedia?ls=nav_multimedia.
71. Quiroga, *Goles y banderas*, p. 171.
72. Ibid., p. 171.
73. Miley, 'Against the Thesis of the "Civic Nation"', p. 17.
74. Stuart Hall, 'Signification, Representation, Ideology: Althusser and the Post-Structuralist Debates', *Critical Studies in Mass Communication*, 2.2 (1985), 99.
75. 'Joan Brossa o la revolta poètica', Fundació Miró, accessed 25 January 2017, http://www.fmirobcn.org/exposicions/122/joan-brossa-o-la-revolta-poetica; 'Manifest groc. Dalí, Gasch, Montanyà i l'antiart', Fundació Miró, accessed 25 January 2017, http://www.fmirobcn.org/exposicions/96/manifest-groc-dali-gasch-montanya-i-lantiart.
76. Edelman, *From Art to Politics*, pp. 143–44.
77. Tàpies, *Complete Writings Volume II. Collected Essays*, p. 107.
78. Michel Foucalt, 'Truth and Power', *The Foucault Reader* (New York: Pantheon, 1984); Minguet Batllori, *Contra la Cooltura; Art i política a Catalunya*, 134.
79. Interview with Toni Tàpies, February 4, 2016.
80. Hall, 'The Question of Cultural Identity', p. 619.
81. Alonso argues that it is the result of a 'thirty-year process of social engeneering of a project' (begining in the 1980s with Pujol and CiU's Catalanism), while Guibernau points to more recent events such as José María Aznar's 'lack of response to demands for greater autonomy', the 2006 Autonomy Statue's revisions, and the high unemployment rate in 2013. Alonso, *El Catalanismo, del Éxito al Éxtasis*, p. 173; Guibernau, 'Catalan Secessionism: Young People's expectations and Political Change', pp. 112–13.
82. Barrio and Rodríquez Teruel, '¿Por qué se han radicalizado los partidos políticos en Cataluña?'
83. Baròmetre d'Opinió Política (BOP). 3ª onada 2012- REO 705, Centre d'Estudis d'Opinió; Baròmetre d'Opinió Política (BOP). 3ª onada 2016- REO 835, Centre d'Estudis d'Opinió.
84. Del Arco Blanco, 'Un paso más allá de la historia cultural: los *cultural studies*', p. 20.

CONCLUSION

> In a world where information circulates through "cool" electronic transfers, there is only "hyperreality," not truth and falsity. This hyperreality looks the same in Los Angeles and Tokyo, London and New York. The vast distances of previous ages have disappeared, as information incessantly pulsates across the globe in nanoseconds.
>
> MICHAEL BILLIG[1]

This investigation has provided evidence as to why Antoni Tàpies became an iconic figure in Catalonia and the sociopolitical circumstances that surrounded his successful career as a working artist. The study has also analysed examples of how different contexts affect the experience of seeing works of art and how political art can impact national thought. Finally, it has defined the relationship between art and politics using the work of Tàpies as a model while broadening the traditional perspective of academic studies concerning this subject. This concluding chapter revisits the initial questions, briefly reflects on cultural policies and the nature of art, and proposes some final questions while suggesting interesting themes for future investigations.

In 'Un paso más allá de la historia cultural: los *cultural studies*' Miguel Ángel del Arco Blanco stated that studying culture 'does not make sense without studying its interaction with politics and historical context in every moment.'[2] He later discussed how the understanding of time in cultural studies is useful for historians to think about history.[3] Without looking at the political and historical circumstances surrounding Tàpies's artwork, in combination with the way his images are able to transform at different intersections through space and time, much of his oeuvre would seem stagnant. As I have argued throughout this investigation, Tàpies's style did not change after the mid 1950s, but the meaning of these artworks is inevitably changeable. Museums cannot present works in an impartial, neutral, or objective fashion, due to numerable factors that ultimately alter and shift meaning because art is a form of communication. Art depends on at least two parties where meaning can become transmuted in the transfer from the artist (via their artwork) to the beholder, "slippage" in semiotics. While it is true that Tàpies's style is tremendously consistent during the second half of the twentieth century and into the twenty-first century, which seems surprising considering the sociopolitical changes that occurred during this period in Spain, his art is far from static. In fact, Tàpies adeptly left meaning up to the viewer. Even though his works may seem repetitive and resolute, he ultimately gave beholders dynamic works that prioritize the observer's liberty and power to decide what those works of art "mean."

Why did Tàpies create this peculiar style and continue to use it incessantly throughout the remainder of his career? The short answer is: this style worked for him and he found no need to change it. It was a style upon which he established his international career as a professional artist and did not fail to generate substantial public for large-scale projects during his lifetime. While few historians question the unchanging nature of Michelangelo's artistic style, for instance, since the early twentieth century there has been a tendency to compartmentalize phases of artistic production amongst modern artists and stylistic movements that is not always necessary.[4] It seems that for a working artist, it would be as difficult (if not more difficult) to maintain the same style during half a century than to change a number of times. Working in the same style is not synonymous with settling within one's comfort zone, because the limitations of that zone are exhaustively explored. The more elaborate answer has to do with space and time. When the epicentre of the art world had just shifted from Paris to New York City after World War II, Tàpies socialized within what was left of shrinking avant-garde artist circles in Europe. His relationship with figures such as Joan Brossa helped him move away from his surrealist compositions of the late 1940s and early 1950s and pushed him towards another sort of style. What art historians now call Informalism was Tàpies's response to a less-than-normal childhood in Barcelona and the equally troubling political circumstances of his early career in Franco's Spain. Tàpies created his particular style under the regime that persecuted the use of Catalan, the artist's first language. He also formed this style at a time when Geometric Abstraction was no longer in the limelight of contemporary art shows. Abstract Expressionism of the New York School was capturing the attention of the world's leading art critics and buyers. Tàpies's generation was the last to have personal contact with the eminent vanguard circles that introduced Cubism, Futurism, Surrealism, and Dada to the world. Tàpies shared a fundamental principle in common with the leaders of each of these previous movements: art is not a mere representation of reality. Instead, it is a platform to think about reality and what exactly reality entails. Tàpies dedicated his entire career to producing works that would engage with the society in which he lived. At times that meant taking up issues concerning Catalan language and identity, but not always. His works also addressed experimentations within the context of contemporary art and social injustices that were reported in the global media. Tàpies continued to work into the early years of the twenty-first century without modifying his style. However, much had changed since he first began his artistic career in post-Civil War Spain. After the death of Franco in 1975 and the transition to democracy, it was no longer necessary for Tàpies to veil his political opinions that he often expressed via his works of art. Despite this dramatic transformation, his artworks maintained a stern continuity with his previous compositions. This tremendous consistency ultimately demonstrated two points: that Tàpies was convinced that he had figured out the best way to communicate his ideas and that the inevitable contextual changes would give his artworks the dynamism that they otherwise lacked.

For example, the surface of *Forma negra sobre quadrat gris* (1960) looks similar to many of the artist's Matter Paintings. The rough texture and gloomy palette ultimately reflect the deficiency of the previous two decades, a dark and difficult era for many Spaniards under Franco's dictatorship. On the other hand, this same canvas can be understood in an entirely different manner. That small, dark gap at the bottom could be a keyhole into another world. It could be the portal to a fantastical space of lush gardens and colours, but we may never find out. We the viewers are provoked to imagine what lies beyond. When the artist said that he wanted his works to be like a springboard, this is exactly what he meant. They are not solutions to problems, nor are they unilateral encryptions. They are more like good adjectives, provoking feelings and describing the realm in which Tàpies lived, both real and imagined. The open-endedness of Tàpies's works ultimately privileges the beholder, giving them power and freedom to explore what the work could mean. For this reason, there was no need for Tàpies to change his style. His methods remained remarkably consistent, although those who look at his works are bound to change in space and time.

Why did Tàpies's artwork become iconic in Catalonia? Part of the reason that his artistic career began to soar in the 1970s was due to the style he created throughout the 1950s and 1960s. Beginning with the Matter Paintings, Tàpies's semi-abstract works captured the attention of an international audience eager to discover something new and different. The artist's contracts with Martha Jackson Gallery in New York City and Gallery Maeght in Paris assured his foreign exposure while important commissions from local political institutions augmented Tàpies's visibility in Catalonia. Tàpies's success within the international art scene paralleled his career on the local level. However, Barcelona is where Tàpies gained his iconic status and where politicians sought to project him as a model citizen. His early career demonstrated that he sought peaceful defiance against the Franco regime.

After the transition to democracy, he continued to work in the same fashion, privileging non-traditional aesthetics, experimental and everyday materials, and tactile surfaces. Via Fundació Antoni Tàpies, gallery shows, and public commissions, the artist simultaneously exhibited both unprecedented works and works that deal with Catalonia. His oeuvre became iconic for two reasons. The first is that he developed his signature style at a time when art professionals were caught in a strange state of flux, not yet having fully embraced the American abstract expressionists nor completely having let go of the geometric abstraction that was popular in interwar Europe. Tàpies and his Matter Paintings gave critics and gallery owners something different to think about. His unique style would be written into the constructed history of art for its innovative yet familiar quality. In the realm of progressive artists of the twentieth century, Tàpies's work became iconic for his style and willingness to separate himself from the dwindling surrealist movement. Second, in addressing topics concerning Catalonia, Tàpies became beloved amongst important Catalan nationalists seeking to disseminate and legitimate the idea of a common history, language, culture, and identity shared throughout the region. Both the Generalitat de Catalunya and the Ajuntament de Barcelona worked to establish and maintain Tàpies's iconic images as representations of Catalan culture and global acclaim. The Generalitat's most important commission glorifies medieval texts, originally written in Catalan, and occupies a prominent position of tremendous media exposure in the autonomous government's headquarters in Barcelona. The Ajuntament de Barcelona, on the other hand, leaned towards Tàpies's less subjective works, supporting projects that did not necessarily contain exclusively Catalan content. Nevertheless, both institutions greatly contributed to the success, financial stability, and iconic status of Tàpies's works and the realization of the Fundació Antoni Tàpies. Furthermore, although to a much lesser extent, the Spanish government represented Tàpies as a model to promote Spain's diversity and modernity.

In the spring of 2014, the Museo de Bellas Artes de Bilbao exhibited Tàpies's *L'esperit català*. The large painting that the collector María Josefa Huarte donated to the University of Navarra in 2008 was on loan to the Basque museum. *Eldiario. es* published an article about the showing of the work titled '*Bilbao muestra el Tàpies más comprometido políticamente con el catalanismo*' [Bilbao shows the Tàpies's piece most politically committed to Catalanism].[5] The title is curious for the way it emphasized Bilbao (the place) as opposed to the actual museum showing the work. The city itself is the agent in the title, not the Museo de Bellas Artes nor Tàpies. The title also claims that *L'esperit català* is profoundly Catalanist, without providing any sort of clarification to what, exactly, that means. Although the article recognizes that the artwork was created in 1971, there is no distinction between the *catalanisme* of the early 1970s and that of the twenty-first century. This could lead viewers to misinterpret the artwork. What was created as a protest against the cultural backwardness of the Franco dictatorship was reported in *eldiario.es* as a straightforward symbol of Catalan nationalism in 2014. However, the political options (including separation from Spain and further autonomy within Spain) that surround twenty-first century Catalanist movements share little in common with the year in which Tàpies made this work. Savvy beholders will not conceive of this artwork as a cry in support of separation from Spain. However, its 2014 exhibition in Bilbao may have led certain viewers to believe that it was (and is) an artwork that supports the separatist movement via its colours, symbols, words, and style. Regardless of how individuals come to understand the 'meaning' of this work of art, as an object it has come to form part of the visualization of a Catalan nation.

In *Goodbye Spain?* Kathryn Crameri discussed how contemporary documentaries mimic 'recognizable patterns' of historic myths concerning Catalonia.[6] These films trigger feelings quickly and their format allows for rapid, mass dissemination, as opposed to the generations that traditional tales and fables take to develop via storytelling. The three documentaries that she analysed push for an independent Catalonia.[7] Crameri also discussed the importance of the arts in the independence movement. 'Cultural products are vital in this process not just because of their ability to disseminate the myth but also because of the way they speak to sentiment, in a way that history on its own cannot.'[8] Artworks such as *L'esperit català* and *Les quatre cròniques* work in a similar fashion, using historic material to trigger emotive responses ultimately linking historic material (real or fictional) to feelings. The arts, or 'cultural products,' create attitudes that, in turn, affect political actions. For this reason, the relationship between art and politics is a valuable field for investigation, especially when identities are concerned. Because of the sentimental nature of an individual's identity, and the way they 'personalize' the nation, the visual arts provide one of many ways in which these feelings become internalized, transformed, or questioned.[9]

The article in *Eldiario.es* claimed that *L'esperit català* was Tàpies's most politically committed work to Catalanism. On the day of the artist's death, Artur Mas similarly stated 'Tàpies was the artist with the most radically Catalan thoughts, expressions, and references.'[10] I want to emphasize that both of these statements are opinions. In the case of Mas, it was more than a mere opinion; it was a statement to appropriate the figure of Tàpies and his work, aligning the artist with his party's nationalizing agenda, as Jordi Pujol had done in the 1980s and 1990s. The way in which individuals experience works of art, as I have discussed in previous chapters, depends on many factors external to the actual artwork itself. In Bilbao in 2014 it is possible that *L'esperit català* seemed like Tàpies's most Catalanist work. However, one could argue the same for his 2006 cover illustration for the *Estatut d'Autonomia de Catalunya*, among others that also directly address Catalan language, history, traditions, heroes, etc. Ultimately, the 'most committed' is that which resonates the strongest with the emotive and intellectual nature of the viewer, something that can change over time and through space.

Returning to the question regarding how Tàpies's art relates to Catalan nationalism, after having examined his style, public works, and late exhibitions, I would like to draw some conclusions. Tàpies's ambivalent style enabled him to address sensitive topics (recall *A la memòria de Salvador Puig Antich*) under Franco's dictatorship without causing the regime to persecute him. Support from local politicians and political institutions helped form the artist's iconic status as an exemplary Catalan patriot. Tàpies's foundation and his public works in and around Barcelona helped solidify his prominent status in the history of Catalan art. Museums like MNAC also sought to bolster the artist's reputation, within a narrative that brought together centuries of artistic works from the region. Finally, Catalan nationalists from Jordi Pujol to Artur Mas have recognized the artist's commitment to Catalan culture, putting Tàpies on a pedestal as a model citizen. His art has never specifically addressed separation from Spain. However, it could have been difficult *not* to interpret words like 'liberty' scratched into the surface of his painting exhibited in Bilbao in 2014 without conjuring the secessionist movement, Mas's referendum, or the radicalization of political parties in Catalonia. 'Liberty,' in Tàpies's 1971 *L'esperit català*, had nothing to do with independence from Spain. It was a cry for democracy and freedom from political authoritarianism, not for Catalonia's liberation from Spain.[11] It is natural to connect objects from the past with the present or recent past; images have the ability to trigger emotions and memories quickly, sometimes making it difficult to situate objects historically. Montserrat Guibernau discussed one of the bonds between feelings and Catalan nationalism in 'Nationalism and Intellectuals in Nations Without States,' stating that 'emotional arguments in contemporary Catalan nationalism still hold live images of either their own or loved one's experiences which may include: torture, imprisonment, exile, proscription, and the lack of freedom to cultivate their vernacular language and culture.'[12] However, it is important not to confuse the distinction between images and art of the past with matters and ideologies of the present.

Much has changed since Tàpies painted *L'esperit català*. Beyond the scope of Spain's most significant political transformation since the onset of the Civil War in 1939, the role of art in society has also changed since the mid 1970s. One no longer needs to actually go to an exhibition in order to see pictures. In fact, we do not even need to wait for the morning paper to catch a glimpse of the latest artistic trends. Electronic media makes images available and reproducible, instantly, across the globe. This does not mean that seeing a digitized version of an artwork such as *L'esperit català* produces the same effect as seeing it hanging in a museum. However, the nature of the practice and reception of art has significantly changed due to the omnipresence of images in electronic format that is now considered normal in 'Western' cultures. Furthermore, serious art is also competing for what Jorge Luis Marzo deemed 'culture to make culture' in 'La era de la degradación del arte y de la política cultural en Cataluña.'[13] His examination of the politics of cultural administration in Catalonia concluded: 'we have fattened a cultural policy that has wound up devouring culture itself.'[14] He went on in the same text to state that instead of supporting cultural activities and professionals, Catalonia's politics have made culture a *product* of its policies, reinforcing his idea of a 'culture to make culture.' Marzo suggested that administrators working in the cultural sector ought to focus less on controlling content and more on keeping up with new technology that can help to preserve and make culture available to a wider public in a variety of formats. The same idea is applicable beyond Catalonia. However, this seems to be an increasingly difficult task to carry out in capitalist societies regardless of their geographical location. Once an image becomes accessible online, it enters into an indefinite space without classification or context. As Billig stated, globalization has created a new way of life, 'there is only "hyperreality," not truth and falsity'.[15] This hyperreality does not change the basic human instinct to communicate, however it does change the manners in which we do. Culture and artistic expression change over time, the way we experience things also changes with time. Artistic institutions often seek to conserve and protect works of art, to educate the public about their creators and the circumstances of their existence; they stimulate thought and cultivate knowledge through the transmission and exhibition of culture in order to help others better understand its present and historical value.

Part of the difficulty in comprehending the value of art is due to its sensational qualities. Words, in comparison to images, often appear easier to perceive. However, this is not just because we think of words as having a single, fixed meaning. We are simply more accustomed to thinking about words than we are about pictures. Education is the first step to becoming more attuned to visual communication, and how formal characteristics (colour, line, shape, style, texture, facture, etc.) can create meaning. Victoria Combalía expressed this topic in her call for the need of higher quality artistic education as a response to negative reviews of Tàpies's *Monument homenatge a Picasso*. Combalía understood that the criticism of the work stemmed from a lack of knowledge of contemporary art, a problem that other European countries did not tend to encounter, she argued.[16] The solution to this problem is simple: educate children in the arts; teach them about artistic practices, trends, materials, and how to read visual languages. Joan M. Minguet Batllori proposed a new system, beginning with primary school and continuing through post-secondary education, in which students would be exposed to 'the critical instruments to face the convulsed visuality of our times.'[17] For both Combalía and Minguet, the focus was not to praise all works of art. Instead, both urged for a rethinking of the Catalan public education system so that beholders would be better equipped to read, interpret, and think critically about art and visual culture.

Before proposing some final questions and future areas for investigation, I want to return to one of the first images I mentioned. It is a moving picture that is equally (or more) committed to Catalanism than any of Tàpies's other works. *Pintura romànica i barretina* is a solemn representation that takes up themes of time, violence, history, and *Catalanisme*. The sociopolitical circumstances under which Tàpies created the work in 1971 shared little in common with its 2013–2014 exhibition, as the cover piece of MNAC's *A Visit to the Romanesque: In Company of Antoni Tàpies*. The artwork's open-endedness contributed to its relevance decades after its design. However, this feature simultaneously leaves the artwork exposed to interpretations that may have little to do with the political perspective with which Tàpies was working with during the early 1970s. Beyond forming part of an exhibition that situates the artist in a line of respected Catalan painters, *Pintura romànica i barretina* invites viewers to think about what the picture should (or should not) represent. In November 2012, the Wilson Initiative published an online magazine including an image that resonates with Tàpies's red hat hanging from a rope.[18] An enormous Catalan flag takes up the majority of the photograph. In the foreground we see the head and shoulders of an anonymous figure in the centre that is wearing a *barretina*. The age and gender of this person is unknown. Some ten meters away stands a row of people who are helping to hold up the other side of the flag, making sure it does not touch the ground. Behind the first row of people is a crowd, waving more than twenty smaller *senyeras* and *estelades*. The image cuts off the mob of people, however it is clear that the same scene continued far beyond the frame. Both Tàpies's *Pintura romànica i barretina* and this photograph share two important things in common: they highlight the *barretina* in the foreground as something special and unique to Catalonia, and they have been politicized in order to represent an idea. MNAC sought to make a connection between Tàpies and its Romanesque collection, proposing the idea that Tàpies is part of a shared cultural tradition linked to the Catalan territory of the twenty-first century Autonomous Community. The Wilson Initiative, which was composed of nine academics who have advocated for the rights of the citizens of Catalonia to vote for independence 'without fear or threats, and with as much information as possible,'[19] used the photograph as a means of showing collaboration and solidarity amongst those who they believe are deserving of the opportunity to vote. Both these images could, in the future,

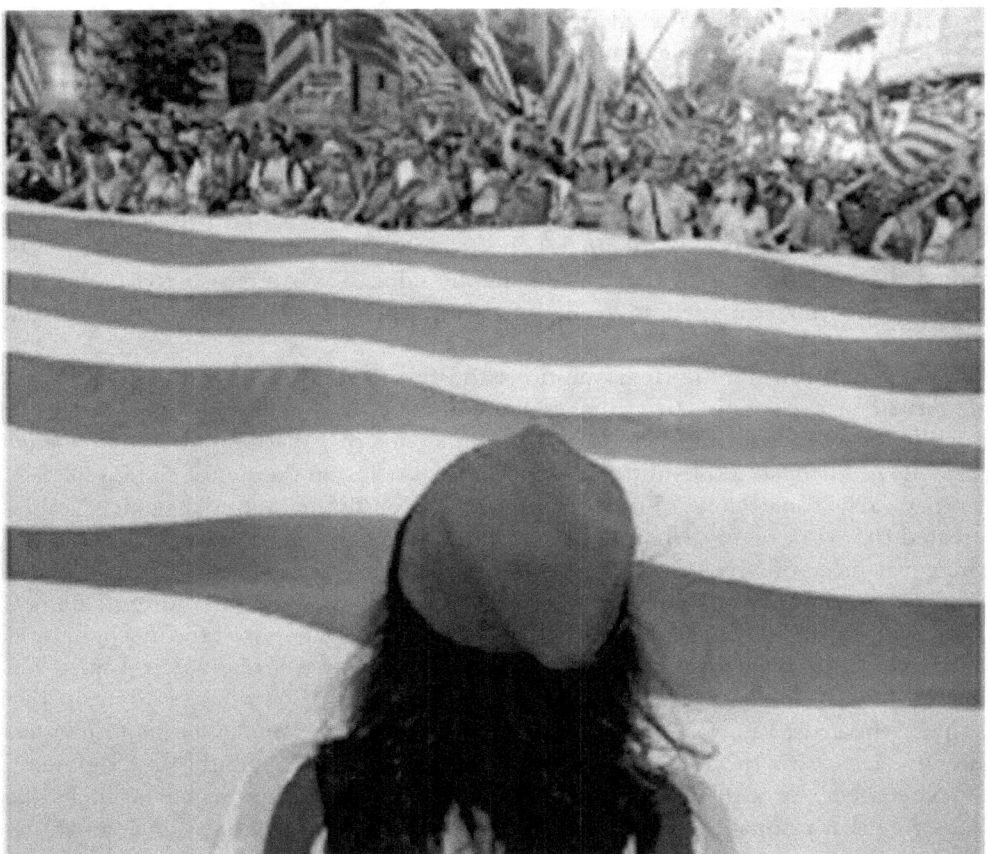

Fig. C.1. Photograph from the Wilson Initiative online magazine, 2012

be moulded in order to illustrate other ideas. However, their original format and presentation ought not to be forgotten. The same goes for all works of art.

How will we read Tàpies's images differently in the future, for example on the celebration of his would-be hundredth birthday in December 2023? How will the future leaders of Catalonia (as an independent nation, autonomous community, or otherwise) project Tàpies as a historic figure? What sort of 'stipulating' will contribute to his legacy as a great Catalan painter, and what details will be left behind?[20] These are rhetorical questions, however, it is likely that as various circumstances change over time, so too will the exhibition and perception of Tàpies's artworks along with his image as a Catalan icon. Part of Tàpies's allure as an avant-garde artist and as an advocate for Catalan identity, had to do with his ability to make others think. He took up social material and spun it in a way that forces viewers to reflect, because his images are not easy to read. *The New York Times* quoted the artist in his obituary, 'my illusion is to have something to transmit... if I can't change the world, at least I want to change the way people look at it.'[21] The images that Tàpies put forward work in order to open up conversations, debates, and further discussions. They also form part of contemporary Catalan culture, which is both directly and indirectly imbued with politics.

When I asked Toni Tàpies to describe his father and his greatest professional achievements, he responded that his dad was 'passionate, hard-working, persistent, and convinced with what he was doing.'[22] He was a driven artist with a clear social and political vision of the world, which he expressed via his works of art. As a whole, his works demonstrate each of these characteristics. Toni reflected on his father's accomplishments in and beyond Catalonia:

> I think that in general you can say that the presence of my father's oeuvre in the art of the second half of the twentieth century is something that is indisputable. If someone wants to write the history of art [...] they would have to talk about my father, and this is not easy. It is not easy for an artist to have the genius and creativity to be recognized amongst the great number of artists from around the globe. In addition, his perseverance and his desire to work and communicate, to send a message to the world of hope in reality, to try to help humanity to overcome adversity, fear, uncertainty, is something that he intended to do from the outset. No artist has been able to fix the problems of the world, but at least I think it is important to try to do so.[23]

Toni's words echo those of his father, published in *The New York Times* article. The point of creating and recreating his ideas in visual terms was always a deeply personal exercise for Tàpies. His objectives were not tangible but ideological. He wanted to change the way his beholders envisioned the world and he achieved this through visual art.

Pepe Serra and Joan Guitart also had similar responses when I asked each of them to reflect on Tàpies's greatest achievement. Serra stated, 'his career; he was continually present, continually working and constantly experimenting.'[24] MNAC's director went on to express his esteem for the artist's radicalism, his international reputation, and unique personal language. He acknowledged the fact that it may take some more time for society (beyond the realm of the culture sector) to come to recognize the value of Tàpies's pictorial language. Nevertheless, he proclaimed that Tàpies was 'the most important artist of the second half of the twentieth century in Spain, for me, and without a doubt in Catalonia.'[25] Guitart said, 'Tàpies's greatest achievement was *la coherencia*, in his works of art as well as his discourse.'[26] *La coherencia*, in this case could be translated as the coherence or consistency of the artist. Both would be indicative of Guitart's positive view of Tàpies and the cohesive nature of his work.

Manuel Borja-Villel, like the artist's son and Pepe Serra, found that Tàpies's 'work is fundamental in order to understand other works of art created during the second half of the twentieth century.'[27] Perhaps, however, art historian Katherine Jentleson most accurately captures Tàpies's greatest achievement through her statement linking the artist to one of Picasso's most remarkable pieces: 'Even in the most desolate periods of Franco-era Spain, there was life after *Guernica*.'[28]

The objectives of this investigation are specifically oriented towards the works of Antoni Tàpies, but they also seek to provide an exemplary perspective for future studies concerning the relationship between art and politics, especially nationalism and national identity. Nationalist ideologies have profound effects on artistic creation, while art also impacts political movements. The relationship between art and nationalism in Catalonia is bilateral. Tàpies created works of art that were often in response to social and political issues and events; he used art as a means of expressing his ideas. Public exhibitions and commissions tied many of his works directly to the world of politics. Tàpies, through the support of the Generalitat de Catalunya, the Ajuntament de Barcelona, the Spanish state, and a number of cultural institutions, built a visual language that addresses both national identity and ideology. That language was reinforced and, at times, contested. It looked very different from that of Joan Miró, yet the two men shared similar ideas. Future visualizations of Catalonia will also be juxtaposed to the works of these two artists. Differing historical circumstances will shape the ways in which new visual languages will be developed and perceived, yet they will always be a product of a political nature and will affect the viewer's understanding of what is 'normal'.

The success of *Les quatre cròniques* and failure of the original *Mitjó* project are a testament to the fragile relationship between art and politics. Tàpies's political art had (and continues to have) the potential to impact national ideologies, particularly in the context of contemporary exhibitions. In Catalonia, major events shape the creation of art and, as part of a wider culture that is increasingly visual, art plays a role in the shifting definition of what it means to be or feel Catalan. As Barrio and Rodríguez Teruel outlined, 'the stability and change in the party system and the stability and change in the electorate are related but not mutually equivalent.'[29] In other words, Catalonia's party system does not exactly correlate with its voters' opinions, but they are related. Citizens' thoughts are directly related, however, to the ways in which they come to personalize the nation. Part of that personalization comes from the visual realm, including works of art. Crameri stated in *Goodbye Spain?*, the 'relation between Catalan politics and civil society is both complex and reciprocal'.[30]

This investigation sketches a general model that shows how politics have a direct impact on the creation of what Tàpies, amongst others, considered 'good' art, as a form of culture that deliberately and relentlessly engages with social and political life. This sort of art, via its exhibition, has the ability to heighten emotions and alter conceptions concerning contemporary issues, which affect the way that citizens view the world. Thoughts and feelings generated through art are not always passive; they can and do transform both real and imagined realities. While further analysis is necessary in order to better understand the nature of such complexities in and beyond Spain, the social role of art makes it inseparable from politics and it can tell us much about the iceberg that lies beneath the surface of the glistening water that conceals the mass below.

Notes to the Conclusion

1. Billig, *Banal Nationalism*, p. 131.
2. Del Arco Blanco, 'Un paso más allá de la historia cultural: Los *cultural studies*', p. 2.
3. Ibid., p. 15.

4. The Museum of Modern Art (MoMA), founded in Manhattan in 1929, exemplified this sort of strict classification system under the leadership of its first director, Alfred H. Barr Jr.
5. 'Bilbao muestra el Tàpies más comprometido políticamente con el catalanismo', *eldiario.es*, 9 April 2014, accessed 9 January 2015, http://www.eldiario.es/cultura/Bilbao-Tapies-comprometido-politicamente-calatanismo_0_247775813.html.
6. Crameri, *Goodbye Spain?: The Question of Independence for Catalonia*, Kindle loc. 2243.
7. Ibid., 2256.
8. Ibid., 2256.
9. Quiroga, 'The Three Spheres', p. 693.
10. 'Artur Mas: "Tàpies ha sido el artista más radicalmente catalán en su pensamiento, su expresión y sus referentes."'
11. Recall the slogan 'Llibertat, amnistia, i Estat d'Autonomia' [Liberty, Amnesty, and Statute of Autonomy] developed at the 1971 Assemblea de Catalunya advocating for political reforms in Spain. See Appendix A.
12. Guibernau, 'Nationalism and Intellectuals in Nations Without States', p. 24.
13. Jorge Luis Marzo, 'La era de la degradación del arte y de la política cultural en Cataluña'. *Soymenos*, 2012. Accessed 11 January 2016, https://soymenos.files.wordpress.com/2012/06/la_degradacion_del_-arte_en_catalunya1.pdf, p. 33.
14. Ibid., p. 33.
15. Billig, *Banal Nationalism*, p. 131.
16. Combalía, 'Un monumento polémico', p. 22.
17. Minguet Batllori, *Contra la Cooltura: Art i política a Catalunya*, p. 69.
18. Wilson Initiative, Online Magazine, 7 November 2012, accessed 12 January 2016, http://www.wilson.cat/en/revista-digital.html, p. 10.
19. Ibid., p. 1.
20. Sontag, *Regarding the Pain of Others*, p. 86.
21. Grimes, 'Antoni Tàpies, Spanish Abstract Painter, Dies at 88'.
22. Interview with Toni Tàpies, 4 February 2016.
23. Ibid.
24. Interview with Pepe Serra, 27 June 2016.
25. Ibid.
26. Interview with Joan Guitart, 12 July 2016.
27. Ceus, 'Tàpies, más allá de la pintura'.
28. Jentleson, 'Antoni Tàpies'.
29. Barrio and Rodríquez Teruel, '¿Por qué se han radicalizado los partidos políticos en Cataluña?', p. 5.
30. Crameri, *Goodbye Spain?: The Question of Independence for Catalonia*, Kindle loc. 1203.

APPENDIX

*English translation of interview with Toni Tàpies in
Barcelona on February 4, 2016*

Emily Jenkins (EJ): How would you describe your father using five adjectives?

Toni Tàpies (TT): Five adjectives... I will tell you some things that are not necessarily adjectives. He was a hard-working artist; work was very important to him, he approached his work as if he were a professional in another sector, he worked every day, sometimes including the weekends, because art was his life and job, he was a very hard worker.

He was, at the same time, very passionate, what he did he did with passion... what more can I say? Well, he was very convinced with what he worked on, he had clear ideas about what he wanted, and what he needed to do, he always had. I suppose when he was younger, he was more insecure, but he always knew that he had ideas to express and he had to express them with his artwork.

He was a culturally cultivated person, he came from a bourgeois family, but his father was quite concerned with culture, although surprisingly like my father, in a self-taught way, because he studied law at university until his final year, then he abandoned the degree. My grandfather wanted him to be a lawyer like himself, but my father did not agree. Remarkably, he taught himself, because he did not even attend art school. He became versed in a great deal of cultural areas, not just artistic or visual culture, but also music and literature; he truly enjoyed watching films and reading books.

Finally, the last characteristic I would say was his passion for collecting. He liked to collect from different periods and cultures. He loved to collect books, antique books, although he had many contemporary books as well. He also enjoyed collecting artworks, from artists whom he considered to be masters as well as primitive African art, pre-Columbian art, Asian art, Indian art, Native American art, a little from the whole world throughout history, from Egypt as well, this was his great passion.

Passionate, hard-working, persistent, and convinced with what he was doing.

EJ: As director of the Gallery Toni Tàpies, have you thought of how you would like future generations to learn about and value the work of your father as an artist and as a person?

TT: Well, actually the institution I think will have more of an impact in this area, in order to show his work, his thoughts, his character, is the Fundació Tàpies. My father wanted to create this foundation, not just to preserve some of his own works that he donated, but also to create a library that includes his own books and the rest has expanded over time. He wanted it to be a centre where other artists could show their works, so that it would be an active centre, not simply dedicated to his works like a mausoleum, but a lively space that would have a long future.

My gallery is doing, and has done, the work it could. I opened it more than twenty years ago. At first it was oriented to show graphic works, prints, and lithographs from a number of different artists. Later, it became a gallery representing various artists, maybe fifteen artists, not just Spanish artists, from other countries as well. However, since my father's death in 2012, I had to concentrate on his legacy, the control of his intellectual property, the management of certifications and authentication of his artworks. For this reason, I have toned down the activity in the gallery, concentrating basically on his artwork. We have small exhibitions, like the one on display now, but with an irregular program (as we also manage the works on loan to other galleries and clients with interests in purchasing specific works).

EJ: Currently, you are not representing any other artists... nor in the future?

TT: No, no I do not believe so.

EJ: In 1976 your father wrote 'when an artist finds their voice, they must execute it with continuity'.[1] During and after the transition, the stylistic consistency that your father maintained in his artworks seems remarkable, considering the magnitude of sociopolitical changes that were happening in Spain. I do not want to say that he did not change as an artist, but particularly with regard to his style after the mid 1950s, the continuity of his works is rather impressive. Do you agree? I wanted to ask because there are art historians that like to create temporal separations, often corresponding to decades, and I do not think that is correct — his works have continuity.

TT: Exactly, I agree. Evidently an artist (particularly an artist like my father) who worked for more than fifty years straight, five decades of work, clearly goes through an evolution. Perhaps in the 1950s and 1960s is when he was most concerned with establishing his language, and once he had solidified it, he probably felt that he had more freedom, especially during his last decades, in the sense that sometimes he would make a more classical work or another that would seem more contemporary, I suppose he had a more open style. It is true that during the time you speak about, during the political transition and during Franco's dictatorship, he always defended democratic values and during the times when it was difficult or impossible to express political opinions in Spain, because there was a dictator and the police would come and put you in jail, his way of expressing himself was often through his paintings. Perhaps during those years his works contained more political connotations, sometimes quite obvious, later perhaps a little more diluted, but he always had social and political convictions that he defended from the beginning to the end, and I think that you can see that throughout his entire oeuvre.

EJ: In 1976, your father made a poster for the PSUC and in the same year he published that it is not necessary to enter or exit a political party if you carry it with you.[2] Did he exclusively support the PSUC at this time? What about after the party's dissolution in 1987?

TT: My father was never a militant of any political party because he wanted to maintain his liberty of thought. What happened is that during the Franco dictatorship the PSUC in Catalonia was a very active party, very active in the defence of democracy, very active in the defence of social rights, and very active in defending the recuperation of regional autonomy of the Catalan nation as well; my father agreed with all of these causes, and while he never officially joined the party, he did have good friends who participated in the clandestine group during this period. They sometimes asked him if he would make a poster, or donate an artwork to sell to help finance the organization, and he always did. Later, once democracy was established, the PSUC changed, everything had changed, now it does not even exist, people that were in the PSUC are now in another party. But at that time, the PSUC was like the centre of the resistance, in favour of democracy for Catalonia in Spain.

EJ: In 1981, during an inauguration in Paris, Jordi Pujol named your father among the great artists of the region (Tàpies being the youngest of the list)[3] and in 2012 Artur Mas said, 'his style has stayed forever associated with an especially genuine form of expressing Catalan identity'.[4] Did your father express opinions about the CiU, Pujol, or Mas?

TT: I do not think that my father publicly spoke about any of these figures specifically, I think that he respected politicians that did their jobs; today I am not sure what he would think after everything that has happened, especially revolving around the Pujol family, I suppose that he would be a little disappointed while waiting to see what actually happened, but in that moment he believed that politicians were just doing their jobs and that, in a way, they defended Catalonia's autonomy, although I suppose that he would consider these parties a little conservative for his own way of thinking. But I do not think he publicly expressed such opinions concerning this topic -- in private it is another question. He did not like the coalition very much, and once democracy was re-established, he would express his thoughts concerning particular politicians in private.

EJ: On the day following the death of Joan Miró (25 December 1983), your father published in *La Vanguardia* about Miró's world. He said it formed part of 'a new vision of the world, a way of understanding life, a way of living more fully and justly, with which goes included, evidently, both our individual and national liberty. And it is not surprising that in this sentiment, Miró was profoundly tied to the need to defend our Catalan spirit, our liberties, our culture'.[5] What would 'national liberty' have meant for your father in 1983? And later on?

TT: I would say that for my father in 1983, just as before, defending Catalonia's national liberty was, in a way, practically synonymous with defending democracy in Spain; because historically Catalonia was a nation led by a monarchy, but a rather advanced monarchy for the time, because it was a sort of parliamentary monarchy, there was a parliament, the king was king, but there was the parliament of citizens that could somehow counter the power of the king. Later, when the Bourbon dynasty came to power, it was lost and a central absolute monarchy was established in Spain, and all that was lost. For my father, when he defended the recuperation of national rights in Catalonia, it was similar to defending the recuperation of democracy not only in Catalonia but also in Spain, with a model that is an historic model that could have also been an ideal model for Spain. I suppose that a republic (for him) was the most normal option, at least a parliamentary monarchy, like it exists today, although some problems need to be solved.

EJ: In 2003 Montserrat Guibernau said something similar, that the works of Miró, Gaudí, Dalí, Tàpies, and Casals have been converted into symbols of Catalan identity.[6] Do you agree?

TT: Well, yes, this tends to happen, and more so in a small country like Catalonia that is still fighting to affirm its identity. When figures emerge like Miró, my father, like Casals, like Gaudí, there is a tendency to use them a bit as a projection of our culture. This has been done, and I suppose it will continue to be done, they are taken as models, to make a statement about having a powerful culture. They have used the name of Tàpies, of Gaudí, and a series of other figures to project this image of Catalonia.

EJ: *Les quatre cròniques* was originally for another room in the palace of the Generalitat but it was relocated. Do you know why?

TT: I do not remember, I cannot tell you exactly. It was a commission that he made for the Generalitat, I cannot tell you if it was planned for another room, it is possible, it is in the room where the Catalan government meets, it always appears on the news.

EJ: There is a photograph of your father signing a contract for the mural; do you know any of the specific conditions of the commission or if they asked him to use that subject?

TT: No, no, the subject no. They asked if he would make a mural and he chose the topic of the four historic chroniclers of Catalonia. I suppose that it seemed correct to him that this particular subject was adequate for the situation, but they did not ask him to make the art specifically about this theme.

EJ: It was simply for a specific space...?

TT: Yes, he made something for the space.

EJ: In the foundation there is a white box full of photocopies of press articles about *Mitjó*, the whole process and quantity of political interventions seem absurd as it was, to begin with, the direction of MNAC's idea to commission the work. Do you remember how your father reacted when politicians, institutions, and the media were debating the project? How did he feel?

TT: Yes, I remember that. The worst he felt since the moment that MNAC asked him to make a project for the *Sala Oval*, and when he presented his small model (which still exists, the sock), was when someone from MNAC said that they had not asked Tàpies to make anything, that he made the model because he wanted to, and the project ended there. If he made something it was because they asked him to make something, not because he had the idea of doing something there, it is absurd. He felt bad about this because it seemed like someone said that he was presenting a project that nobody sought him out to do, and that is not true. Later I think he became a little entertained reading the number of stories that were printed in newspapers, the majority were ridiculous, that in a way show the cultural and artistic level of this country, when in other countries this sort of project would be something normal that nobody would remark about to such an extent. Here it turned into a hot topic of the press, the television, they made jokes and published cartoons.

EJ: It is curious that you say this because *The New York Times* published something about *Mitjó*, and it projected Barcelona as more sophisticated than the United States precisely for having this sort of public debate about the project. However, I agree more with you, that it was at a level....

TT: ...yes it was a very low level, to me the polemic always seemed correct, but they ended up saying hurtful, atrocious things. Public sculpture is always polemic because not everyone likes it, there are neighbours that live nearby and they could be bothered by new projects while others will never see the sculpture, sometimes they obstruct access; I remember Richard Serra's sculptures, for example, that became controversial simply because they created a barrier between neighbours, or they were even seen as dangerous. Public sculptures are always going to be polemic, but the debate that occurred here with *Mitjó* was with extremely low levels of artistic analysis.

EJ: As a poet and a gallery owner, how do you see the role of politicians in relation to contemporary art?

TT: The role of politicians concerning contemporary art is minor, fairly irregular and not always at a high level. Politicians in general tend to use art for their own agenda — artists should be careful not to fall into their hands. Sometimes particular artists can become of interest, for example when we talked about the PSUC, my father did have affinity for the party, and there was a synergy between them in order to obtain something better. Today, I think artists ought to maintain a distance from politics, because if they do not they end up losing their liberty, I do not mean to say that as individuals they cannot have political opinions, but I think that maintaining a concrete separation, because as I say, with some exceptions, generally politicians in this country do not understand very much about contemporary art.

EJ: Your father made a cover for the Statute of Autonomy of Catalonia (2006). Do you know if he had been asked to do it or if it was simply something he wanted to do?

TT: Normally when he made this type of thing it was because someone asked him to. Yes, yes, this was a commission.

EJ: His artworks, as well as his writing, privilege ambiguity and they often give the individual the opportunity to think and reflect. At the same time, there are works that show his support to certain initiatives. It is clear that he was an anti-Francoist. Would you have considered him always as a Catalanist, and what did Catalanism mean for him?

TT: We spoke about this a bit, to defend Catalanism (for him) was to defend a model of understanding political life in a country where absolute power did not exist, instead there had been a parliament that could counteract the absolute power of a king. This was the case in Catalonia during the Middle Ages, Catalonia was one of the first countries to have a constitution, to defend this was to defend, at that time, something that did not yet exist in Spain, and in this sense my father was a Catalan nationalist.

EJ: Do you remember if he had an opinion about the reconstruction of *Les Quatre Columnes* in 2010?

TT: No, I do not think so. He was quite old, he probably only read about it in the media. I suppose that he would have thought that it was a positive act to recover the monument, but I do not remember that we spoke much about this topic.

EJ: In 2013 Google created a doodle dedicated to Tàpies using an image of one of his artworks. Did you know the company was going to do so beforehand?

TT: No, no, it was a surprise.

EJ: Curious, is it legal to do that?

TT: Yes, yes it is curious... well I imagine that Google should have asked for rights to use the image, but I found out about the doodle the day that it appeared, they (employees of the foundation) called me telling me to look at Google, I looked and saw it, it was the chair. I did not know beforehand.

EJ: Did he express opinions about the separatist movement in Catalonia? Would your father have participated in 9N?

TT: Today? I am not sure. For my father what was important, in his time, was that Spain would return to a democratic country, with a parliament, that could be more or less equivalent to other European countries, and that would respect Catalonia's autonomy, as it was for some years, later there was an involution, from Madrid which intended to recover aspects that had already been ceded to Catalonia. Today, and all of this concerning 9N, which he did not live because it was after his death, I am truly not sure what he would think. I personally think that it is a shame not to have previously found a system that would allow for the different nations that form part of Spain to be united, focusing more on what unifies than on what separates us. This has not been possible and Madrid's government is primarily at fault, it has always tried to denigrate the Catalan language, including in many instances humiliating Catalan culture, and we are paying for this, it is a pity. I think that my father would have said that it is a shame, that we could have better solved this issue from the outset so that we would not have to be in this situation, this is what I imagine he would think now.

EJ: The Museu Nacional d'Art de Catalunya used the artwork *Pintura romànica i barretina* (1971) as a cover for the exhibition publications for *A Visit to the Romanesque: In Company of Antoni Tàpies*. What do you think about this artwork and the exhibition?

TT: It is an amusing canvas; he took a Romanesque piece, with little value and made this intervention, sort of like a tribute to a certain era of Catalan history. For him, Romanesque Catalan art had always had a large impact and MNAC has some examples of tremendous importance here, possibly the most important in any museum in Barcelona.

EJ: And the exhibition *Tàpies. From Within* a few months before?

TT: This was an exhibition with a lot of artworks, part of which was shown in the foundation and another at MNAC. Later there was a slightly reduced version that was shown in Miami, at the Perez Museum. Personally, I think that there were probably too many artworks in this exhibition, but it was the criteria of the commission and evidently, I respect their decisions.

EJ: Do you think it was because of the space (the rooms they had chosen) or did they simply want to show more examples of each moment? It started with his oldest artworks and followed chronologically...

TT: I do not think it was a problem of space. Personally, if I were to do an exhibition like this, I would have been more selective; I would have put up fewer pieces with a little more space for each one.

EJ: And the exhibition that the Guggenheim organized in 2013 (the same year), I am curious if Bilbao was chosen for any particular reason, because he had more experience in New York, as he had various exhibitions there. Maybe it was to facilitate the transport of the artworks...

TT: This was all about the Guggenheim Bilbao, they asked to have an exhibition of objects and sculptures, and they did it there, they never offered us the option to do it in New York.

EJ: Finally, what do you believe was your father's greatest professional achievement?

TT: I think that in general you can say that the presence of my father's oeuvre in the art of the second half of the twentieth century is something that is indisputable. If someone wants to write the history of art of the second half of the twentieth century, they would have to talk about my father, and this is not easy. It is not easy for an artist to have the genius and creativity to be recognized amongst the great number of artists from around the globe. In addition, his perseverance and his desire to work and communicate, to send a message to the world of hope in reality, to try to help humanity to overcome adversity, fear, uncertainty, is something that he intended to do from the outset. No artist has been able to fix the problems of the world, but at least I think it is important to try to do so.

Notes

1. Tàpies, *La realidad como arte*, 85.
2. Ibid., 84.
3. Pujol, *Discurso en la sede la UNESCO en París*, 115–17.
4. 'Artur Mas: "Tàpies ha sido el artista más radicalmente catalán...."'
5. Tàpies, *La realidad como arte*, 266.
6. Guibernau, 'Nationalism and Intellectuals in Nations without States', 25.

BIBLIOGRAPHY

Archives

Arxiu Fotogràfic de Barcelona, Ajuntament de Barcelona
Arxiu Històric de la Ciutat de Barcelona, Ajuntament de Barcelona
Arxiu i Biblioteca, Fundació Antoni Tàpies
Arxiu i Biblioteca, Museu d'Art Contemporani de Barcelona
Biblioteca Nacional de España
Biblioteca y Centro de Documentación, Museo Nacional Centro de Arte Reina Sofía

Bibliography

116 icones turístiques de Catalunya, ed. by the Departament d'Empresa i Coneixement (Barcelona: Generalitat de Catalunya, 2010)

ABC, 23 March 1974, <http://hemeroteca.abc.es/nav/Navigate.exe/hemeroteca/madrid/abc/1974/04/23/001.html> [accessed 5 September 2016]

ACHE, JOSEP, 'Tàpies dóna a Sabadell un símbol', *Diari de Sabadell*, 17 June 1995. Photocopy consulted in the Fundació Tàpies Library, Barcelona

AGUILAR DÍAZ, CARMEN, ET AL., *Historia del Arte 2, Bachillerato* (Madrid: Santillana, 2009)

AGUSTÍ, ANNA, JACQUES DUPIN, and MIQUEL TÀPIES, *Tàpies. Obra completa. Volum 4art. 1976–1981* (Barcelona: Polígrafa and Fundació Antoni Tàpies, 1995)

AGUSTÍ, ANNA, NURIA ENGUITA MAYO, and MIQUEL TÀPIES, *Tàpies. Obra completa. Volum 8è. 1998–2004* (Barcelona: Polígrafa and Fundació Antoni Tàpies, 2006)

ALBERCH, RAMON, 'Un menú diario en el Archivo Histórico', *El Periódico*, 24 June 1992. Photocopy consulted in the Fundació Tàpies Library, Barcelona

ALCOBERRO, A., ET AL., *Història: Ciències Socials, 4 ESO* (Barcelona: Teide, 2008)

ALONSO, MARTÍN, *El Catalanismo, del Éxito al Éxtasis* (Barcelona: El Viejo Topo, 2014)

ALÓS, ERNEST, 'La tierra de los mil "Tàpies."' *El Periódico*, 12 February 2012. Photocopy consulted in the Fundació Tàpies Library, Barcelona

ALEMANY, LUIS, 'Tàpies para escépticos', *El Mundo*, 7 February 2012, <http://www.elmundo.es/elmundo/2012/02/07/cultura/1328613795.html> [accessed 23 August 2015]

ÁLVAREZ JUNCO, JOSÉ, *Mater Dolorosa: La idea de España en el siglo XIX* (Madrid: Taurus, 2001)

ÁLVAREZ JUNCO, JOSÉ, JUSTO BERAMENDI, and FERRÁN REQUEJO, *El nombre de la cosa: Debate sobre el término nación y otros conceptos relacionados* (Madrid: Centro de Estudios Constitucionales, 2005)

AMAT, JORDI, *Largo proceso, amargo sueño: Cultura y política en la Cataluña contemporánea* (Barcelona: Tusquets Editores, 2018)

ANDERSON, BENEDICT, *Imagined Communities: Reflections on the Origin and Spread of Nationalism* (New York: Verso, 2006)

ANDRADE, JUAN, *El PCE y el PSOE en (la) transición: La evolución ideológica de la izquierda durante el proceso de cambio poñítico* (Madrid: Siglo XXI de España, 2012)

Anfosso, 'La destrucción del confort como homenaje a Picasso', *Diario de Barcelona*, 9 February 1982. Photocopy consulted in the Fundació Tàpies Library, Barcelona

Anholt, Simon, *Competitive Identity: The New Brand Management for Nations, Cities and Regions*, Basingstoke: Palgrave Macmillan, 2007

Anguera i Nolla, Pere, *Els precedents del catalanisme. Catalanitat i anticentralisme: 1808–1868* (Barcelona: Empuries, 2000)

Antón, Jacinto, 'Antoni Tàpies, un artista deslumbrante', *El País*, 6 February 2012, <http://cultura.elpais.com/cultura/2012/02/06/actualidad/1328557005_302756.html> [accessed 29 August 2016]

'Antoni Tàpies abofeta al realismo: "Es pintura facilona para nuevos ricos,"' *ABC*, 11 June 1993, p. 12

'Antoni Tàpies galardonado con el Príncipe de Asturias de las Artes por su "riesgo creativo y capacidad innovadora,"' *ABC*, 19 May 1990, p. 61, <http://hemeroteca.abc.es/nav/Navigate.exe/hemeroteca/sevilla/abc.sevilla/1990/05/19/061.html> [accessed 13 June 2016]

Apostua, Luis, 'Calcetin con millones', *Navarra Hoy*, 9 February 1992

Archilés, Ferran, 'Lenguajes de nación, Las "experiencias de nación" y los procesos de nacionalización: propuestas para un debate', *Ayer*, 90 (2013): 91–114

Arco Blanco, Miguel Ángel del, 'Un paso más allá de la historia cultural: Los *cultural studies*', in *Por una historia global: El debate historiográfico en los últimos tiempos*, ed. by Teresa María Ortega López (Granada: Universidad de Granada, 2007)

Armstrong, John A, *Nations before Nationalism* (Chapel Hill, NC: The University of North Carolina Press, 1982)

Aronczyk, Melissa, *Branding the Nation: The Global Business of National Identity* (Oxford: Oxford University Press, 2013)

'Artur Mas: "Tàpies ha sido el artista más radicalmente catalán en su pensamiento, su expresión y sus referentes,"' *El Periódico*, 6 February 2012, <http://www.elperiodico.com/es/noticias/ocio-y-cultura/artur-mas-sido-artista-mas-radicalmente-catalan-pensamiento-expresion-sus-referentes-1393521> [accessed 10 January 2016]

Àtremis, 'Visca el mitjó', *Diari de Barcelona*, 11 February 1992. Photocopy consulted in the Fundació Tàpies Library, Barcelona

'El Ayuntamiento de Barcelona concede a Antoni Tàpies la medalla de oro de la cuidad', *El País*, 29 February 1992. Photocopy consulted in the Fundació Tàpies Library, Barcelona

Balcells, Albert, *Catalan Nationalism* (New York: St. Martin's Press, 1996)

Balfour, Sebastian, *Dictatorship, Workers, and the City: Labour in Greater Barcelona since 1939* (Oxford: Clarendon Press, 1989)

Balfour, Sebastian and Alejandro Quiroga, *The Reinvention of Spain* (Oxford: Oxford University Press, 2007)

Balibar, Etienne and Immanuel Wallerstein, *Race, Nation, Class: Ambiguous Identities* (New York: Verso, 1991)

'Barral dice que la poémica del calcetín beneficia al MNAC', *La Vanguardia*, 10 September 1992. Photocopy consulted in the Fundació Tàpies Library, Barcelona

Barral i Altet, Xavier, 'Coherència tapiana', *Avui*, 7 January 1997. Photocopy consulted in the Fundació Tàpies Library, Barcelona

Barrio, Astrid and Juan Rodríguez Teruel, '¿Por qué se han radicalizado los partidos políticos en Cataluña? El sistema de partidos y el auge del soberanismo (1999–2012)'. <https://www.academia.edu/6792494/_Por_qu%C3%A9_se_han_radicalizado_los_partidos_pol%C3%ADticos_en_Catalu%C3%B1a_El_sistema_de_partidos_y_el_auge_del_soberanismo_1999_2012_> [accessed 4 January 2021]. Originally published in French as Astrid Barrio López and Juan Rodríguez Teruel. 'Pour quelles raisons les partis

politiques en Catalogne se sont-ils radicalisés?: Le système des partis et la montée du souveranisme (1999–2012), *Pôle Sud*, 40 (2014): 99–120
BERAMENDI, JUSTO, 'Cataluña y el derecho a decidir', *Ayer*, 99 (2015), 276–80
BERAMENDI, JUSTO G., RAMÓN MAIZ, and XOSÉ MANOEL NÚÑEZ SEIXAS, eds, *Nationalism in Europe: Past and Present* (Santiago de Compostela: Xunta de Galicia, Universidade de Santiago, 1994)
BEREZEN, MABEL, 'Politics and Culture: A les Fissured Terrain', *Annual Review of Sociology*, 23 (1997), 361–83
BERGER, STEFAN, LINAS ERIKSONAS and ANDREW MYCOCK, eds, *Narrating the Nation: Representations in History, Media and the Arts* (New York: Berghahn Books, 2008)
BERRY, NICOLE, 'Antoni Tàpies at Dia:Beacon', AccessibleArt.com, 24 June 2009
BHABHA, HOMI K, *Nation and Narration* (New York: Routledge, 1990)
'Bilbao muestra el Tàpies más comprometido políticamente con el catalanismo', *eldiario.es*, 9 April 2014, <http://www.eldiario.es/cultura/Bilbao-Tapies-comprometido-politicamente-calatanismo_0_247775813.html> [accessed 9 January 2015]
BILLIG, MICHAEL, *Banal Nationalism* (London: Sage, 1995)
Boletín Oficial del Estado, 10 December 2013, <https://www.boe.es/boe/dias/2013/12/10/pdfs/BOE-A-2013-12886.pdf> [accessed 15 June 2016]
BONET, BLAI, *Tàpies* (Barcelona: Polígrafa, 1964)
The Book of Deeds of James I of Aragon: A Translation of the Medieval Catalan Llibre dels fets, trans. by Damian Smith and Helen Buffery (Aldershot: Ashgate, 2003)
BORDES, JORDI, 'Sabadell, tercera cuitat d'Europa que té una escultura de Tàpies', *El 9 Nou*, 17 June 1995. Photocopy consulted in the Fundació Tàpies Library, Barcelona
——'Tàpies instal·la a Sabadell la seva primera obra fora de Barcelona', *El 9 Nou*, 13 June 1995. Photocopy consulted in the Fundació Tàpies Library, Barcelona
BORJA-VILLEL, MANUEL JOSÉ, 'Antoni Tàpies: The "Matter Paintings"' (unpublished doctoral dissertation, City University of New York, 1989)
——*Fundació Antoni Tàpies* (Barcelona: Edicions de l'Eixample, 1990)
El Born Centre Cultural, <http://elborncentrecultural.barcelona.cat/el-centre/> [accessed 26 January 2016]
El Born Centre de Cultura i Memòria, <http://elbornculturaimemoria.barcelona.cat/en/the-center/> [accessed 25 January 2017]
BORRÁS, MARIA LLUÏSA, 'Antoni Tàpies o una nueva cultura', *Destino*, 12 June 1971, pp. 60–61.
BOSWELL, DAVID and JESSICA EVANS, eds, *Representing the Nation: A Reader. Histories, Heritage and Museums* (London: Routledge, 1999)
BRASS, PAUL, ed., *Ethnic Groups and the State* (London: Croom Helm, 1985)
——*Ethnicity and Nationalism: Theory and Comparison* (New Delhi: Sage, 1991)
BREUILLY, JOHN, *Nationalism and the State*, 2nd edition (Manchester: Manchester University Press, 1993)
BRUBAKER, ROGERS, *Nationalism Reframed: Nationhood and the National Question in the New Europe* (Cambridge: Cambridge University Press, 1996)
BRUNET I CID, FERRAN, 'The Economic Impact of the Barcelona Olympics Games, 1986–2004', Centre d'Estudis Olímpics, 2002, <http://olympicstudies.uab.es/pdf/wp084_eng.pdf> [accessed 1 September 2015]
CABAÑAS BRAVO, JOSÉ MIGUEL, 'La primera Bienal Hispanoamericana de Arte: arte, política y polemica en un certamen internacional de los años cincuenta' (unpublished doctoral thesis, Universidad Complutense de Madrid, 1991)
CACHO VIU, VICENTE, *El nacionalismo catalán como factor de modernización* (Barcelona: Quaderns Crema, S.A., 1998)

———ed., *Els modernistes i el nacionalisme cultural (1881–1906)* (Barcelona: La Magrana, 1984)
Calleja, J. M., *Poesía visual catalana* (Santander: Aula de Letras de la Universidad de Cantabria, 2010)
Cañizares, María Jesús, 'Guerra en el ayuntamiento por la nueva fachada del Liceu', *Crónica*, 31 March 2016, <http://www.cronicaglobal.com/es/notices/2016/03/guerra-en-el-ayuntamiento-por-la-nueva-fachada-del-liceu-35846.php> [accessed 15 July 2016]
Casanellas, Pau, *Morir matando: El franquismo ante la práctica armada, 1968–1977* (Madrid: Catarata, 2014)
Castello, Enric, ed., *La Mediatización del conflict politico: Discursos y narrativas en el contexto español* (Barcelona: Laertes, 2012)
Castells, Luis, ed. *Del territorio a la nación: Identidades territoriales y construcción nacional*. (Madrid: Biblioteca Nueva, 2006)
Catoir, Barbara, *Conversations with Antoni Tàpies* (Munich: Prestel-Verlag, 1991)
Ceus, Barbara, 'Tàpies, más allá de la pintura', *El País*, 18 May 2009. <https://elpais.com/diario/2009/05/18/cultura/1242597611_850215.html> [accessed 4 January 2021]
Chipp, Herschel B., *Theories of Modern Art* (Berkeley: University of California Press, 1996)
Cien años de cultura catalane (1880–1980) (Dirección General del Patrimonio Artístico, Madrid: Ministerio de Cultura, 1980)
Cirici, Alexandre, 'Antoni Tàpies o l'art del món no dit', Tàpies exhibition catalogue (Barcelona: Galeria Maeght, 1981)
——— *Tàpies: 1954–1964* (Barcelona: Gustavo Gili, 1964)
——— *Tàpies: Testimoni del silenci* (Barcelona: Polígrafa, 1970)
Cirlot, Juan-Eduardo, *Tàpies* (Barcelona: Omega, 2000)
Combalía, Victòria, *Tàpies* (Barcelona: Poligrafa, 1986)
——— *Tàpies: Los genios de la pintura española* (Madrid: Sarpe, 1988)
———'Un monumento polémico', *El País*, 21 March 1983. Photocopy consulted in the Fundació Tàpies Library, Barcelona
Combalía, Victoria and Amador Vega, eds, *Mística y creación en el siglo XX* (Barcelona: Herder, 2006)
Conversi, Daniele, 'Art, Nationalism and War: Political Futurism in Italy (1909–1944)', *Sociology Compass*, 3.1 (2009), 92–117
——— *The Basques, the Catalans and Spain: Alternative Routes to Nationalist Mobilisation* (Reno and Las Vegas: University of Nevada Press, 1997)
———'The Smooth Transition: Spain's 1978 Constitution and the Nationalities Question', *National Identities*, 4.3 (2002), 223–44
Corredor-Matheos, José, *Antoni Tàpies: Materia, signo, espíritu* (Barcelona: Polígrafa, 1992)
Crameri, Kathryn, 'Banal Catalanism?', *National Identities*, 2 (2000), 145–57
——— *Goodbye Spain?: The Question of Independence for Catalonia* (East Sussex, England: Sussex Academic Press, 2014)
Culla i Clará, Joan B., *El catalanisme d'esquerra (1928–1936)* (Barcelona: Curial, 1977)
Dia Art Foundation, 'Antoni Tàpies: The Resources of Rhetoric', <http://www.diaart.org/exhibitions/introduction/9> [accessed 4 November 2015]
Dies de transició Salvador Puig Antich: Dotze hores de vida: L'execució de Puig Antich. Directed by Francesc Escribano. Televisió de Catalunya and Vernal Media, 2006.
Domènech, A. *Història de l'Art: Vitrall 2, Batxillerat* (Barcelona: Teide, 2009)
Dowling, Andrew, *Catalonia Since the Spanish Civil War: Reconstructing the Nation* (Portland, OR: Sussex Academic Press, 2013)
Duarte, Ángel, 'El catalán en su paisaje: Algunas notas sobre los usos del imaginario del paisaje catalán, y catalanista, en el primer franquismo', *Historia y Política*, 14 (2005), 165–90
Dupin, Jacques, *Matiere d'infini* (Tours: Farrago, 2005)

―――'Devant Tàpies', *Derrière le Miroir*, 168 (November 1967). Photocopy consulted in the Fundació Tàpies Library, Barcelona
'Duran: "Que hi hagi mitjó no és decisiu pel museu"', *Diari de Barcelona*, 23 April 1992. Photocopy consulted in the Fundació Tàpies Library, Barcelona
EDELMAN, MURRAY, *From Art to Politics: How Artistic Creations Shape Political Conceptions* (Chicago: The University of Chicago Press, 1995)
EDENSOR, TIM, *National Identity, Popular Culture and Everyday Life* (Oxford: Berg, 2002)
ENGUITA MAYO, NURIA, *Los carteles de Tàpies y la esfera pública* (Barcelona: Fundació Antoni Tàpies, 2007)
ERRÁZURIZ, JAVIERA, 'El movimiento estudiantil madrileño durante el curso 1975–1976: Auge y agotamiento de un actor fundamental en lucha contra el franquismo', *Ayer* 99 (2015): 199–224
ESCOBAR, JESÚS, *La Plaza Mayor y los orígenes del Madrid barroco* (San Sebastián: Nerea, 2007)
ESCRIBANO, FRANCESC, *Compte enrere: La història de Salvador Puig Antich* (Barcelona: Edicions 62, 2001)
ESTEBAN DE VEGA, MARIANO, and DOLORES DE LA CALLE VELASCO, eds, *Procesos de nacionalización en la España contemporánea* (Salamanca: Universidad de Salamanca, 2010)
FERNÁNDEZ, DAVID. 'Galán gana 7,4 millones entre sueldo y acciones al frente de Iberdrola en 2013'. *El País*, 21 February 2014, <http://economia.elpais.com/economia/2014/02/21/actualidad/1392991404_982190.html> [accessed 27 January 2016]
FERNÁNDEZ, JOSEP-ANTON, 'Becoming Normal: Cultural Production and Cultural Policy in Catalonia', in *Spanish Cultural Studies: An Introduction*, ed. by Helen and Jo Labanyi (Oxford: Oxford University Press, 1995), pp. 342–46.
―――*El malestar en al cultura catalana: La cultura de la normalització, 1976–1999* (Barcelona: Editorial Empúries, 2008)
FIGUEROLA-FERRETTI, LUIS, 'El arte en Madrid: La pintura actual de Tàpies', *Goya*, 184 (January–February 1985): 46–55
FISHMAN, GEORGE, 'Antoni Tàpies elevates consciousness and conscience in PAMM exhibit', *Miami Herald*, 13 March 2015, <http://www.miamiherald.com/entertainment/visual-arts/article14061947.html> [accessed 23 March 2015]
'Fons municipal d'art contemporani', <http://www.santboi.cat/Publi089.nsf/CC37DDC9 7C4288B6C1257A85002BD319/$FILE/INVENTARI%20FONS%20MUNICIPAL%20 D'ART%20CONTEMPORANI.pdf> [accessed 27 August 2015]
FONTOVA, ROSARIO, 'La sala oval del Palau Nacional se abrirá en el 92', *El Periódico*, 17 December 1991
FOSTER, HAL, ROSALIND KRAUSS, YVE-ALAIN BOIS, BENJAMIN H. D. BUCHLOH, *Arte desde 1900: Modernidad antimodernidad posmodernidad* (Madrid: Ediciones Akal, 2006)
FOUCALT, MICHEL, 'Truth and Power', *The Foucault Reader* (New York: Pantheon, 1984)
FRADERA, JOSEP MARÍA, *Cultura nacional en una sociedad dividida: Cataluña 1838–1868* (Madrid: Marcial Pons, 2003)
FRADERA, JOSEP MARÍA and ENRIC UCELAY DA CAL, eds, *Noticia nova de Catalunya* (Barcelona: Centre de Cultura Contemporánia, 2005)
FRANZKE, ANDREAS, *Tàpies* (Barcelona: Polígrafa, 1992)
FREEMAN, JUDI, *Picasso and the Weeping Women* (Los Angeles: Los Angeles County Museum of Art, 1994)
Fundació Antoni Tàpies, <http://www.fundaciotapies.org/site/spip.php?rubrique65> [accessed 14 November 2015]
FUNDACIÓ JOAN MIRÓ, 'Joan Brossa o la revolta poètica', <http://www.fmirobcn.org/exposicions/122/joan-brossa-o-la-revolta-poetica> [accessed 25 January 2017]
―――'*Manifest groc. Dalí, Gasch, Montanyà i l'antiart*', <http://www.fmirobcn.org/exposicions/96/manifest-groc-dali-gasch-montanya-i-lantiart> [accessed 25 January 2017]

'La Fundación Antoni Tàpies abre sus puertas', *ABC*, 7 June 1990, 146. <http://hemeroteca.abc.es/nav/Navigate.exe/hemeroteca/madrid/abc/1990/06/07/146.html> [accessed 13 June 2016]

'La Fundació Tàpies, en la corda fluixa', *Ara*, 6 June 2015. <https://www.ara.cat/cultura/Fundacio-Tapies-corda-fluixa_0_1370863098.html> [accessed 4 January 2021]

GABRIEL, PERE, *El catalanisme i la cultura federal: Història i política del republicanisme popular Catalunya el segle XIX* (Reus: Fundació Josep Recasens, 2007)

GAECÍA-SEDAS, PILAR, *Joaquím Torres-García i Rafael Barradas: Un diáleg escrit, 1918–1928*. (Barcelona: Publicacions de l'Abadia de Montserrat, 1994)

GALERIA JOAN PRATS, *Antoni Tàpies: 40 anys del col·laboració* (Barcelona: Polígrafa, 2004)

GALFETTI, MARIUCCIA, *Tàpies: Obra gráfica, 1937–1978* (Barcelona: Gustavo Gili, 1980)

GALLEGO, FERRAN, *El mito de la transición: La crisis del franquismo y los orígenes de la democracia (1973–1977)* (Barcelona: Crítica, 2008)

GARCÍA ROVIRA, ANA MARÍA, eds, *España, ¿nación de naciones?* (Madrid: Marcial Pons, 2002)

GARUT, JOSÉ MARIA, *Dos siglos de pintura catalane: XIX y XX* (Madrid: Ibérico Europa de Ediciones, D.L., 1974)

GASCH, SEBASTIAN, *Tàpies* (Madrid: Dirección General de Bellas Artes, 1971)

GELLNER, ERNEST. *Nationalism* (New York: New York University Press, 1997)

—— *Nations and Nationalism* (Oxford: Blackwell, 2006)

Generalitat de Catalunya, 9N 2014 <http://www.participa2014.cat/resultats/dades/ca/escr-tot.html> [accessed 25 January 2016]

——BARÒMETRE D'OPINIÓ POLÍTICA (BOP), 3ª onada 2012- REO 705, Centre d'Estudis d'Opinió, <http://ceo.gencat.cat/ceop/AppJava/pages/estudis/categories/fitxaEstudi.html?colId=3;4308&lastTitle=Bar%F2metre+d%27Opini%F3+Pol%EDtica%3BBar%F2metre+d%27Opini%F3+Pol%EDtica+%28BOP%29.+3a+onada+2012> [accessed 7 March 2016]

——BARÒMETRE D'OPINIÓ POLÍTICA (BOP), 3ª onada 2016- REO 835, Centre d'Estudis d'Opinió. <http://ceo.gencat.cat/ceop/AppJava/pages/home/fitxaEstudi.html?colId=6008&lastTitle=Bar%F2metre+d%27Opini%F3+Pol%EDtica.+3a+onada+2016> [accessed 25 January 2017]

——Enquesta sobre context polític a Catalunya. 2015- REO 806, Centre d'Estudis d'Opinió. <http://ceo.gencat.cat/ceop/AppJava/pages/home/fitxaEstudi.html?colId=5649&lastTitle=Enquesta+sobre+context+pol%EDtic+a+Catalunya.+2015> [accessed March 7, 2016]

——ESTADÍSTIQUES CULTURALES DE CATALUNYA. FEBRUARY 2015. <HTTP://DADESCULTURALS.GENCAT.CAT/WEB/.CONTENT/SSCC/GT/ARXIUS_gt/Estad_culturals_Catalunya_2015.pdf> [accessed 27 January 2016]

——LEY 17/1990, 2 DE NOVIEMBRE, DE MUSEOS, <HTTP://DOGC.GENCAT.CAT/ES/PDOGC_canals_interns/pdogc_resultats_fitxa/?action=fitxa&documentId=59538&language=es_ES> [accessed 22 January 2016]

——PREÁMBULO (Autonomy Statute), <http://web.gencat.cat/es/generalitat/estatut/estatut2006/preambul/index.html> [accessed 9 October 2015]

'La Generalitat "pide" consejo sobe una obra de Tàpies', *Segre*, 25 January 1992. Photocopy consulted in the Fundació Tàpies Library, Barcelona

'La Generalitat se opone al calcetín de Tàpies', *La Vanguardia*, 6 February 1992. Photocopy consulted in the Fundació Tàpies Library, Barcelona

GENIOLA, ANDREA, 'Erudición y particularismo: sobre la oferta "regional" franquista', *VII Encuentro de investigadores del Franquismo*, ed. by D. Lanero Táboas, A Cabana Iglesia, and V. Santidrián Arias. (Santiago de Compostela: n.p., 2011)

GEORGE, ALEXANDRA, *Constructing Intellectual Property* (Cambridge: Cambridge University Press, 2012)
GIMFERRER, PERE, *Tàpies and the Catalan Spirit* (Barcelona: Polígrafa, 1975)
GIORI, PABLO, 'Castells, sardanes i toros: Les disputes culturals dels nacionalismes durant el franquisme'. *Segle XX: Revista Catalana d'historia*, 7 (2014), 13–32
—— 'Cataluña, nación y medios: La construcción del espacio nacional de comunicación (1978–2014)', *Revista internacional de Historia de la Comunicación*, 3.1 (2014), 119–39
Gobierno de España, Ministerio de Hacienda y Administraciones Públicas: Estadísticas 2006–2015: Presupuestos Generales del Estado Consolidados 2015. <http://www.sepg.pap.minhap.gob.es/sitios/sepg/es-ES/Presupuestos/Estadisticas/Documents/2015/01%20Presupuestos%20Generales%20del%20Estado%20Consolidados.pdf> [accessed 30 January 2016]
GONZÁLEZ, VICENTE, 'El pintor barcelonés no figuraba en la lista de artistas preseleccionados', *La Vanguardia*, 19 May 1990. <http://hemeroteca.lavanguardia.com/preview/1990/05/19/pagina-37/33022907/pdf.html?search=Premio%20Pr%C3%ADncipe%20de%20Asturias%20Antoni%20T%C3%A0pies> [accessed 28 August 2016]
GONZÁLEZ-FERNÁNDEZ, ÁNGELES, ed., *Ayer 99: Las transiciones ibéricas* (Madrid: Asociación de Historia Contemporánea and Marcial Pons, 2015)
GRAELL, VANESSA, 'Muere Tàpies a los 88 años', *El Mundo*, 7 February 2012. <http://www.elmundo.es/elmundo/2012/02/06/cultura/1328557633.html> [accessed 29 August 2016]
GRAHAM, HELEN and ANTONIO SANCHEZ, 'The Politics of 1992', in *Spanish Cultural Studies: An Introduction*, ed. by Helen Graham and Jo Labanyi (Oxford: Oxford University Press, 1995), pp. 406–18
GRAHAM, HELEN and JO LABANYI, eds, *Spanish Cultural Studies: An Introduction* (Oxford: Oxford University Press, 1995)
GRANJA SÁINZ, JOSE LUIS DE LA, JUSTO G. BERAMENDI, and PERE ANGUERA, *La España de los nacionalismos y las autonomías* (Madrid: Síntesis, 2001)
GREELEY, ROBIN, 'Nationalism, Civil War and Painting: Joan Miró and Catalanisme in the 1930's'. Paper presented at The University of Michigan, 1996
—— 'Painting Mexican Identities: Nationalism and Gender in the work of María Izquierdo', *Oxford Art Journal*, 23.1 (2000), 51–72
—— *Surrealism and the Spanish Civil War* (New Haven: Yale University Press, 2006)
GRIMES, WILLIAM, 'Antoni Tàpies, Spanish Abstract Painter, Dies at 88', *The New York Times*, 6 February 2012, <http://www.nytimes.com/2012/02/07/arts/design/antoni-tapies-spanish-abstract-painter-dies-at-88.html?_r=0> [accessed 13 January 2016]
GUGGENHEIM BILBAO, 'Antoni Tàpies. From Object to Sculpture (1964–2009)', <http://tapies.guggenheim-bilbao.es/en/exhibitions/introduction/> [accessed 18 November 2015]
GUIBERNAU, MONTSERRAT, *Catalan Nationalism: Francoism, Transition and Democracy* (London: Routledge, 2004)
—— 'Catalan Secessionism: Young People's expectations and Political Change', *The International Spectator: Italian Journal of International Affairs*, 49.3 (July 2014), 106–17
—— 'Nationalism and Intellectuals in Nations without States: The Catalan Case', in *Working Papers 222* (Barcelona: Institut de Ciències Polítiques i Socials, 2003). <https://www.icps.cat/archivos/WorkingPapers/wp222.pdf?noga=1> [accessed 4 January 2021]
—— *Per un catalanisme cosmopolita*. Barcelona: Angle, 2009
—— 'Secessionism in Catalonia: After Democracy', *Ethnopolitics*, 12.4 (2013), 368–93
GUIBERNAU, MONTSERRAT and JOHN HUTCHINSON, eds, *Understanding Nationalism* (Cambridge: Polity Press, 2001)
GUSTÀ HERNÁNDEZ, JAIME, 'El calectín de Tàpies', *La Vanguardia*, 18 March 1992. Photocopy consulted in the Fundació Tàpies Library, Barcelona

HALL, STUART, 'Creolization, Diaspora, and Hybridity in the Context of Globalization', *Creolité and Crolization*, Documenta11_Platform3. Ostfildern-Ruit (2003), 185–98
—— *Critical Dialogues in Cultural Studies* (New York: Routledge, 2007)
—— 'The Problem of Ideology-Marxism without Guarantees', *Journal of Communication Inquiry*, 10 (June 1986), 28–44
—— 'The Question of Cultural Identity', in *Modernity: An Introduction to Modern Societies*, ed. by Stuart Hall (Cambridge, MA: Blackwell, 1996)
—— ED., *Representation: Cultural Representations and Signifying Practices* (London: Sage, 1997)
—— 'Signification, Representation, Ideology: Althusser and the Post-Structuralist Debates', *Critical Studies in Mass Communication* 2:2 (1985): 91–114
HALL, STUART and PAUL DU GAY, eds, *Questions of Cultural Identity* (London: Sage, 1997)
HARGREAVES, JOHN, *Freedom for Catalonia? Catalan Nationalism, Spanish Identity and the Barcelona Olympic Games* (Cambridge: Cambridge University Press, 2000)
HAUPT, GERHARD, MICHEL LÖWY, and CLAUDE WEILL, *Les marxistes et la question nationale (1894–1914)* (Paris: Maspero, 1974)
HENSBERGEN, GIJS VAN, *Guernica: The Biography of a Twentieth-Century Icon* (New York: Bloomsbury Publishing, 2004)
HERB, HUNTRAM H. and DAVID H. KAPLAN, *Nested Identities: Nationalism, Territory, and Scale* (Lanham, MD: Rowman & Littlefield Publishers, 1999)
HEREDIA, MARTINE, *Tàpies, Saura, Millares: L'art informel en Espange* (Paris: Presses Universitaires Vincennes, 2013)
HIERRO, MARÍA JOSÉ, 'Crafting Identities in a Multinational Context: Evidence from Catalonia', *Nations and Nationalism*, 21.3 (2015), 461–82
HOBSBAWM, E. J., *Nations and Nationalism Since 1780: Programme, Myth, Reality* (Cambridge: Cambridge University Press, 1992)
HOBSBAWM, ERIC and TERENCE RANDER EDS, *The Invention of Tradition* (New York: Cambridge University Press, 1983)
HOLGUÍN, SANDIE, *Creating Spaniards. Culture and National Identity in Republican Spain* (Madison, WI: The University of Wisconsin Press, 2002)
Homenaje a Joan Brossa (Oviedo: Asociación de Deseñadores Gráficas de Asturias, 2000)
HOMS, NURIA and MANUEL J BORJA-VILLEL, *Tàpies: Obra gráfica, 1995–2011* (Barcelona: Gustavo Gili, 2014)
HROCH, MIROSLAV, *Social Preconditions of National Revival in Europe: A Comparative Analysis of the Social Composition of Patriotic Groups Among the Smaller European Nations* (Cambridge: Cambridge University Press, 1985)
Instituto Cervantes, <http://www.cervantes.es> [accessed 29August 2016]
Instituto Nacional de Estadística. Encuesta de empleo del tiempo 2002–2003, <http://www.ine.es/daco/daco42/empleo/dacoeet.htm> [accessed 29 June 2016]
J.LL.D., 'La plaza de Cataluña de Sant Boi de Llobregat nace como "símbolo permanente de la catalanidad y la democracia"', *El País*, 14 March 1983. Photocopy consulted in the Fundació Tàpies Library, Barcelona
JENKINS, BRIAN and SPYROS A. SOFOS, eds, *Nation and Identity in Contemporary Europe* (London: Routledge, 1996)
JENTLESON, KATHERINE, 'Antoni Tàpies: An Artist's Odyssey in the Age of Franco' *Artinfo*, 2 July 2009. Photocopy consulted in the Fundació Tàpies Library, Barcelona
JONES, DANIEL E., 'Pujol y la construcción de un espacio catalán de comunicación. Interacciones entre instituciones políticas y empresas mediáticas (1980–2003)', *Ámbitos*, 16 (2007), 499–524
JULIÁN, INMACULADA, 'Presentación de doctor honoris a Antoni Tàpies', Barcelona, 22 June 1988

KING, EDWARD and EASTMAN JOHNSON, 'The Value of Nationalism in Art', *The Monthly Illustrator*, 4.14 (June 1985), 265–68
KRAUSS, ROSALIND and MARGIT ROWELL, *Joan Miró: The Magnetic Fields* (New York: Solomon R. Guggenheim Museum, 1972)
LAITIN, DAVID D., 'Linguistic Revival: Politics and Culture in Catalonia', *Comparative Studies in Society and History*, 31.2 (April 1989), 297–317
LANG, COLIN, 'Antoni Tàpies: The Resources of Rhetoric', *Art Forum*, May 2009
LENORE, VÍCTOR, *Indies, Hipsters y gafapastas: Crónica de una dominación cultural* (Madrid: Capitán Swing, 2014)
LESCAZE, LEE, 'Mr. Tàpies's Unmatched Sock', *The Wall Street Journal*, 22 July 1992, A10
LINDHOLM, CHARLES. *Culture and Authenticity* (Oxford: Oxford University Press, 2008)
LLOBERA, JOSEP, 'The Role of Commemorations in (Ethno)Nation-Building: The Case of Catalonia', in *Nationalism and the Nation in the Iberian Peninsula*, ed. by Clare Mar-Molinero and Angel Smith (Oxford: Berg, 1996)
LÓPEZ PACAL, RAMÓN and MIGUEL CABO VILLAVERDE, eds, *De la idea a la identidad: Estudios sobre nacionalismo y procesos de nacionalización. Estudios en homenaje a Justo Beramendi* (Granada: Comares, 2012)
LUBAR, ROBERT, 'Antoni Tàpies's Recent Works' (New York: Pace Gallery, 1993)
—— 'Joan Miró before "The Farm," 1915–1922: Catalan Nationalism and the Avant-garde' (unpublished doctoral dissertation, New York University, Graduate Scool of Arts and Science, 1988)
—— 'Miró's Luinguistic Nationalism', in Robert S. Lubar, Joaquim Molas, Clara Janés i Pere Gimferrer, *Cent Anys de Miró, Mompou i Foix* (Barcelona: Universitat de Barcelona, 1994)
—— 'Miró's Mediterranean: Conceptions of a Cultural Identity', in *Joan Miró: 1893–1993* (Barcelona: Fundació Joan Miró, 1993)
—— 'Tàpies. New York', *The Burlington Magazine*, 137.1105 (April 1995), 271–73
LUNA, JOAQUÍN, 'Tàpies recibió sin ningún recelo la Medalla de Oro de la Generalitat', *La Vanguardia*, 7 October 1983. Photocopy consulted in the Fundació Tàpies Library, Barcelona
MALET, ROSA MARIA, *Los carteles de Tàpies* (Barcelona: Poligrafa, 1984)
MALET, ROSA MARIA and MIQUEL TÀPIES, *Tàpies Affiches* (Paris: Cercle d'art, 1988)
'Maragall no intervendrá en la decisión sobre el "calcetín" de Tàpies'. *El País*, 8 February 1992. Photocopy consulted in the Fundació Tàpies Library, Barcelona
MARÍN MEDINA, JOSÉ, *Tàpies: Meditaciones, 1976* (Madrid: Ediciones Rayuela, 1976)
MARTÍ, DAVID, 'The 2012 Catalan Election: The First Step Towards Independence?' *Regional and Federal Studies*, 23.4 (2013), 506–16
MARTÍNEZ FIOL, DAVID, 'La construcción mítica del "onze de setembre" en la cultura política del catalanismo durante el siglo XX', *Historia y Política*, 14 (2005), 219–44
MARTÍNEZ-HERRERA, ENRIC and THOMAS JEFFERY MILEY, 'The Constitution and the Politics of National Identity in Spain', *Nations and Nationalism*, 16 (2010), 6–30
MARZO, JORGE LUIS, *Arte Moderno y Franquismo: Los orígnes conservadores de la vanguardia y de la política artística en España* (Girona, 2006). <https://www.soymenos.net/arte_franquismo.pdf> [accessed 4 January 2021]
—— 'La era de la degradación del arte y de la política cultural en Cataluña', *Soymenos*, 2012, https://soymenos.files.wordpress.com/2012/06/la_degradacion_del_-arte_en_catalunya1.pdf [accessed 11 January 2016]
MAR-MOLINERO, CLARE and ANGEL SMITH, eds, *Nationalism and the Nation in the Iberian Peninsula: Competing and Conflicting Identities* (Oxford: Berg, 1996)
MASSOT, JOSEP, 'Tàpies: l'ética de la pintura, L'artista català mor als 88 anys al seu domicili de Barcelona'. *La Vanguardia*, 7 February 2012, p. 28

—— 'El vicepresidente del MNAC se opone a la escultura del calcetín'. *La Vanguardia*, 23 January 1992. Photocopy consulted in the Fundació Tàpies Library, Barcelona
MAYO, NURIA ENGUITA, SANDRA FORTÓ, NÚRIA HOMS, and PILAR PARCERISAS. *Los carteles de Tàpies y la esfera pública* (Barcelona: Fundació Antoni Tàpies, 2006)
MAYHEW, JONATHAN, 'Valente/Tàpies: The Poetics of Materiality', *Anales de la literatura española contemporánea*, 22.1/2 (1997), 91–102
MCCARTHY, DAVID, *American Artists Against War (1935–2010)* (Oakland: University of California Press Books, 2015)
MCROBERTS, KENNETH, *Catalonia: Nation Building Without a State* (Oxford: Oxford University Press, 2001)
MEES, LUDGER, 'Emociones en política. Conceptos, debates y perspectivas analíticas' *Emoción e identidad nacional: Cataluña y el País Vasco en perspectiva comparada*, ed. by Géraldine Galeote, Maria Llombart Huesca, and Maitane Ostolaza (Paris: Édicions Hispaniques, 2015), pp. 25–45
MÉNDEZ RAMOS, ABRAHAM, 'En torno a un "calcetín"', *El Observador*, 7 March 1992. Photocopy consulted in the Fundació Tàpies Library, Barcelona
MICHONNEAU, STEPHANE, *Barcelona, memoria i identitat: Monuments, commemoracions i mites* (Barcelona: Eumo, 2002)
MIHELJ, SABINA, *Media Nations: Communicating Belonging and Exclusion in the Modern World* (New York: Palgrave Macmillan, 2011)
MILEY, THOMAS JEFFREY, 'Against the Thesis of the "Civic Nation": The Case of Catalonia in Contemporary Spain', *Nationalism and Ethnic Politics*, 13.1 (2007), 1–37
MILEY, THOMAS JEFFREY and ROBERTO GARVÍA, 'Conflict in Catalonia: A Sociological Approximation'. *Genealogy*, 3.56 (2019), 1–27
MINDER, RAFAEL, 'Catalonia Overwhelmingly Votes for Independence From Spain in Straw Poll', *The New York Times*, 9 November 2014, <http://www.nytimes.com/2014/11/10/world/europe/catalans-vote-in-straw-poll-on-independence-from-spain.html> [accessed 25 January 2016]
MINGUET BATLLORI, JOAN M., *Contra la Cooltura; Art i política a Catalunya* (Barcelona: Edicions Els Llums, 2015)
MIQUEL SOBRER, JOSEP, *Catalonia: A Self-Portrait* (Bloomington: Indiana University Press, 1992)
'El MNAC no decidirá sobre el "calcetín" de Tàpies hasta después de las elecciones', *El País*, 25 February 1992. Photocopy consulted in the Fundació Tàpies Library, Barcelona
'MNAC, Museu Nacional d'Art de Catalunya', Mission statement, renovation plans, and year 2000 goals, Metropolitan Museum of Art, Thomas J. Watson Library, Copy from the University of Connecticut library (Storrs campus)
MOIX, LLÀTZER, 'Tàpies reinvindica el arte como vehículo de reflexión en su monumental obra para la UPF'. *La Vanguardia*, 6 December 1996, <http://hemeroteca.lavanguardia.com/preview/1996/07/28/pagina-41/33957519/pdf.html?search=Sala%20de%20Reflexi%C3%B3n%20T%C3%A0opies> [accessed 9 June 2016]
MOLINA APARICIO, FERNANDO, *Mario Onaindia (1948–2003): Biografía patria* (Madrid: Biblioteca Nueva, 2012)
MOLINA, FERNANDO and JOSÉ ANTONIO PÉREZ, *El peso de la identidad: Mitos y ritos de la historia vasca* (Madrid: Marcial Pons, 2015)
MOLINERO, CARME, COORD., *La Transición treinta años después* (Barcelona: Península, 2006)
MOLINERO, CARME and PERE YSÀS, *Els anys del PSUC: el partit de l'antifranquisme (1956–1981)* (Barcelona: L'Avenç, 2010)
—— *La cuestión catalana: Cataluña en la transición española* (Barcelona: Crítica, 2014)
MONTANER, JOSEP MARIA, 'El Pavelló de Catalunya a l'Expo de Sevilla', in *Textos Originals en Catalá*, <http://www.raco.cat/index.php/Catalonia/article/viewFile/107212/166299> [accessed 8 December 2014]

Montgomery, Ken, 'Banal Race-thinking: Ties of Blood, Canadian History Textbooks and Ethnic Nationalism', *Paedagogica Historica*, 41.3 (2005), 313–36
Moore- Gilbert, Bart, *Postcolonial Theory: Contexts, Practices, Politic* (New York: Verso, 1997)
Moreno Luzón, Javier, ed., *Construir España: Nacionalismo español y procesos de nacionalización* (Madrid: Centro de Estudios Políticos y Constitucionales, 2007)
Mori, Norihide, 'The Image and the Real: A Consideration of Sartre's Early Views on Art', *Aesthetics*, 16 (2012), 11–24
Moure, Gloria. *Tàpies: Objectos del tiempo* (Barcelona: Polígrafa, 1994)
'Muere en Barcelona el artista Antoni Tàpies', *El Periódico*, 6 February 2012, <http://www.elperiodico.com/es/noticias/ocio-y-cultura/muere-genio-del-informalismo-antoni-tapies-1393283> [accessed 29 August 2016]
Muñoz Mendoza, Jordi, *La construcción política de la identidad española: ¿Del nacionalcatolicismo al patriotism democrático?* (Madrid: Centro de Investigaciones Sociologicas, 2012)
Muriel Ladrón de Guevara, Xavier Cóller, and Daniel Romaní, 'The Image of Barcelona '92 in the International Press' (Barcelona: Centre d'Estudis Olimpics UAB, 1995), <http://olympicstudies.uab.es/pdf/wp105_eng.pdf> [accessed 8 December 2014]
Museo Nacional Centro de Arte Reina Sofía, 'Dalí: All of the Poetic Suggestions and All of the Plastic Possibilities', <http://www.museoreinasofia.es/en/exhibitions/dali-all-poetic-suggestions-and-all-plastic-possibilities> [accessed 21 November 2015]
Museu d'Art Contemporani de Barcelona Collection, <http://www.macba.cat/en/rinzen-1461> [accessed 25 September 2015]
Museu d'Historia de Catalunya, <http://www.en.mhcat.cat/> [accessed 26 January 2016]
The Museu Nacional d'Art de Catalunya (Barcelona: Generalitat de Catalunya, 2009)
Museu Nacional d'Art de Catalunya, Official Institutional Objectives (Barcelona: Generalitat de Catalunya, 2005)
—— 'The Museum', <http://www.museunacional.cat/en/museum> [accessed 20 January 2016]
—— 'Tàpies. From Within', http://museunacional.cat/en/tapies-within-3 [accessed 21 July 2014]
Nairn, Tom, *The Break-up of Britain: Crisis and Neo-Nationalism* (London: New Left Books, 1977)
Navarro Arisa, Juan José, 'El Ayuntamiento de Barcelona cede a Tàpies un edificio que albergará la fundación del artista', *El País*, 14 March 1987, <http://elpais.com/diario/1987/03/14/cultura/542674807_850215.html> [accessed 28 August 2016]
Nistal González, Fernando, *El papel del Partido Comunista en la Transición* (Madrid: Centro de Estudios Políticos y Constitucionales, 2015)
Norotzky, Viviana, 'Selling the Nation: Identity and Design in 1980s Catalonia', *Design Issues* 25.3 (Summer 2009): 62–75
Núñez Seixas, Xosé Manoel, 'La región y lo local en el primer franquismo', *Imaginarios y representaciones de España durante el franquismo* (Madrid: Velázquez, 2014), pp. 127–54
'A Obiols no le gusta el calectín', *Segre*, 8 February 1992. Photocopy consulted in the Fundació Tàpies Library, Barcelona
Official Statistics Website of Catalonia, 'Generalitat Public Sector: Budget. 2010–2015', <http://www.idescat.cat/pub/?id=aec&n=683&lang=en> [accessed 27 January 2016]
Olivar, Marcial, *The Art Museum of Catalonia, Barcelona*, trans. by James Brockway (New York: Meredith Press, 1968)
Onieva, Antonio J., *A New Complete Guide to the Prado Gallery* (Madrid: Editorial Mayfe, S.A., 1966)

Ors i Rovira, Eugeni d' (Xenius), *La Veu de Catalunya* (Barcelona: 1899–1937, Biblioteca de Catalunya), <http://www.bnc.cat/esl> [accessed 28 March 2013]

Osma, Guillermo de, *Ismos: Arte de Vanguardia (1910–1936) en España* (Madrid: Galería Guillermo de Osma, 1993)

Oxford Dictionaries, <http://www.oxforddictionaries.com/definition/english/visualize> [accessed 21 September 2015]

Ozkirimli, Umut, *Contemporary Debates on Nationalism: A Critical Engagement* (New York: Palgrave Macmillan, 2005)

Palacios, David, 'En el interior de la capilla laica de Tàpies', *La Vanguardia*, 5 June 2016, <http://www.lavanguardia.com/local/barcelona/20160602/402225411601/capilla-laica-tapies-upf-reflexion.html> [accessed 9 June 2016]

Panyella, Jordi, *Salvador Puig Antich, caso abierto* (Barcelona: Lectio, 2015)

Palau, Maria, 'El gran artista i pensador', *El Punt Avui*, 7 February 2012, <http://www.elpuntavui.cat/cultura/article/19-cultura/504330-el-gran-artista-i-pensador.html> [accessed 29 August 2016]

Parcerisas, Pilar, 'Una cambra per al silenci', *Avui*, 6 February 1997

'El parlamento de Cataluña aprueba el nuevo Estatuto'. *El País*, 30 September 2005, <http://elpais.com/elpais/2005/09/30/actualidad/1128068217_850215.html> [accessed 29 August 2016]

Pasamar, Gonzalo, '¿Cómo nos han contado la Transición? Política, memoria e historiografía (1978–1996)', *Ayer*, 99 (2015), 225–49

Penrose, Roland, *Tàpies* (Barcelona: Polígrafa, 1977)

Permanyer, Lluís, *Tàpies i les civilización orientals* (Barcelona: EDHASA, 1983)

—— *Tàpies y la nueva cultura* (Barcelona: Polígrafa, 1986)

Petrescu, Diona, ed., *Altering Practices: Feminist Politics and Poetics of Space* (London: Routledge, 2007)

Picazo, Glòria, 'Tàpies: vestigis d' alló que existí', *Nous Horitzons*, 83 (March– May 1983), 30–31

'El PP s'oposa a la instal·lació del mitjó de Tàpies al Palau Nacional', *Avui*, 28 January 1992

Prado, Benjamín, 'Dalí el fascista', *El País*, 8 July 2004, <http://elpais.com/diario/2004/07/08/madrid/1089285859_850215.html [accessed 21 November 2015]

Prat de la Riba, Enric. *La nacionalidad catalana* (Barcelona: Aymá, 1982 [1906])

Preziosi, D. and C. Farago, eds, *Grasping the World: The Idea of the Museum* (Aldershot: Ashgate, 2004)

'Proyectos y realización del monument a Picasso, de Tàpies', *Belles Arts*, Bulletí de la Facultat de Belles Arts de la Universitat de Barcelona (April–May 1983)

Pujol, Jordi, 'Discurso en la sede la UNESCO en París, con motivo de la Exposición *Catalunya Avui*', 23 March 1981

—— *Catalunya-Espanya* (Madrid: Espasa-Calpe, 1996)

Quaggio, Giulia, *La cultura en transición: Reconciliación y política cultural en España, 1976–1986* (Madrid: Alianza, 2014)

Quiroga Fernández de Soto, Alejandro, *Goles y banderas: Fútbol e identidades nacionales en España* (Madrid: Marcial Pons Historia, 2014)

—— *Haciendo españoles: La nacionalización de las masas en la dictadura de Primo de Rivera (1923–1930)* (Madrid: Centro de Estudios Políticos y Constitucionales, 2008)

—— 'Michael Billig en España: Sobre la recepción de Banal Nationalism', in *Pensar con la Historia desde el siglo XXI*, ed. by Pilar Folguera and others (Madrid: Universidad Autónoma de Madrid, 2015), pp. 4185–02

—— 'The Three Spheres: A Theoretical Model of Mass Nationalization: The Case of Spain', *Nations and Nationalism*, 20.4 (2014), 683–700

QUIROGA, ALEJANDRO and FERNANDO MOLINA, 'National Deadlock. Hot Nationalism, Dual Identities and Catalan Independence (2008–2019)', *Genealogy*, 4.15 (2020), 1–18
RAILLARD, GEORGES, *La syllabe noire de Tàpies* (Marsella: André Dimanche Éditeur, 1994)
—— *Tàpies* (Paris: Maeght Éditeur, 1976)
RANCIÉRE, JACQUES, *The Politics of Aesthetics: The Distribution of the Sensible* (London: Continuum, 2004)
RASSEL, LAURENCE, *Tàpies From Within 1945–2011* (Barcelona: Fundació Antoni Tàpies, 2013)
——AND OTHERS, *En record d'Antoni Tàpies*. Ateneu Barcelonès, Barcelona, 3 March 2012. <https://traces.uab.cat/record/116365?ln=ca> [accessed 4 January 2020]
'Repsol dona a la Fundació Museo d'Art Contemporani la obra Rinzen, de Antoni Tàpies', Repsol press release, 17 December 1998, <http://www.repsol.com/es_es/corporacion/prensa/notas-de-prensa/ultimas-notas/donacion_de_la_obra_rinzen_a_la_fundacio.aspx> [accessed 14 September 2015)
'Un restaurante crea un a encuesta-sortea sobre el "calcetín" de Antoni Tàpies', *El País*, 18 June 1992
RICHARDS, MICHAEL, *After the Civil War: Making Memory and Re-making Spain Since 1936* (Cambridge: Cambridge University Press, 2013)
RIQUER, BORJA DE, 'La Catalunya autonómica 1975–2003', vols 9 and 10, *La Història de Catalunya*, ed. by Pierre Vilar, 62, 2003
——DIR., *Història, política, societat i cultura dels Països Catalans* (Barcelona: Enciclopèdia Catalana, 1996–1999)
——*Identitats contemporànies: Catalunya i Espanya* (Vic: Eumo, 2000)
——*Lliga Regionalista (1898–1904)*. Barcelona: Ed. 62, 1977)
——'Social and Economic Change in a Climate of Political Immobilism', in *Spanish Cultural Studies: An Introduction*, ed. by Helen Graham and Jo Labanyi (Oxford: Oxford University Press, 1995), pp. 259–70
RIQUER, BORJA DE, JESUS M. RHODES, and JOSEP TERMES, 'El nacionalismo catalan', *Cuadernos de Historia* 16.89 (Madrid: Groupo 16, D.L., 1985)
RISPA, RAUL, CESAR ALONSO DE LOS RIOS, and MARIA JOSE AGUAZA, eds, *Expo'92 Sevilla: Architecture and Design* (New York: Abbeville Press, 1993)
RIUS ULLDEMOLINS, JOAQUIM, 'Política cultural e hibridación de las instituciones culturales: El caso de Barcelona', *Revista Española de Ciencia Política* 29 (July 2012): 85–105
ROBINSON, WILLIAM H., JORDI FALGÁS, and CARMEN BELEN LORD, eds, *Barcelona and Modernity: Picasso, Gaudí, Miró, Dalí* (New Haven: Yale University Press, 2006)
ROE, JEREMY, *Tàpies* (New York: Parkstone Press Ltd., 2006)
ROHRER, JUDITH, 'A Theme for Reflection: The Recent Work of Antoni Tàpies', *Arts Magazine* (December 1975). Photocopy consulted in the Fundació Tàpies Library, Barcelona
ROMA, VALENTÍN, *Tresors del Palau de la Generalitat de Catalunya — 2* (Barcelona: Generalitat de Catalunya, Museu Nacional d'Art de Catalunya, 2001)
ROOD, GREGORY, DIR., *Tàpies*, BBC and TVE Catalunya, 1990
ROSENBERG, HAROLD, 'Rosenberg on Violence in Art and Other Matters', *Artscanada* 26 (February 1969): 32
ROTHKO CHAPEL, <http://rothkochapel.org/index.php?option=com_content&view=article&id=3&Itemid=6> [accessed 18 September 2015]
ROVIRA I VIRGILI, ANTONI, *Nacionalisme i federalisme* [1912–1932] (Barcelona: Reeds, 1982)
SAFRAN, WILLIAM and RAMÓN MAIZ, eds, *Identity and Territorial Autonomy in Plural Societies* (London and Portland: Frank Cass, 2000)
'Sala de Reflexión en la Universidad Pompeu Fabra. Barcelona', *On* 180 (1997): 90–95

SALA, MARIA, 'El calcetín de Tàpies', *El Periódico*, 18 February 1992. Photocopy consulted in the Fundació Tàpies Library, Barcelona
SALAT, JORDI, *Les quatre columnes catalanes* (Barcelona: Llibres de l'Índex, 2005)
SALVAT PAPASSEIT, JOAN, ed., *Arc-Voltaic*, Arxiu de Revistes Catalanes Antigues, February 1918, <http://www.bnc.cat/digital/arca/index.html> [accessed March 10, 2013]
SANTOS TORROELLA, R., 'Primera Piedra', *La Vanguardia*, 5 April 1983
SARTORIUS, NICOLÁS and ALBERTO SABIO ALCUTÉN, *El final de la dictadura: La conquista de la democracia en España: noviembre de 1975–junio de 1977* (Madrid: Temas de Hoy, 2007)
SARTRE, JEAN-PAUL, 'The Unprivileged Painter: Lapoujade', *Essays in Aesthetics* 60–77 (New York: Citadel Press, 1963)
SAZ CAMPOS, ISMAEL, *España contra España: Los nacionalismos franquistas* (Madrid: Marcial Pons, 2003)
SCHUMACHER, EDWARD, 'Sculptures Are Changing the Look of Barcelona', *The New York Times*, 4 September 1990, <http://www.nytimes.com/1990/09/04/arts/sculptures-are-changing-the-look-of-barcelona.html> [accessed 27 August 2016]
SCOTT, JAMES C., *Domination and the Arts of Resistance* (New Haven: Yale University Press, 1990)
SERRA, CATALINA, 'El "calcetín" de Tàpies existe', *El País*, 17 February 2010, <http://elpais.com/diario/2010/02/17/catalunya/1266372439_850215.html> [accessed 14 November 2015]
——'El Pintor Antoni Tàpies gana el Premio Príncipe de Asturias de las Artes', *El País*, 13 May 1990, http://elpais.com/diario/1990/05/19/cultura/643068006_850215.html [accessed 31 August 2015]
——'El MACBA instala la pieza que Tàpies presentó en la Bienal de Venecia', *El País*, 18 December 1998, <http://elpais.com/diario/1998/12/18/cultura/913935604_850215.html> [accessed 14 September 2015]
——'Tàpies, immortal', *Ara*, 7 February 2012, <http://www.ara.cat/cultura/Tapies-immortal_0_641935882.html> [accessed 29 August 2016]
——'TVE- Cataluña y la BBC colaboran en un documental sobre Tàpies', *El País*, 28 June 1990, <http://elpais.com/diario/1990/06/28/radiotv/646524002_850215.html> [accessed 19 June 2016]
SERRANO, IVAN, 'Just a Matter of Identity? Support for Independence in Catalonia', *Regional and Federal Studies*, 23.5 (2013), 523–45
SERRANO, M. LÓPEZ, *Palacio Real de Madrid* (Madrid: Editorial Patrimonio Nacional, 1967)
SHAPIRO, IAN, *Politics Against Domination* (Cambridge, MA: The Belknap Press of Harvard University, 2016)
SMITH, ANTHONY D., *Chosen Peoples: Sacred Sources of National Identity* (Oxford: Oxford University Press, 2003)
——'Culture, Community and Territory: The Politics of Ethnicity and Nationalism', *International Affairs*, 72.3 (July 1996), 445–58
—— *The Ethnic Origins of Nations* (Oxford: Basil Blackwell, 1986)
—— *Nacionalismo y modernidad: Un estudio crítico de las teorías recientes sobre nacionales y nacionalismo* (Madrid: Itsmo, 2000)
—— *National Identity* (London: Penguin, 1991)
—— *Las teorías del nacionalismo* (Barcelona: Península, 1976)
SOLE I SABATÉ, J. M., *La represión franquista en Cataluña 1938–1953* (Barcelona: Edicions 62, 1985)
SONTAG, SUSAN, *Regarding the Pain of Others* (New York: Farrar, Straus, and Giroux, 2003)
SÒRIA, JOSEP MARIA, 'Naixement i mort de l'Assemblea de Catalunya', *La Vanguardia*, 6 November 2011

Stanford Encyclopedia of Philosophy, <http://plato.stanford.edu/entries/nationalism/> [accessed 7 December 2015]
STAPELL, HAMILTON, *Remaking Madrid: Culture, Politics, and Identity After Franco* (New York: Palgrave Macmillan, 2010)
TAPIÉ, MICHEL, *Antoni Tàpies* (Milan: Fratelli Fabbri, 1969)
——*Avec Antoni Tàpies* (Paris: Derrière le Miroir, 1967)
'Tàpies: 75 años de creación'. *ABC*, 20 December 1998, p. 83. <http://hemeroteca.abc.es/nav/Navigate.exe/hemeroteca/sevilla/abc.sevilla/1998/12/20/083.html> [accessed 13 June 2016]
'Tàpies, adiós al gran renovador del arte español'. *ABC* (Sevilla), 7 February 2012, p. 1
'Tàpies, descalzo', *ABC de las artes* 90 (December 1993). <http://hemeroteca.abc.es/nav/Navigate.exe/hemeroteca/m> [accessed 9 September 2015]
Tàpies: Desde el Interior 1945–2011, ed. by MNAC and the Fundació Antonio Tapies (Madrid: La Fabrica, 2013)
Tàpies, els anys 80 (Barcelona: Ajuntament de Barcelona, 1988)
Tàpies: Extensions de la Realidad (Milan: Gruppo Edit. Fabbri, 1990)
Tàpies: Retrospectiva, Exposición enmarcada en el programa 'Arte español para el exterior' (Madrid: Dirección General de Relaciones Culturales y Cientificas, 2004)
TÀPIES, ANTONI, *Antoni Tàpies (Obra 1956–1976)* (Barcelona: Fundació Joan Miró, 1976)
——*L'art contra l'estètica* (Barcelona: Ariel, 1970)
——*L'art i els seus llocs* (Madrid: Editorial Siruela, 1999)
——*Art i espiritualitat* (Barcelona: Universidad de Barcelona, 1988)
——*En blanco y negro* (Barcelona: Galaxia Gutenberg, 2008)
——*The Complete Works Volume 1. 1943–1960* (Barcelona: Ediciones Polígrafa and Fundació Antoni Tàpies, 1988)
——*The Complete Works. Volume 2. 1961–1968* (Barcelona: Ediciones Polígrafa and Fundació Antoni Tàpies, 1990)
——*The Complete Works. Volume 3. 1969–1975* (Barcelona: Ediciones Polígrafa and Fundació Antoni Tàpies, 1992)
——*The Complete Works. Volume 4. 1976–1981* (Barcelona: Ediciones Polígrafa and Fundació Antoni Tàpies, 1996)
——*The Complete Works. Volume 5. 1982–1985* (Barcelona: Ediciones Polígrafa and Fundació Antoni Tàpies, 1998)
——*The Complete Works. Volume 6. 1986–1990* (Barcelona: Ediciones Polígrafa and Fundació Antoni Tàpies, 2002)
——*The Complete Works. Volume 7. 1991–1997* (Barcelona: Ediciones Polígrafa and Fundació Antoni Tàpies, 2003)
——*The Complete Works. Volume 8. 1998–2005* (Barcelona: Ediciones Polígrafa and Fundació Antoni Tàpies, 2005)
——*Complete Writings Volume I. A Personal Memoir: Fragments for an Autobiography*, trans. by Josep Miquel Sobrer (Barcelona: Fundació Antoni Tàpies, 2009)
——*Complete Writings Volume II. Collected Essays*, trans. by Josep Miquel Sobrer (Barcelona: Fundació Antoni Tàpies, 2009)
——*Pequeña historia de Antoni Tàpies* (Barcelona: Mediterrània, 2013)
——*La práctica de l'art* (Barcelona: Ariel, 1970)
——*La realidad como arte: Por un arte moderno y progresista* (Murcia: Comisión de Cultura del Colegio Oficial de Aparejadores y Arquitectos Técnicos, 1989)
——*Tàpies In Perspective* (Barcelona: Museu d'Art Contemporani de Barcelona and Actar, 2004)
——*El tatuaje y el cuerpo: Antoni Tàpies conversaciones con Manuel Borja-Villel* (Barcelona: Rosa Cúbica, 2005)

TATE, 'Matter Painting', <http://www.tate.org.uk/learn/online-resources/glossary/m/matter-painting> [accessed 17 May 2015]

TEIXIDOR, JOAN, *Antoni Tàpies: Fustes, papers, cartons i collages* (Barcelona: Sala Gaspar, 1964)

TERMES, JOSEP and JORDI CASASSAS, *El Futur del Catalanisme* (Barcelona: Ediciones Proa S.A., 1997)

THISSE, ANNE-MARIE, *La creación de las identidades nacionales: Europa: siglos XVIII–XX* (Vigo: Ézaro, 2010)

'El tripartito y CiU dan luz verde al Estatut tras un acuerdo sobre financiación y enseñanza pública', *El País*, 29 September 2005. <http://elpais.com/elpais/2005/09/29/actualidad/1127981820_850215.htm> [accessed 29 August 2016]

TUBAU, CAROLINA, DIR., *Te de Tàpies*, Televisió de Catalunya, 2009

UNIVERSITAT POMPEU FABRA, 'A Brief History of a Young University', <https://www.upf.edu/universitat/en/presentacio/historia.html> [accessed 8 December 2015]

VALASKIVI, KATJA, *Cool Nations: Media and the Social Imaginary of the Branded Country* (London and New York: Routledge, 2016)

VÁZQUEZ MONTALBÁN, MANUEL, *Sabotaje olímpico* (Barcelona: Planeta, 1993)

'Vicens: Guitart no puede vetar el calcetín', *La Vanguardia*, 7 February 1992. Photocopy consulted in the Fundació Tàpies Library, Barcelona

VIDAL CASTAÑO, JOSÉ ANTONIO, *La memoria reprimida: Historias orales del maquis* (Valencia: Universidad de Valencia, 2004)

VILA-SAN-JUAN, SERGIO, 'Antoni Tàpies recibe el premio Príncipe de Asturias de las Artes', *La Vanguardia*, 19 May 1990, <http://hemeroteca.lavanguardia.com/preview/1990/05/19/pagina-37/33022907/pdf.html?search=Premio%20Pr%C3%ADncipe%20de%20Asturias%20Antoni%20T%C3%A0pies> [accessed 28 August 2016]

VILLABONA, RAFAEL, 'Solé Tura: "El 'calcetín' de Tàpies no me entusiasma demasiado"', *El Observador*, 5 February 1992. Photocopy consulted in the Fundació Tàpies Library, Barcelona

WEBER, EUGEN, *Peasants into Frenchmen: The Modernization of Rural France 1870–1914* (London: Chatto and Windus, 1977)

WEIBEL, PETER, ANDREA BUDDENSIEG, and RASHEED ARAEEN, *Contemporary Art and the Museum: A Global Perspective*, ed. by Andrea Buddensieg and Peter Weibel (Ostfildern: Hatje Cantz, 2007)

WILLIAMS, JAMES H. ED., *(Re)Constructing Memory: School Textbooks and the Imagination of the Nation* (Boston: Sense, 2014)

WILLIAMS, ROBERT, *Art Theory: An Historical Introduction* (Malden, MA: Wiley-Blackwell, 2009)

Wilson Initiative, <http://www.wilson.cat/en/> [accessed 7 August 2013]

ZINN, HOWARD, *Artists in Times of War* (New York: Seven Stories Press, 2003)

INDEX

ABC 5, 18, 72, 74, 84–85, 116
Ajuntament de Barcelona 2, 8, 20, 55–59, 61, 67, 70, 72, 78, 80–81, 88–89, 101, 138, 153–54, 160
Alemany, Luis 39
Anderson, Benedict 12, 15, 135
Andrade, Juan 45
Antón, Jacinto 116
Apostua, Luis 67, 89
Appadurai, Arjun 102
Archilés, Ferran 16, 115, 135
Arco Blanco, Miguel Ángel del 16, 63, 115, 147, 151
Assemblea de Catalunya 37, 39, 44, 95, 103
Avui 1, 18, 45, 76–77, 84, 87, 116

Balfour, Sebastian 3, 21, 40, 86, 100, 115
Barral, Xavier 82, 87
barretina 13–14, 28–29, 35, 74, 84, 95–96, 98, 123, 147, 157
Barrio, Astrid 142, 146, 160
Beramendi, Justo 143
Berger, Stefan 12–13, 15
Bhabha, Homi 15, 97–99
Billig, Michael 12–13, 15, 94–96, 99, 105–06, 135, 138, 140, 151, 156
Bohigas i Guardiola, Oriol 80
Borja-Villel, Manuel 4–6, 29, 85, 112, 159
Borrás, Maria Lluïsa 41
Breckenridge, Carol A. 102
Brereton, Laurie 126
Brossa, Joan 9, 16, 27–29, 32–34, 51, 72, 144, 152

Candidatura d'Unitat Popular (CUP) 142
Catalan language 70, 74–75, 88, 99, 111, 143, 152, 155, 168
Catalan nationalism 3–4, 12, 54, 70, 93–94, 100, 103, 106, 123, 131, 134, 136, 140–41, 145–46, 154–55
Catoir, Barbara 6, 29, 34, 98
Centre d'Estudis d'Opinió 17, 131, 141, 147
Combalía, Victoria 18, 57, 156–57
Convergència Democràtica de Catalunya (CDC) 11, 70, 80, 142–43
Convergència i Unió (CiU) 8, 53, 64, 69, 70, 72–75, 83, 88–89, 103, 109, 114, 118, 132, 142–43, 165
Conversi, Daniele 3, 10–11, 15, 140
Crameri, Kathryn 3, 95–96, 140–42, 154, 160

Dada/dadaist 1, 28, 152

Dalí, Salvador 1, 3, 37, 109, 112, 124–25, 134–35, 144, 166
Dau al Set 28–29, 51, 72, 139
Dia:Beacon 2, 18, 111–13, 122, 139–40
Diada 42, 59–60, 133
Dowling, Andrew 3, 70, 73
Duarte, Ángel 20
Duran i Farell, Pere 80–82

Edelman, Murray 2, 15, 102, 104, 138, 144
Edensor, Tim 13, 15, 94, 100
Enguita Mayo, Nuria 6, 18, 110
Esquerra Republicana de Catalunya (ERC) 3

Figuerola-Ferretti, Luis 52
Foix, J.V. 6
Fundació Antoni Tàpies 2, 4, 6, 17–18, 20, 55, 60–61, 67, 70–73, 76, 83, 86, 89, 110–11, 121, 131, 153, 154
Futurism 10–11, 152

Gasch, Sebastian 6, 52, 64, 144
Gaudí, Antoni 1, 3, 6, 134, 166
Gellner, Ernest 12, 15
Generalitat de Catalunya 2, 8, 18, 60, 67, 72, 89, 132, 138, 153, 160
Gifreu, Josep 136
Gimferrer, Pere 6–7, 37, 51, 53
Giori, Pablo 35
Goya, Francisco 9, 18, 104, 111
Greeley, Robin 4, 31
El grup de Taüll 121
Guardans, Ramon 80, 82, 84
Guggenheim Museum Bilbao 2, 18, 109, 122–24, 126, 137, 139, 169
Guibernau, Montserrat 3, 70, 134, 141–42, 155, 166
Guitart, Joan 11, 18–19, 27, 68, 72, 80–82, 159
Gustà Hernández, Jaime 78

Haacke, Hans 113
Hall, Stuart 22, 115, 124, 139, 144, 146
Heidemarie, Uhl 134
Hobsbawm, E.J. 12, 15
Hugo, Victor 10, 114

Informalism 4, 14, 27, 34, 152
Iniciativa per Catalunya Verds (ICV) 86
Instituto Cervantes 2, 110–11, 126

Jentleson, Katherine 1, 159
Jones, Daniel E. 120

Krauss, Rosalind 29

Lenore, Víctor 125
Lescaze, Lee 82
Llobera, Josep 133
Llorens, Tomàs 53
Lubar, Robert 4–5, 15, 22, 31
Luengo Teixidor, Félix 123

Malevich, Kazimir 1, 38, 59
Maragall, Pasqual 57, 60, 70, 80, 83, 103
Marí, Antoni 86
Mariscal, Javier 5
Martínez-Herrera, Enric 143
Marzo, Jorge Luis 156
Mas, Artur 2, 69, 103, 109, 132, 133, 135, 147, 155, 165
Matter Paintings 5, 7, 27, 34, 36–37, 84, 89, 152–53
McCarthy, David 10–11, 15
Mees, Ludger 13, 134
Mihelj, Sabina 16, 98
Miley, Thomas J. 143–44
Minguet Batllori, Joan M. 136–38, 145, 157
Miró, Joan 1–7, 13–15, 20, 27–34, 36–39, 41, 45, 51–56, 59, 61, 72, 74, 80, 98, 100, 104, 111–12, 123, 134–35, 144, 160, 165–66
Molina, Fernando 4, 74, 94
Molinero, Carme 3, 40
Museo Nacional Centro de Arte Reina Sofía (Reina Sofía) 5, 19, 112, 124–25
Museu d'Art Contemporani de Barcelona (MACBA) 17, 18, 33, 84–85, 101
Museu Nacional d'Art de Catalunya (MNAC) 2, 8, 11, 13, 18–19, 21, 75–76, 78, 80–83, 102, 109, 114, 116–23, 126, 131, 134, 136, 138–40, 144, 147, 155, 157, 159, 166–67, 169

Nairn, Tom 15
national identity 2, 3, 9, 13, 31–32, 35, 44, 56, 88, 93–95, 100, 104, 126, 131–33, 136, 138, 141, 143, 146, 160
nationalization 4, 10, 16, 70, 74, 88, 131, 134, 140
New York Times 18–19, 76, 116, 132, 148, 158–59, 167
Noucentisme/noucentista 20, 31–32, 103, 117, 119, 137
Núñez Seixas, Xosé Manoel 35

Obiols, Raimon 80
Olympic Games (1992) 8, 60, 67, 75, 78, 82–83

El País 6, 18, 57, 60, 72, 80, 103, 112, 114, 116
Partido Comunista de España (PCE) 40–41, 45
Partido Popular (PP) 78, 103, 109
Partido Socialista Obrero Español (PSOE) 56, 109
Partit Comunista de Catalunya (PCC) 45

Partit Socialista Unificat de Catalunya (PSUC) 40, 43–45, 105, 110, 126, 165, 167
Partit dels Socialistes de Catalunya (PSC) 8, 56, 59–60, 80, 83, 89, 103, 109, 114
Permanyer, Lluis 5, 6, 18, 54
Picasso, Pablo 1, 7, 9, 19–20, 56–61, 63, 70, 78, 111–12, 116, 126, 156, 159
Prado, Benjamín 125
Puig Antich, Salvador 41–43, 62, 155
Puig i Cadafalch, Josep 117–18
Pujol, Jordi 1, 8, 51, 53, 60, 69–70, 72–75, 103, 109, 120, 126, 136, 155, 165
Punt Diari 18, 76–77, 84

Quiroga, Alejandro 3–4, 13, 15, 22, 74, 94, 96, 100, 115, 131–35, 143, 145

Rancière, Jacques 10
Rassel, Laurence 5–6
Rauschenberg, Robert 1, 59, 133
Richards, Michael 35
Riquer, Borja de 3, 35
Rodríguez Fominaya, Álvaro 123
Rodríguez Teruel, Juan 142, 146, 160
Rood, Gregory 18, 73

Sala, Maria 78
Santos Torroella, Rafael 57
Schumacher, Edward 19
Scott, James C. 14–15, 41, 63, 145
Second Spanish Republic 20, 35, 37, 43
senyera 44, 95, 99, 123, 134, 157
separatism/separatist movement 7, 94–95, 131, 142–43, 154, 168
Serra, Pepe 18–19, 82, 121, 159
Serra, Richard 123, 167
Shapiro, Ian 142
Smith, Anthony D. 3
Solé Tura, Jordi 80
Sontag, Susan 131, 133, 135
Stapell, Hamilton 54
Sunyer, Joaquim 20, 104–05
Surrealism/surrealist 1, 4–5, 27–29, 31–34, 36, 117, 125, 152–53

Tàpies, Antoni:
  artworks:
    7 de novembre 40, 103
    11 de setembre 42–43, 59–60, 62
    ACC 1 Art Català Contemporani 39
    Blanc amb deus creus 37–38
    La bota i el mitjó 62–63
    Cadira i roba 133–34
    Complement miraculós 70
    Creu de paper de diari 29
    Creu ocre i blanc sobre marró 37–38

Forma negra sobre quadrat gris 152
Gran díptic roig i negre 62
Gran pintura amb X i + 37–38
Efecte de drap 42–43
Empremta de tisores 39
L'escala 112–13
L'esperit català 21, 43–45, 154–56
Gran campana (Sabadell) 85–86, 101
A la memoria de Salvador Puig Antich 42–43, 62, 155
Mitjó 62–63, 76–84, 89, 102, 104, 106, 114, 116, 136- 37, 160, 166–67
Monument homenatge a Picasso 56–60, 70, 78, 156
Mural Universal Exposition (Seville 1992) 73–74, 76, 93, 98, 101, 104
Núvol i cadira 72, 78, 88, 114
Parla, parla 116
Pintura romànica i barretina 13–14, 74, 93, 95–96, 121, 157, 169
Portada de Estatut d'Autonomia de Catalunya 9, 103–04, 155
PSUC: per Catalunya, la Democràcia i el Socialisme 44–45
Les quatre cròniques 21, 68–70, 74, 93, 99–100, 140, 147, 154, 160, 166
Rinzen 84–85, 101, 105
Sala de reflexió 86–88, 102
Els solcs 28
Tela i tisores 38–39
Terra i pintura 34
documentaries and film:
   En record d'Antoni Tàpies 18

Tàpies 18, 73, 97
Te de Tàpies 18
exhibitions:
   Antoni Tàpies (obra 1956–1976) 52–53
   Antoni Tàpies: From Object to Sculpture 122–24, 137
   Antoni Tàpies: The Resources of Rhetoric 111–13, 122
   Galeria Antonio Machon 52
   Galeries Laietanes 4
   Martha Jackson Gallery 52
   The Posters of Antoni Tàpies and the Public Sphere 109–13, 126
   Stradler 52
   Tàpies els anys 80: 55–56, 61–62
   Tàpies. From Within 5, 116–17, 121–24, 141, 169
   A Visit to the Romanesque: In Company of Antoni Tàpies 13, 121, 134, 139, 141, 157, 169
Tàpies, Toni 18–19, 44–46, 54, 68, 83, 103, 106, 117, 122–23, 134–35, 146, 159, 163–70
Todolí, Vicente 123
Torres-Garciá, Joaquín 20
Tubau, Carolina 18

Unió Democràtica de Catalunya (UDC) 70

Valaskivi, Katja 135
La Vanguardia 18, 53–54, 57, 72, 78, 80–81, 115, 165
Vázquez Montalbán, Manuel 75
Vicens, Francesc 80

Ylla-Català, Gemma 123
Ysàs, Pere 3, 40

www.ingramcontent.com/pod-product-compliance
Lightning Source LLC
Chambersburg PA
CBHW082246220526
45469CB00009B/2892